Contents

Introduction

This book is intended to help you do everything necessary to achieve the highest possible grade in the Edexcel AS Applied ICT qualification. You have to produce electronic portfolios of evidence for Units 1 and 2 and take a practical examination in Unit 3. This book provides all necessary guidance together with plenty of suggestions of areas for you to do your own research. Whilst the book provides many examples and details you will need to do your own research when building your portfolio.

Unit 1

In this Unit the book provides full descriptions of many aspects of the information age. These are intended to help you to make sure that you cover all necessary topics and give you ideas for your own research. There are also hints and tips to help improve the presentation and content of the final product. Read through the examples and follow your own interests in order to make the ebook personal to you.

Unit 2

In this Unit you have to study a transactional web site of your own choice in order to understand the processes behind ecommerce web sites. On the CD is software to allow you to make a fully functional commercial web site. If you experiment with this you will have a better understanding of all aspects involved in running such a site. You will also need to produce a simple database. Chapters 2.8 and 2.9 provide all the practical help you need to do this.

Unit 3

This Unit provides all the background you need in order to understand how knowledge workers use ICT to help make decisions. Examples are provided to allow you to practice the skills you will need in order to achieve your best performance in the short time allowed in the practical examination.

UNIT 1
The information age

The Information Age

Aims

- To examine the technologies used in the Information Age.
- To examine some of the opportunities created by the Information Age.
- To look at some of the challenges created by the Information Age.
- To learn about how information can be represented digitally.

The Internet

Few innovations in any field have developed as quickly as the Internet. In the space of about twenty years, it has become a vital part of modern life for many people. It puts us in touch with vast amounts of information, it can save us effort, time and money. However, not everyone is willing or able to take advantage of its immense benefits. Also, like any other powerful resource, it has its drawbacks which we have to learn to cope with.

What is the Internet?

The Internet is an *infrastructure*. This means it provides a platform on which many different useful activities can take place. The Internet can be looked at rather like a country's road system. A road system consists of a variety of roadways which are maintained by different organisations (the local authorities, the highways commission and private owners). The roadways enable all sorts of users to move people and a huge variety of goods short and long distances. The Internet allows information to be moved from one computer to another.

The Internet started as a way of connecting a number of universities in the USA. In 1968, the US Department of Defense Advanced Research Project Agency (ARPA) proposed this link as a fail-safe way of providing communications. For the first time, users on one site could log on to computers on remote sites. This network was called ARPANET.

More sites joined in and it was not long before hundreds of separate networks were able to communicate.

www.computerhistory.org/exhibits/internet_history/

Connections

The Internet is an infrastructure made from connected devices called *nodes*. These are usually computers which are connected to each other by cables or radio links. Hardware devices called *routers* are used to direct signals along suitable pathways.

Organisations called Internet Service Providers (ISPs) give users access to the Internet. They often provide many added value services too, such as web page hosting, chat rooms and news reports.

> **ACTIVITY**
>
> Collect some information about an ISP and write a report about its services.
>
> Your report should include:
>
> ● the name of the ISP;
> ● the cost of a subscription;
> ● the facilities available;
> ● any limits on its use;
> ● how the ISP advertises its services.

Nobody owns the Internet. Different parts may be owned by service providers, but the Internet as a whole belongs to no individual. However, there are certain groups that make decisions about communication standards in the interest of all users.

Uses

The Internet is used for three main purposes:

► **email**: Sending of messages over the Internet is for many people, the most valuable aspect of the Internet. This will be examined later in Chapter 1.2.
► **The World Wide Web**: This is the collection of billions of web pages that can be accessed by anyone connected to the Internet. Web pages are interpreted and displayed on a computer by using web browser software such as Microsoft's Internet Explorer, Netscape Navigator or Mozilla Firefox.
  The usefulness of web pages has increased very rapidly, making the Web a practical way for providing information as well as doing business.
► **File transfer**: The Internet provides a convenient way to transmit data files of all types to anywhere in the world. During this course, your work will be transferred in this way, from school to the examination board and to the examiner.

Why the Internet is so successful

The Internet is a powerful and reliable extension to previously existing communication methods. It has worked so well because of a number of key decisions and trends.

Costs

The cost of computer equipment has been steadily falling for a number of years. This has enabled millions of people and businesses to 'buy into' the developing technologies.

Programming and file standards

The adoption of standards has enabled computers of different types to communicate with each other. It does not matter whether you are using a PC, an Apple or a mainframe, there is always a way to connect to the Internet.

► **Identifying nodes**: Internet nodes are identified in a standard way. Each device has a unique address in the format a.b.c.d where a, b, c and d are numbers in the range 0 to 255. These are called IP addresses and identify where data is to be routed. An IP address looks something like this: 192.168.122.55. Every computer on the Internet has its own number; it's a bit like a phone number, every one is different.

► **Communication protocols**: Protocols are the rules that govern how devices communicate with each other. The most important set of protocols is called TCP/IP (Transmission Control Protocol / Internet Protocol).

The DNS (Domain Name System) translates IP addresses, which are difficult to remember, into recognisable domain names. There are many Domain Name Servers on the Internet which carry out this conversion automatically.

► **HTTP (Hypertext Transfer Protocol)**: This set of rules controls how web pages are set up and interpreted by browsers.

► **FTP (File Transfer Protocol)**: This is the set of rules that ensures that data files are transmitted without error.

► **HTML (Hypertext Markup Language)**: This is the standard for defining web pages. All web pages have at their heart simple text files that use special *tags* in order to control how a browser interprets and displays the page. The simplicity of HTML is important in allowing all types of computers to interpret web pages in the same way. Below is an example of HTML code:

```
<html>
<head>
<meta http-equiv="Content-Language" content="en-gb">
<meta http-equiv="Content-Type" content="text/html;
charset=windows-1252">
<meta name="GENERATOR" content="Microsoft FrontPage 4.0">
<meta name="ProgId" content="FrontPage.Editor.Document">
<title>This is a start</title>
<meta name="Microsoft Theme" content="expeditn 011">
</head>

<body bgcolor="#FFFFFF" background="images/exptextb.jpg"
text="#000000" link="#993300" vlink="#666600"
alink="#CC3300">

<!--mstheme--><font face="Book Antiqua, Times New Roman,
Times"><!--mstheme--></font>

<h1 align="center"><!--mstheme--><font face="Book Antiqua,
Times New Roman, Times" color="#660033">The Airport<!--
mstheme--></font></h1>
<!--mstheme--><font face="Book Antiqua, Times New Roman,
Times">
<p> </p>
<p align="center"><map name="FPMap0">
```

► **PDF (Portable Document Format)**
This is a document standard developed by the Adobe Corporation which allows the transmission of documents in a form so that they are displayed exactly as in the original.

► **JPEG – Joint Photographic Experts Group**
This is a standard of image file compression that allows images to be transmitted rapidly and displayed in any browser.

► **Java**
Java is a programming language that is ideally suited to the Web environment. It allows programs to be written that can be partially compiled to files known as *byte code*. Programs supplied in byte code can be run in any browser and do not need to be specially compiled to run on any particular operating system.

Other important standards have also developed to allow the increasing use of multimedia on the Internet. MPEG (Moving Pictures Experts Group) is a common standard for transmitting moving images and Macromedia Flash takes this capability even further.

Redundancy

Redundancy means building in more capability than is actually needed. The nodes on the Internet are connected by many different routes. This means that if there is a break in one communication link, there will be an alternative route for the data.

■ **Figure 1.1**

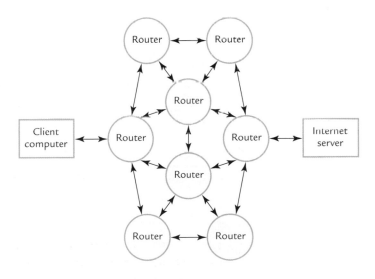

www.grc.com/dos/PacketRouting.htm

This link has more information available about how data is routed over the Internet.

Fast data transmission rates

The usability of the Internet depends upon an adequate data transmission rate. Increasing numbers of Internet users now have access to *broadband* technologies. These permit transmission rates of at least 500 kbits per second. With broadband, the Internet is an acceptable medium for the transmission of large documents, images and sound files.

ACTIVITY
● Use the Internet to look up five Internet service providers.
● Produce a table comparing the connection speeds that they offer.

Multimedia

Multimedia brings together a variety of communication methods. A multimedia presentation is likely to contain some of these elements:

▶ text;
▶ still images;
▶ moving pictures;
▶ animations;
▶ sound.

Multimedia is a popular way to get across messages to an audience. This is because a combination of methods is more likely to be:

▶ understandable (some points are better explained in diagrams or animations);
▶ memorable (a presentation with impact is more likely to be remembered);
▶ interesting (a variety of stimuli keeps the audience interested);
▶ consistent (a message repeated to different groups can be run and re-run, always containing the same message delivered in the same way).

Who uses multimedia?

The answer to this is nearly anyone whose job is to communicate.

■ Figure 1.2

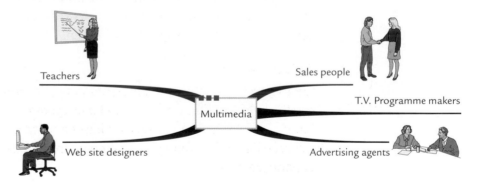

Multimedia software

There is plenty of software that is capable of playing a multimedia presentation. In particular, any web browser has the capability to run multimedia, by invoking 'plug-in' applications that can run in a window. Modern operating systems have multimedia software bundled as part of the package. For example, Windows XP comes with various utilities such as a DVD player, a sound recorder and a media player.

Software to make presentations is also common these days. For example Microsoft Office contains PowerPoint which most PC users have used from time to time in order to make presentations. PowerPoint allows the easy creation of slide shows that contain:

PLUG-IN: A software add-on that adds a new feature to an existing software package.

- ► bullet lists;
- ► movies;
- ► sounds;
- ► animated text and graphics;
- ► transitions from one point or one slide to the next;
- ► hyperlinks.

■ Figure 1.3

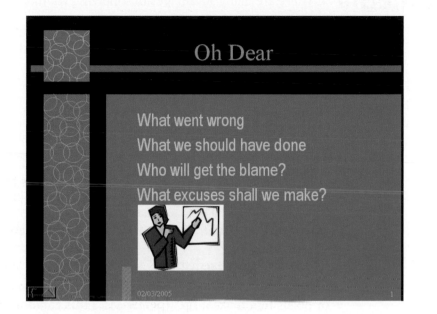

Uses of multimedia

Presentations and talks

MS PowerPoint presentations can be used to illustrate a talk or lecture. In this case, the speaker will control the progress of the slides by clicking a mouse or a remote control. Such presentations are usually projected on a screen so that many people can see them.

Advertising

Another very common use of presentations is in free-running screen-based displays. These are getting more and more common as a means of advertising. Multimedia displays can be seen on buses and trains, where passengers can see a succession of slides and movies ranging from news clips to public service announcements.

■ Figure 1.4

Some supermarkets display advertisements continually running over their goods in order to attract shoppers' attention.

Training

Many training courses are now supplied on CD or DVD so that users can follow exactly the same course wherever they are.

There are many advantages to supplying training in this way:

▶ It can be interactive.
▶ It can include audio and video clips.
▶ It can include demonstration files.
▶ CDs are lighter and easier to distribute than books.

Technical issues

Multimedia files are often very large. A single screenshot in colour takes over 1 MB of storage. A movie needs at least 25 frames per second in order to display smoothly. Sound files contain vast amounts of information. These issues pose problems for the storage and transmission of multimedia presentations. Downloading a web site that uses images or movies can be very slow which is frustrating for a user. There are various ways of overcoming these problems.

Quality and resolution

An image or movie can be reduced in quality by limiting the number of dots or pixels that make it up. In some cases this can be acceptable in order to reduce download time.

Many web sites display moving images in small windows in order to reduce the amount of data that has to be sent.

Compression

There are various ways that image and movie files can be compressed so that less time is taken to download them and less storage space is needed to store them.

Compression means that not all the detail is stored. For example, in an image, instead of storing 1000 identical pixels of blue sky, the value for 'blue' is stored plus the value 1000. Alternatively, certain parts of an image can be stored at a lower resolution than others. The software that displays the presentation must be able to restore the data to the original form (usually 'on the fly'). This can cause a perceptible delay when playing back. You may have noticed a delay on digital television when a new screen is selected. This is caused by the decompression of the received signal.

Compression will be examined in more detail on page 80.

Broadband

What is broadband?

The rate at which data is transmitted is sometimes referred to as the bandwidth. It is measured in bits per second (bps). The higher the transmission rate the better the network performance. One kilobit per second is 1 kbps: that is 1000 bits per second (or more correctly 1024 bits per second).

The bandwidth can be increased by making the connecting medium carry more than one channel of data simultaneously. This technique is called broadband and it allows vastly more data to be transmitted across a serial connection than with a narrowband connection.

Many users are connected to the Internet with modems that are capable of delivering only 56 kbps. However, across the world, more and more users are connecting to the Internet with broadband links. This makes the Internet even more useful. Broadband is one of the reasons why downloading music files from accredited web sites (as well as by using peer-to-peer services) is now a viable proposition.

Modern broadband connections have bandwidths measured in megabits per second (i.e. 1 million bits per second).

When a user connects to the Internet, the bandwidth makes a big difference to the quality of the experience. The performance of the older serial modems can be so slow. This is a real nuisance when downloading web sites with pictures. In the case of moving images, the performance can be completely unusable.

MODEM: A modem (modulator demodulator) is a device that changes a computer's digital signals into the varying voltages (analogue signals) used by most PSTNs (Public Service Telephone Networks) and back again. Even today, many Internet users still use slow (56 kbps) modems.

> Data can be transmitted serially or in parallel.
>
> Parallel transmission uses several wires to carry the data. Often eight parallel wires are used together so that 8 bits (1 byte) can be transmitted at a time. Parallel cables are expensive and bulky.
>
> Serial transmission needs only one line or wire. The data bits flow one after another. This potentially slows down transmission. The rate of transmission can be improved by increasing the frequency of the bit stream or by arranging for the carrier to contain more than one channel. This is a way of allowing more bits to transmit simultaneously.
>
> Serial transmission is cheaper than parallel transmission because only one line is used.

Types of broadband

Broadband performance can be delivered in a variety of ways. They all require some means of digital transmission.

ISDN (Integrated Services Digital Network)

This is a dial-up service that provides a digital link. As the network is digital so a modem is not needed to convert the signals. An ISDN link is dialled-up by the computer when required and the subscriber is charged accordingly. When the session is finished, the line is given up. ISDN links can commonly deliver download speeds of up to 128 kbps.

Leased line

Some users need long sessions connected to the Internet. Many companies, universities and schools need to keep their networked users connected all day long. In this case, it is not economic to be charged by the time connected. It makes more sense to pay a higher fee for an always-open connection with no additional timing charges. Leased lines can be hired at different connection rates: 10 Mbps is common.

ADSL (Asymmetric Digital Subscriber Line)

This service is becoming more common as an economical way of delivering broadband to small users such as individual homes. It makes use of part of the carrying capacity of an existing analogue telephone line by sending digital signals along it. A special modem is required and it can deliver transmission speeds of up to 2 Mbps. At the moment, not all areas can receive ADSL services.

The connection is called asymmetric because the bandwidth is not divided equally between uploading and downloading. Typically, more bandwidth is given to downloading because most home users will receive much more data than they will send.

Cable

Subscribers to cable television and phone services can have a broadband connection which makes use of a cable television channel. This is capable of providing very high bandwidths.

> **ACTIVITY**
>
> Using presentation software produce a presentation to explain to someone the advantages of broadband for Internet access.

Wireless connections

Computers are particularly useful as communications devices, allowing the transfer and sharing of data ever more widely and quickly. Most organisations and even many homes now have networks in order to link computers together.

Making networks can be awkward. Wiring a building can be very expensive and sometimes difficult. Wired networks also lack flexibility. It can be a nuisance finding an access point if you want to work at different locations in a building or even beyond it.

To solve the problem of mobility, more and more connections are wireless. These use radio waves to carry the data transmissions in the same way as mobile telephone networks, but over much shorter distances

Wireless LANs

A LAN is a Local Area Network. That is a network confined to one site.

It is often easier to set up a LAN (Local Area Network) by attaching a radio transceiver to each computer which communicates with a radio access point installed somewhere within radio range. This access point can be connected by a router to a server or linked to a conventional wire LAN.

Advantages of wireless LANs

Users can set up their computers wherever they want within range of an access point and have access to all the facilities of the network.

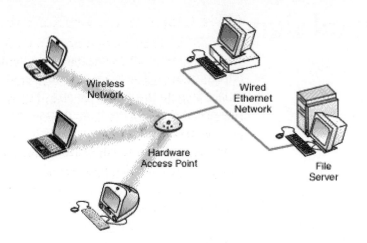

■ **Figure 1.6** Diagram showing relationship between computers, access points and servers

When used in the home, wireless LANs are a cheap and relatively easy way to allow working in any room or in the garden. They also avoid the need for drilling and laying cables.

Disadvantages of wireless LANs

They tend to be a lot slower than wired LANs. This may not be a problem if the amount of network access is limited, but if a wireless LAN is used to connect a lot of workers or a class of students, the performance may be unacceptable.

The signal is only useable over a short distance; the makers often claim distances of up to 800 m. However that is in a field; in a building, the walls reduce the quality of the signal quite quickly.

There are also security issues with wireless LANs. Anyone with a wireless enabled PC and within range can pick up the radio signals and possibly gain access to private data. In reality, this problem can be avoided by the proper configuration of the LAN and by use of encryption techniques, but a surprising number of companies do not have even this basic degree of protection.

WiFi

Many public places now provide wireless Internet access for a small charge. Places like railway stations, coffee bars, hotels and pubs are now offering wireless connections to people on the move.

WiFi is of great benefit to people who have to work while on the move. It lets them use the Internet for all the usual reasons as well as providing a way of communicating with their office network.

WiFi is by no means universally available. You have to be within range of a WiFi *hot spot*. In big cities, this can mean that there are lots of places where you can get access, but it does depend on how many organisations have decided to create hot spots. At the time of writing, coverage in London is quite good but there are many parts where signals are not available. Vienna is known to have comprehensive coverage.

To use this type of system usually requires a subscription to the service being provided, although some places have pay as you go arrangements.

PDAs (Portable Digital Assistants) are popular as they are much smaller than a laptop and have facilities to access the Internet, and therefore email, when on the move.

Digital signals

The digital revolution has had a big impact on many aspects of entertainment. There are several reasons for this.

Digital data is made from only 0s and 1s. A bit is simply a choice between two options: yes or no, true or false, 1 or 0, or, crucially, on or off. A switch can be on or off, there is no halfway state. One switch can therefore represent a decision: yes or no. It can also represent the numbers 0 or 1. This means that when it is copied or transmitted, each bit is either dealt with correctly or it is not. All sorts of checks can be built into copying and transmitting processes in order to check for errors. If a zero is received when a 1 is expected, the bit only needs to be switched. The result of this is that digital data is copied exactly and it can be transmitted with no errors. This is very different from analogue systems, where copying and transmitting signals always resulted in a degradation of a signal.

■ Figure 1.7

But if you take a word-processed file and copy it to a disk, then copy the copy, you can repeat this until you get fed up! There will be absolutely no degradation of the data. This is because each time you copy it the computer creates a new file.

Digital phones and TV

Broadband technology allows hundreds of separate channels to be transmitted on a single carrier. This allows an enormous amount of information to be transmitted and made sense of with limited investment. Broadband digital technology allows thousands of phone calls to be transmitted simultaneously on one carrier radio wave. Without this, it would not be possible for millions of mobile phone users to use their phones at the same time. It also allows hundreds of TV channels to be beamed into your home via cable or satellite connection. The quality is reliable too because digital data suffers from less interference than analogue signals.

Another benefit of this huge amount of data that can be carried is that in some cases, TV can be made interactive. Eventually, it will be possible to choose more and more TV on demand as there will be many different choices available at the same time. Already, you can select different views of a sporting event. The Formula 1 Channel allows you to view the race from the trackside, the pit lane or from the driver's cockpit.

■ Figure 1.8

Some digital news channels let you choose which of the day's big stories you want to watch.

■ Figure 1.9

Transforming information

The ability to transfer and transform information is really at the heart of the digital age.

Digital information

As we have seen, data that is held in computer systems is all digital. It is made up of 0s and 1s; in other words, binary representation. A single memory location in a computer's memory holds eight bits, each being set as a 0 or a 1. That is all. There is no other system for storing data in digital computers. This simplicity has made digital storage and processing so effective. A set of bits makes up a pattern that can mean anything we want it to mean.

Numbers

Take the binary pattern 01000001.

This can represent the decimal number 65. If the computer system 'knows' that the pattern is supposed to represent a number, it will be ready to perform calculations on it.

Text

However, we also need to store text when we are word processing or setting up a web site. The pattern 01000001 can then be used to represent the letter 'A'. This is making use of a coding system called ASCII (American Standard Code for Information Interchange). There are other code systems that let a computer code for any character in any language.

Look at the activities of the Unicode organisation at http://www.unicode.org/

Formatting codes

When we use a word processor, we want to store more than just the text, so other bit patterns are embedded into the files we make to show the software not just what to display, but *how* to display it.

**e-book
Text1.doc**

ACTIVITY

Load the file *Text1.doc* into a word processor. This is a Microsoft Word document of a a simple piece of text.

Close it and load it into MS Notepad. MS Notepad is not capable of interpreting the MS Word formatting codes so it displays them instead. They look like a load of gobbledegook.

Text1.rtf is a Rich Text Format file. It is the same document but the formatting codes are simpler. They can be read by many different pieces of software. Load this into MS Notepad. It still won't look right but you may be able to spot the codes that turn on the bold characters.

Load the .rtf file into MS WordPad and it will display properly.

Take a look at the different amounts of storage that these files occupy on the disk.

Other files

Any form of information can be encoded digitally, not just words and numbers, but sounds, images and movies. This allows us to manipulate it in any way we want using a huge variety of different types of software.

Examples of transforming data

Information technology can make us better communicators. This is because of the powers that we have to present information in different ways. We have seen how multimedia presents many opportunities for communicating in new and striking ways.

Presenting numerical data

A computer makes it easy to manipulate numerical data so that we can use it to make the point that we want. Suppose that the residents of a village, where the speed limit is 40 mph think that most traffic is speeding as it passes by. This can be checked by installing a sensor and recording equipment. The software can record all this data and we can study it in a spreadsheet.

■ Figure 1.10

	A	B
1	Time	Speed (mph)
2	9:00	50
3	9:00	55
4	9:01	45
5	9:02	35
6	9:03	30
7	9:04	15
8	9:05	57
9	9:06	58
10	9:06	66
11	9:08	65
12	9:09	45
13	9:10	46
14	9:10	67
15	9:12	30
16	9:13	45
17	9:15	26
18	9:16	65
19	9:18	45
20	9:19	34
21	9:19	23
22	9:21	12
23	9:23	32
24	9:24	55
25	9:26	54
26	9:28	53

This takes a lot of studying to make some sense out of it. Is there a speeding problem or not? It is easy, with spreadsheet software to transform this data and also to make summaries. One quick transformation is to use the numerical data to make a scatter plot.

■ Figure 1.11

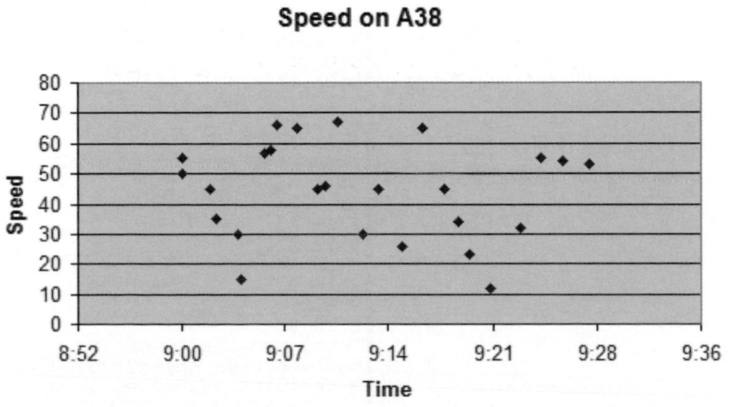

Speed on A38

This is better as it allows us to see that quite a lot of the speed measurements are above 40 mph.

e-book spreadsheet 1.xls

The spreadsheet in the example is on the CD (*spreadsheet1.xls*).

Load the spreadsheet and carry out the following operations:
- make a scatter graph;
- sort the data into speed order.

Import and export

If data is processed by one application and it is needed in another, the format of the data may have to change. Changing data to suit a different application is called exporting data. Similarly, bringing data in that has been prepared in a different package is called importing data. There are always ways to do this so there is never a need to re-enter data that already exists in digital form.

The speed data in the example was collected from a sensor and imported into a spreadsheet. Spreadsheets, just like any other common application, save a lot of embedded data along with the data in the cells. There will be information about the way to display the data, and row and column information. Links to graphs and other sheets also have to go in. If you use Microsoft Excel, the files will be saved, by default in .xls (MS Excel spreadsheet) format. Most common software can recognise xls files and display them to some degree.

If you want to use this data in a database, Microsoft Access is able to import MS Excel files. However, you may want to export the data for use in a mainframe database application that you know nothing about. In that case, you can always use a save as option and save the data as a CSV (comma separated values) file. You will lose all the formatting information, but the basic data will be usable by most other applications. Here is the spreadsheet data saved as a CSV file and displayed using a simple text editor (in this case, MS Notepad).

■ Figure 1.12

```
road speed - Notepad

File  Edit  Format  View  Help
Time,Speed (mph)
9:00,50
9:00,55
9:01,45
9:03,35
9:03,30
9:04,15
9:05,57
9:06,58
9:07,66
9:07,65
9:08,45
9:08,46
9:08,67
9:10,30
9:11,45
9:12,26
9:13,65
9:14,45
9:15,34
9:16,23
9:17,12
9:18,32
9:19,55
9:20,54
9:22,53
Total vehicle count,25
No. vehicles exceeding 40 mph,16
% vehicles exceeding 40 mph,64.00%
```

Sharing information quickly

Digital data is not just easy to transform. It is also easy to send at great speed. There are various technologies that make the transmission of data very rapid:

▶ **Metal cable**: low voltage pulses can be sent as a stream along any conductor. At any particular time, either there is a pulse or there is not (0s and 1s again). Streams of data conducted by cable travel at the speed of light.

■ Figure 1.13

▶ **Fibre-optic cable**: this is a thin transparent fibre that uses total internal reflection to keep a light beam confined within it. The light beam can be modulated (have its frequency altered) to encode data. This too travels at the speed of light.

■ Figure 1.14

▶ **Radio**: where it is difficult or expensive to install cable, radio frequency waves can be modulated to encode digital data. They can be used in a local situation, for example, WiFi or over longer distances such as from a ground station to a satellite. Even larger distances can be covered as in the case of retrieving data from space probes.

■ Figure 1.15

Now that we have the massive infrastructure of the Internet, it is very easy for anyone to share information more or less instantly. There are ever more inventive ways of doing this.

email

This, of course, is a great way to get data files between people. The text of this book was written by one author in one place and emailed to the other for checking. This made it very easy to work collaboratively without wasting any time.

> **Standard ways of working**
> What precautions need to be taken when different people work on the same project via email? How can the careful choice of filename help?

Intranets

An intranet is a private network that uses the same kinds of software that you would find on the public Internet, but only for access internally to an organisation or by people with secure access.

Sometimes, several people need to work together on a project where each member of the team has to see the work in progress of all the others.

CASE STUDY

The *Society Of Digital Information Technicians* is a professional body that sets examinations globally. The senior examiners write the exam papers taken by the students. The examiners live in Australia, Brazil, Peru, Austria, Luxembourg, the USA and the UK. They need to collaborate while developing the exam papers. It is too expensive to fly them all to the board's headquarters in London to meet more than very occasionally. The exam papers need to be kept securely all the time, so email cannot be used. Normal post and courier services are too expensive and slow. The telephone is inconvenient because of time zone differences.

The solution

The exam board has set up a secure area on its intranet. It can be accessed from the Internet using any browser. The examiners can log in, using their unique IDs and passwords. This leads them to a discussion area where files can be uploaded. The only people who have access to this restricted area are the examiner team and the board's officers.

Any member of the team can download the latest version of the exam papers at any time and add comments. Eventually, the Chief Examiner decides that the process is complete and indicates that a particular file is the final version. The board's officers can then check and print the paper.

This process can now be completed in a few weeks when previously it used to take up to six months.

Questions to consider

How do the examiners know which is the latest version of an exam paper?

How can the examiners indicate suggested changes on a paper without deleting previous material?

What disadvantages are there in working collaboratively like this?

Greater interaction with each other and organisations

The digital age has brought many opportunities for people to interact that were not there before. These opportunities affect us both in social and business activities.

Online chat

It is easy to have an online conversation with one or many friends while you get on with other jobs at the computer. The friends can be anywhere, although there may sometimes be time zone problems.

Students can have a chat while doing their work and also they can share ideas. It is easy and quick to send brief messages and files can be sent too. This enables work to be done collaboratively as well as being able to keep in touch with your friends. This is especially useful if you are on vacation from university.

The great thing about this way of communicating is that if you have an 'always-open' broadband connection, there are no additional costs to being online.

■ Figure 1.17

Interacting with businesses

Modern digital technology, and the Internet in particular, makes it easy to interact with businesses. This can be as a customer or as a partner business. When businesses work together, this is called B2B (Business to Business).

DHL is a courier service that sends packages around the world. If an individual or a business has a package to send, it is necessary to first fill in an airway bill.

This airway bill requires the sender's name and address, the recipient's name and address and details of the consignment.

When the consignment is ready, DHL is contacted by phone or on their web site and a courier comes to collect the package.

The courier looks up the three letter IATA code for the nearest airport to the destination of the package. For example, if the package is going to a London address, the code will be LHR (London Heathrow).

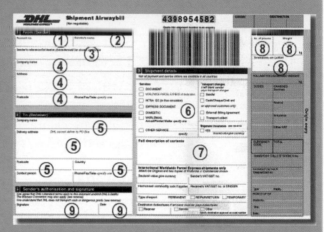

The airway bill has a unique bar code on it and throughout its journey, this will be scanned and tracked. The DHL database keeps an up-to-date record of the package's location.

The customer can check the progress of the package at any time by logging onto DHL's web site and entering the airway bill number.

The DHL database is accessible from anywhere in the world. This level of customer interaction is becoming common in many different businesses and can make life a lot easier. For example, if someone claims not to have received a consignment, the sender can log onto the DHL web site and say, 'Mr John Palmer signed for it yesterday at 14:03'.

DHL Global	DHL Web Shipping	DHL Connect	Site Search

UNITED KINGDOM

Tracking
Tariff and Transit
Fuel Surcharge
Services
Shipping Tools
Information
Press
About DHL
Order Supplies
Open Account

Date	Local Time	Location Service Area	Checkpoint Details
February 03, 2005	15:07	Bristol - UK	Shipment picked up
February 03, 2005	17:30	Bristol - UK	Departing origin
February 03, 2005	19:07	Bristol - UK	Departed from DHL facility in Bristol - UK
February 03, 2005	21:08	East Midlands - UK	Arrived at DHL facility in East Midlands - UK
February 04, 2005	02:09	East Midlands - UK	Departed from DHL facility in East Midlands - UK
February 04, 2005	03:09	Birmingham - UK	Arrived at DHL facility
February 04, 2005	07:55	Birmingham - UK	With delivery courier
February 04, 2005	10:38	Birmingham - UK	Shipment delivered

coursework_tip

This kind of service is common in the information age. You might use an example like this in your project. It is an example of an online service.

Use the Internet to investigate the tracking services offered by this and some other delivery services.

You may find that your school or college has a consignment to send and you can follow it.

Log onto the courier's site from time to time and see the route taken by the consignment. You may be surprised about the route taken.

Many other companies are able to track the progress of orders and thereby give customers reassurance that all is well. Another good example is Amazon. If you order books from Amazon, you can check whenever you like to see whether the order has been logged, assembled or dispatched. It gives you a good idea of when the order will arrive.

Many theatres take bookings online. They are able to use modern digital technology in all sorts of ways to help you make a booking. Apart from showing which performances are available, and the prices of the seats, some provide a seating plan. If you click on a particular seat, you can get an image showing the view of the stage from that seat. This can help a lot in deciding which seats to buy.

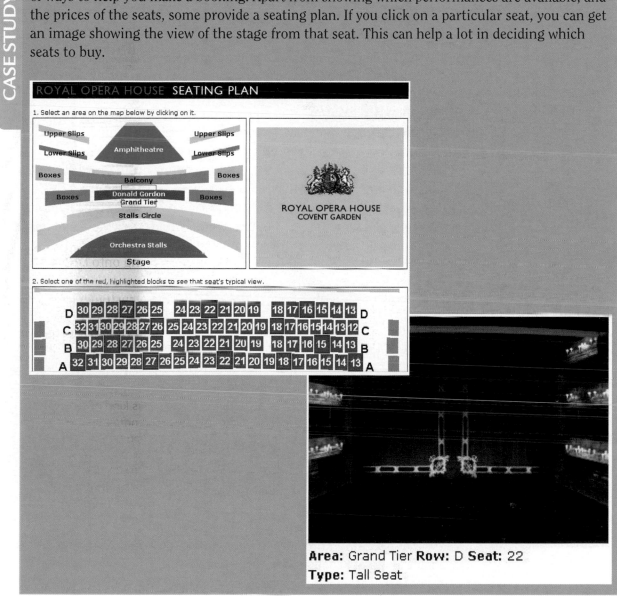

Area: Grand Tier **Row: D Seat:** 22
Type: Tall Seat

Business opportunities large and small

Because the Internet is such a powerful communication tool, it is an ideal medium in which to conduct business. Just as the development of computers really took off in the 1950s as a result of the world of business finding uses for them, it is business that is really driving the most important recent developments on the Internet. All the activities that are being conducted on the Internet are together known as ebusiness or ecommerce.

Already, the number of ways that the Internet is used for business is huge and new ways are being invented all the time.

■ Figure 1.22

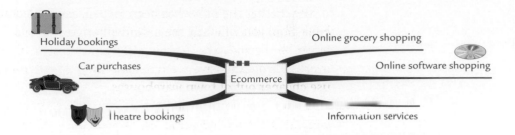

Holiday bookings

Car purchases

Theatre bookings

Ecommerce

Online grocery shopping

Online software shopping

Information services

For a short time, some people thought that ecommerce would be a huge new market and lots of start-up companies (known as dotcoms) encouraged many speculators to invest heavily in the hope of big returns. However, the bubble soon burst because it is not enough just to use the Internet as a way to conduct business, you have to have a solid business behind it providing goods or services that people actually want to buy.

There have been many examples of where online businesses have failed. The usual reason has been that many have been supply-led instead of demand-led. In other words, it is no good saying, 'We have the technology, let's try and sell something'. You have to know that there is a real demand for the goods or services before committing investment.

In 2000, an online university called UKeU was set up by the government in the UK. The idea was that students from all over the world would sign up in order to study online and get a prestigious UK degree. Fifty million pounds of taxpayers' money was spent on the initiative. The project was a failure and eventually collapsed. Money was spent on developing the technology without ever researching whether anybody actually wanted to use the service. Its target was to attract 5600 students in its first year of operation. In fact, fewer than 900 signed up. Fourteen million pounds was spent on developing the technology and £11 m was spent on course development. Also the directors were awarded huge sums in performance related bonus payments (in 2002/3, the sum was more than £100 000). This is just one of very many cases where public sector IT projects have gone wrong, and because they are funded by the taxpayer, market forces cannot kick in as a control.

The companies that have been most successful in ebusiness have been those that have either provided a brand new service that was not previously available and that people find useful, or provide something quicker or cheaper than was previously available.

Below are just a few examples of how ebusiness can fulfil a need and be successful.

Unsold hotel rooms can be sold at the last minute. The Internet allows anyone to search a database and find something suitable very quickly. Some web sites specialise in this kind of thing, for example www.lastminute.com and www.laterooms.co.uk.

Often goods are more expensive in some countries. For example, cars are more expensive in the UK than in continental Europe. The Internet can allow cross-border sourcing, thereby saving customers a lot of money. There are some issues with this kind of buying. For example, a customer living in England, uses an Internet bank account based in France to order goods for delivery to a villa in Spain. Which country's laws apply to this sale?

The Internet can allow customers to have wider choice. If you go into a bookshop, you will only see a limited range of books that the bookshop buyer has decided are likely to sell well. Online booksellers do not have the overheads of expensive premises and they can offer a vast range of books and use cheaper out of town warehouses.

Brand new opportunities also exist. The web site friendsreunited.com has generated entirely new trade by providing a service that was just not possible before mass Internet access became a reality.

ACTIVITY

Ask around your group and your teachers or lecturers to find out how many people have made recent purchases online. Find out what these purchases were. You will probably find that people use online services much more than they used to.

Later in the book, in Chapter 2.2, you will look more closely at a variety of ways in which business is conducted on the Internet.

Virtual communities

The Internet has made it possible for people who are interested in the same thing to post their opinions and thoughts for all to see. These people and the readers make up what can be regarded as a *virtual community*. Something is virtual if it does not physically exist. Because the Internet is worldwide, these virtual communities can cover the planet.

Some virtual communities are based on profession or occupation. One example is on the web site of the *Times Educational Supplement*. Here, teachers can express opinions and seek answers to questions.

■ Figure 1.23

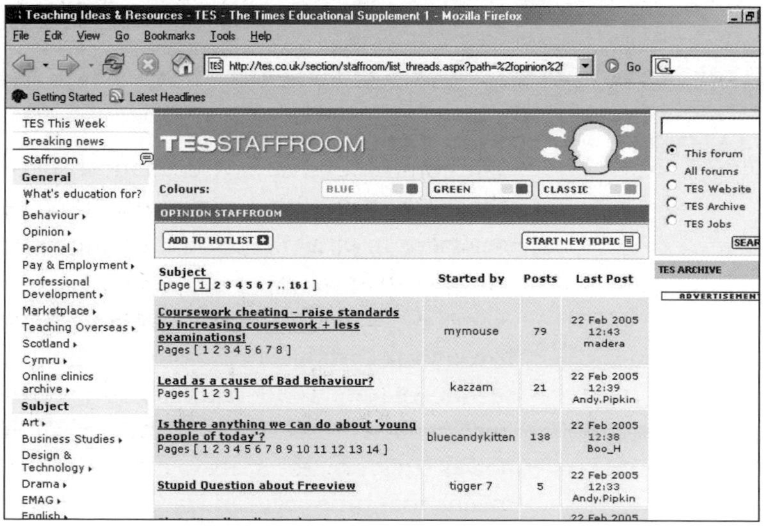

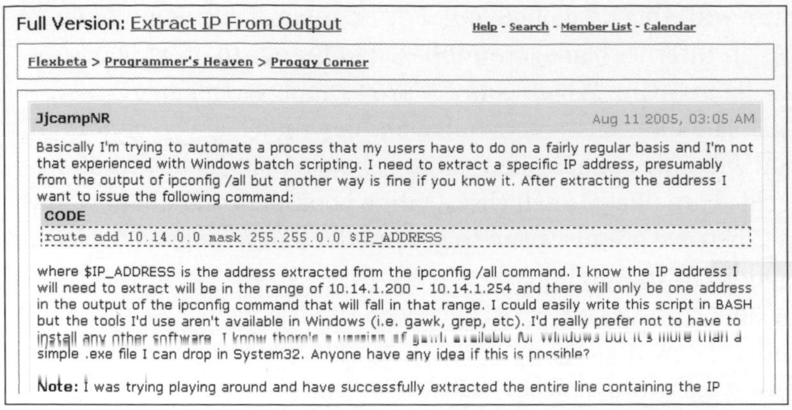

Full Version: <u>Extract IP From Output</u>   <u>Help</u> - <u>Search</u> - <u>Member List</u> - <u>Calendar</u>

<u>Flexbeta</u> > <u>Programmer's Heaven</u> > <u>Proggy Corner</u>

JjcampNR   Aug 11 2005, 03:05 AM

Basically I'm trying to automate a process that my users have to do on a fairly regular basis and I'm not that experienced with Windows batch scripting. I need to extract a specific IP address, presumably from the output of ipconfig /all but another way is fine if you know it. After extracting the address I want to issue the following command:

```
CODE
route add 10.14.0.0 mask 255.255.0.0 $IP_ADDRESS
```

where $IP_ADDRESS is the address extracted from the ipconfig /all command. I know the IP address I will need to extract will be in the range of 10.14.1.200 ~ 10.14.1.254 and there will only be one address in the output of the ipconfig command that will fall in that range. I could easily write this script in BASH but the tools I'd use aren't available in Windows (i.e. gawk, grep, etc). I'd really prefer not to have to install any other software. I know there's a version of gawk available for Windows but it's more than a simple .exe file I can drop in System32. Anyone have any idea if this is possible?

Note: I was trying playing around and have successfully extracted the entire line containing the IP

■ Figure 1.24

Many sites exist where people can ask for and give advice. Asking for technical help is common.

Virtual communities and democracy

Virtual communities make it much easier for people to express their opinions to a wider audience. In the past, people were only able to address a wide audience by attending public meetings or by writing letters to the newspapers. Public meetings inevitably have limited audiences and getting a letter published depends on the space available and the views of the editor.

You will see in Chapter 1.2 how the growth of *blogs* has made it possible for online communities to discuss political issues and extend political debate.

Disadvantages of virtual communities

As always in the fast developing world of the Internet, there are downsides to the development of online communities. The technology has been much used by undemocratic groups and terrorists in order to promote violence on a greater scale than in the past. One example of this is how animal rights campaigners have published the private details of those people who they take a dislike to. This has resulted in acts of violence and harassment by criminally-inclined supporters.

Terrorist groups have coordinated their activities by Internet communications. Supporters in many countries who do not know each other form a virtual community dedicated to violence.

As in many cases, the Internet has made possible degrees of communication that have made a big difference to the way we think and act. It is not surprising that good and bad result from this new freedom.

Technologies that blur the distinction between home and work

The rapid development of digital technology has greatly affected the way we work. Again, we are only just beginning to understand the impact that this has.

Working on the move

If you walk through any reasonably long-distance train these days, you will see lots of people with laptops , busily working on a word-processed document, a presentation or their email. Many Virgin trains now provide a power supply by the seats to cater for this. The portability of the technology means that time spent in travel can be used productively. This, as always, has advantages and disadvantages. It can be more worthwhile than before to make long journeys because the time spent in travelling is no longer 'dead time'. A lot of this book has been written on train journeys. A danger is that in reality we are not just work machines: everybody needs a life as well.

Figure 1.25

Digital technology can increase expectations so that working life intrudes into areas that were once private or into leisure time. Sometimes on long train journeys, it is better to spend your time staring out the window or reading a novel so that you get a break from work.

Working at home (Teleworking)

It is so easy to check emails from home that evenings often become part of the working day. This is all very convenient, but we need to keep things under control so that we are in charge, not the demands of work.

However, with a bit of care and self discipline, the mobility of the technology can be liberating. More and more people work from home *instead* of going to the office. All they need is a computer and an Internet connection and they can have access to email and often their work-based computer network.

Working from home brings great benefits. You work when *you* feel like it, not when the clock tells you to. You do not spend time and money on travel. If you want a break, you can switch off the computer and do something else instead. If you are working from home for a company, your employer can save on office space by rotating the use of desks ('hotdesking'.).

The downside of this (there always is one!) is that it can be just too easy to watch daytime TV or go for a walk. You really need a lot of self-control to make this work. It can be difficult if a family member wants some attention or when the cat insists on flicking her tail across the keyboard! You can also get lonely working from home. You can also miss out on office gossip which can put you at a disadvantage if you don't know what is going on.

Often a compromise is best. Some people work only some of the time from home, maybe one or two days a week. That way they keep in touch with the human side of the work environment but gain some of the freedom that goes with home working.

Mobile phones

Mobile phones have also transformed our working practices. It doesn't matter where you are any more. You can be on a business trip somewhere, but that doesn't stop clients from getting in touch. Call diversion services can route callers to your mobile if someone calls your home or office number. Again, you need to know when to switch off. It is not good when the boss calls with an urgent problem and asks, 'Where are you?' and gets a reply such as, 'I'm on the top of a mountain in the Alps at the moment'. The introduction of mobile phones means that you now call a person rather than a place. A landline is connected to a place such your home, a mobile is not fixed so you can call direct to the person.

Self-service environment

The Internet has put people in direct touch with lots of useful databases. This has cut out the middleman in many useful transactions. We can find things out by ourselves without having to ask others for their help. Apart from increasing our freedom, it also saves time not having always to ask sales people or consultants for their help.

Banking

Internet banking is a good example of how we can now help ourselves to services which we used to have to ask others for. We can now:

▶ check our statements at any time;
▶ transfer money between accounts;
▶ make payments;
▶ set up regular payments;
▶ pay bills.

Online banking is covered more completely in Chapter 1.3.

Shopping

It is no longer necessary to visit the supermarket. Orders can be placed online and the goods delivered to your home. There are certain disadvantages to this, such as not always getting exactly what you want, or you may want to make your own choices from fresh goods. However there are situations where you just don't have time to shop and some people can find it difficult to get out, possibly because they have mobility problems.

> **ACTIVITY**
> ● Use the Internet to look at a major supermarket's web site.
> ● Is the site only used for Internet shopping?
> ● What other uses can you see on their site?

Learning

portfolio_tip

You should not rely only on the Internet for material in your portfolio. There is still a very important place for using more traditional resources such as books, newspapers, magazines and personal contacts. To get high marks for your work you **must** use sources other than the Internet.

There is so much information available to Internet users that the opportunities for learning have never been greater. This too has become almost a 'help-yourself' activity. Students increasingly turn to the Internet as their first option when researching their work: but there are pitfalls. It is easy to plagiarise and this has caused many students to have their work rejected, thereby receiving no exam grade. It can also be difficult to judge whether a source of information is reliable or not. It takes quite a lot of skill and experience to get the best out of what is a completely disorganised resource.

It is increasingly accepted that learning is not just a process confined to school and university. This is not new: people have always needed to learn in order to progress in their jobs, but it is more evident than in the past. Employees are expected to make their own efforts to keep up with changes in their industries and online resources make this easier.

There are plenty of 'teach yourself' resources that cover almost anything you need to know. It is hardly surprising that a lot of these learning resources are about IT itself. You can find endless tutorials on programming languages, networks and web design that have been provided free by a whole host of people. Other resources, more likely linked to a particular qualification may have to be paid for. Still, they all allow access to information with the speed that computers bring and with the benefit that you can use them when it suits you and not just when the classes are running. This is particularly useful to those who are trying to mix their studies with their home commitments, such as parents with young children.

There are lots of useful small-scale aids to learning as well. If you need to learn to type faster, there are many online typing tutorials and practice programs. You can learn foreign languages and hear them spoken correctly.

For many of us, it helps a lot to have a real teacher as well as access to online resources. You should never forget the importance of the human factor. This can be combined with the benefits of online learning if a course is run at a centre. With many of the students using online materials, the teacher can spend more time targeting individual problems.

Privacy

The information age has many implications for the privacy of individuals. This is more of an issue than in the past because information can now be copied very quickly and it is easy to send it anywhere in the world quickly. Because it is so easy to store and manipulate information, many organisations have the incentive to collect information, so there is more information in existence. Collecting information is attractive to businesses because it enables them to understand their market better and also to target advertising more effectively.

> **ACTIVITY**
>
> Collect a week's worth of junk mail and make a list of the organisations that have made use of databases to the target the mail items. Can you find out where the relevant data was first collected?

The downside of businesses collecting all this information is an increase in the amount of intrusive contact that individuals suffer from all sorts of organisations. This is not just restricted to junk mail which, although irritating, can be thrown away. There is also an increase in the number of 'cold calls' where organisations you have never heard of telephone you, usually during a meal or your favourite TV programme. There are laws about the passing on of private information, but they don't seem to stop a lot of information sharing.

Sometimes, you might be refused credit for no apparent reason. A mistake in a database can have very embarrassing and inconvenient consequences.

Collecting information is also attractive to governments. Governments like to control people and the more information they have, the better they can do this. There are sometimes plausible reasons for this. A good information supply might possibly be of use in tracking the activities of terrorists or other criminals. It is also useful in tracking who has paid their taxes. Government agencies have access to business records too, and the driver licensing agency (DVLA) has access to insurance and MOT records. There is always a lingering worry about how much information is there and who can get at it.

Identity cards are able to give the police and other agencies a very quick way of finding out a wide variety of personal details about individuals. Many perfectly law abiding citizens are deeply concerned about the extra powers that identity cards give the state without there being any proof that there are any tangible benefits. This is an ethical issue which has arisen because of the information age.

■ Figure 1.26

Members of the public have access to a surprising amount of personal information. Services such as 192.com can give anyone access to people's names, addresses and telephone numbers. In some countries, criminal records can also be seen.

Most countries have laws that limit the amount of personal data that can be held on individuals and the conditions under which it is kept, such as the UK Data Protection Act 1998. Despite this, many are still concerned that the amount of private information that is freely accessible is unacceptable and is growing. This is one problem that is unlikely to go away and we shall have to adapt to it.

Copyright and legislation

When someone writes something, paints something, writes a computer program, takes a photograph or creates some music, there is an issue of ownership. Who actually owns these creations? The owner is the creator of the item. We say the item is the creator's *intellectual property*. The item is subject to copyright which means that others are not allowed to make copies except under defined circumstances. At the very least, material in the public domain should be acknowledged. However, if the item is stored digitally, as it almost certainly will be, it is easy to copy and pass on.

Technological advances have made copyright issues more of a problem than they used to be. In the past, students, and sometimes teachers, photocopied large sections of books to save money, thereby cheating the author of due income. This reduces the incentive for authors to produce books and other resources. It is so much easier to cheat with digital resources. Materials placed on web sites can be downloaded and copied and also altered in order to pretend that someone else's work is your own.

Even governments have been caught out copying the work of others and pretending that it was officially collected intelligence.

portfolio_tip

Make sure that all the material that you make use of in your portfolio is properly referenced to avoid any suspicion of plagiarism.

The fact that digital data can be copied exactly has made the copying of music a particular copyright problem. Peer-to-peer file sharing services such as Napster allowed users to get perfect quality copies of music which at one stage looked as if it could endanger the whole music business. The emergence of legal download sites has reduced this danger and the sales of online music have in some cases now exceeded the sales of CDs. Modern high capacity storage devices can contain hundreds of songs making it unnecessary even to go to the trouble of burning a CD.

Devices (such as the Apple iPod) now allow you to carry around many hours of entertainment in a small space. A 10 GB device can hold as much as 1000 tracks, the equivalent of several 100 CDs. (These devices also serve as portable storage for other computer files.)

Employment

Nearly every job has changed as a result of the information age. Many old jobs, such as newspaper typesetting, have changed out of all recognition. The skills of setting print in hot lead are no longer needed. However, probably more jobs have been created than lost in the information revolution.

What is undeniable is that nearly everyone has to use IT in some shape or form in their job. You could fill a book with examples, but here are a few. Bus drivers and train ticket clerks sometimes have on-board computers to let them cost tickets to chosen destinations and print tickets.

■ Figure 1.27

A gas engineer, called out to fix an appliance, has a laptop connected by a radio link to headquarters. This can be used to print a bill for the customer, accept online credit card payment and update the gas company's records, look at parts diagrams for the faulty appliance and order the spare parts.

Doctors now usually keep patients' records on computer systems making it easier to see a patient's medical history. These systems have become so useful that they have been expanded to include drug databases, a facility for printing out prescriptions and often an intranet with information for patients. The patient can be given an information sheet to take away with information about his or her condition.

Everybody needs IT skills and those who have a particularly high level of IT skill or a skill that is not common, can command very good salaries. There are many new jobs that are completely IT-focused. There is a great need for specialist IT skills such as networking and database development.

There is a great need for IT support and repair services. IT training is big business as well. A country that has fully embraced the information age has more opportunity for employment than one that has not. This leads to a healthy economy that benefits everyone.

However, IT moves so quickly so these skills become out of date and IT professionals have to invest a lot of effort and often money to keep up with developments. Companies that invest in training their staff tend to do better than those who ignore this need. They also have more satisfied staff who are less likely to move on.

Some jobs have become de-skilled as a result of IT advances. When typewriters were used in offices, a secretary needed to lay out a letter very carefully so that it looked right. To centre a line involved skill. Now a click of a button does it all. A mechanic tuning a car used his skill to listen to the engine, look at the exhaust and make adjustments. Now computer diagnostics tune the car and even log faults.

Digital divide

Most of us have benefited enormously from the information age; even those who do not use IT systems directly. Service has improved in many industries, products are of better quality as the result of computer-controlled engineering. We don't expect new cars to go wrong any more and their service intervals have increased because of the greater precision with which the parts are made.

With cheap computers and easily available connectivity, most people in the economically developed parts of the world who want access to the Internet have now got it. However, there are some people who do not get all the possible benefits from the information age. We call this the digital divide. There are all sorts of reasons why not everyone takes advantage of the benefits of being connected. Some do not have access to the Internet because of where they are located, through ignorance or because they just don't want to get involved.

Chapter 1.4 covers these issues in greater detail.

Online services

Aims

- ■ To examine services available on the Internet.
- ■ To examine the advantages and disadvantages of several online services.

> **coursework_tip**
>
> The research for this section of your portfolio will be mostly Internet-based.
>
> During your research, try to think about the advantages of the services that you are researching.

Many people only use the Internet for browsing the World Wide Web. The Internet has many uses beyond this. This chapter looks at some of the services available to people who have a connection to the Internet.

Online services often give people who can access them an advantage over those who cannot.

Communications

> **coursework_tip**
>
> A good idea for your coursework might be to interview some people about how they make use of the Internet for communications.

The Internet is a worldwide network of computers that are able to communicate with each other. This provides users with a ready-made communications system. Once connected to the Internet, a user has access to a system that will carry messages anywhere at great speed and at little cost.

Email

Email is short for electronic mail; it has been around for many years. Even before the Internet, many company networks had an electronic mail system on them. These systems only worked internally. Email was developed for the ARPAnet shortly after its creation. It is perhaps the most powerful technology used on the Internet today.

Email works using the domain name system, just like web pages. An Internet *domain* has an *email server* associated with it to manage all addresses at that domain.

Each email address is written in the same format: `name@domain`. Each email address must be unique in a particular domain. That is why some people have hotmail addresses like `Paul9876` with numbers added to make the name unique on the hotmail domain.

Here is an example of how an email address is made up.

`Paul@anyserve.net`

The domain here is `anyserve.net` the unique name `Paul` identifies the individual mail account.

DOMAIN NAME SYSTEM: A standard way of defining and naming resources on the Internet. A limited number of domain name suffixes such as .com or .org are available and users can apply to hold a unique name using one of these.

In this simple structure, each domain has a mail server. Big domains may have several servers. These servers look after the accounts for all the users with addresses at that domain. Email servers use the Internet's *domain name system* to look up the *IP address* of another mail server, connect to it and transfer email to it. The receiving server then sorts the mail to the individual mailbox.

Ways to access email

Email is normally accessed in one of two ways:

► using an email package (client-based);
► using a web-based system.

There are many email packages available. Email packages allow you to store received messages to a computer's hard drive and send messages you create.

■ Figure 1.28

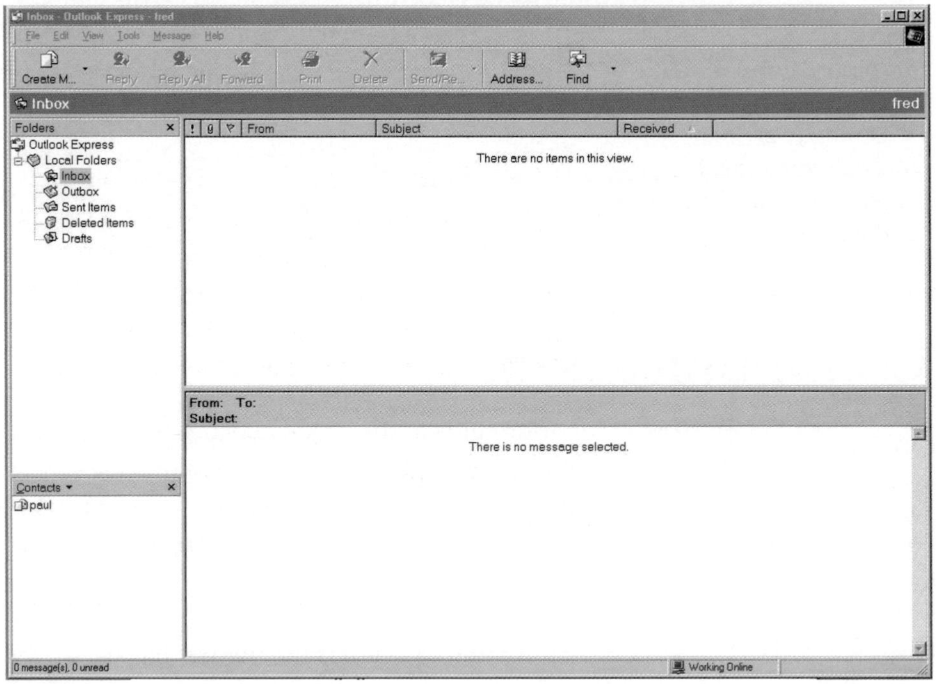

With this type of email package, you set up your computer with details of your account and password. The software links to the server and downloads any email waiting at your mailbox to your computer.

You can prepare emails at any time and save them to send later. This allows a businessperson to prepare emails whilst travelling on the train, read any that were downloaded before leaving the office and reply to them. On return to the office or at home the computer is connected to the Internet and all the outgoing emails are sent at the same time as any new ones are picked up. This is called preparing emails 'offline'.

Another way to access email is to use a web-based service. There are hundreds of free web-based email providers as well as some offered as a subscription service. Hotmail is perhaps the most well known of the free systems.

Using this type of email, you need to be connected to the Internet. You then go to the page for your service and log on. Many of the features of email

> SPAM is unsolicited and unwanted email. It is always a nuisance and getting rid of it can waste hours. It sometimes carries viruses, Trojan horses, spyware and other 'malware' (malicious software) that can damage your data or invade your privacy.

packages are available on this type of service. Most include an inbox, outbox and address books, just like package or client-based systems.

This type of service has the advantage that you can use any computer anywhere in the world to access your email. One disadvantage is that you must be connected to the Internet to use it. A further drawback is that some web-based mail services are very prone to spam. Sometimes a new account will receive spam before the first email is sent. This is because spammers automatically target random names at the well-known email domains.

ACTIVITY

Prepare a presentation to inform an audience about the respective merits of web-based and package-based email systems.

Using email

Most people compose email messages in an informal way. It seems to have become accepted that emails are not normally as formal as letters. Most people start and end emails in a fairly chatty informal way. 'Hi Pete' is acceptable in a business email although it would be regarded as unacceptably casual in a written letter. Many people continue this by not using correct sentence structure or punctuation. However it is important to realise that this is not always appropriate and that there are occasions when an email needs to written as carefully as a letter. If you are contacting a company as a result of a job advertisement on their web site, then a good impression needs to be made from the start. A chatty email would be regarded as unacceptable.

Many companies have rules for their employees to follow when sending emails both within and outside the company. Schools and colleges often have an 'acceptable use' policy.

ACTIVITY

Find out if you school or college has an acceptable use policy.

- Look up examples of 'acceptable use' policies on the Web.
- Write a report describing the features you find in them.

Companies often add a disclaimer to emails like this:

> The views expressed in this email are those of the individual and may not represent company policy or reflect the views of any one else in the company. This email may contain confidential material. If you were not an intended recipient, please notify the sender and delete all copies.
>
> We may monitor email to and from our employees.

Emails have the advantage of being almost instant, and can be sent to many people at the same time. They can also have files attached to them. However, although they may be quick and convenient you cannot send original documents with actual signatures which are often needed for legal documents. You can however send pdf attachments of scanned documents.

Instant messaging

Instant messaging is way of sending and receiving messages in real time while you are online. It is a bit like instant email. The difference is that you are connected to the Internet and logged into the service. When a message is sent to you, it pops up on you screen. You can reply as soon as you want to. MSN is a very popular service of this type (see page 19). The program *Messenger* is built in to Microsoft *Windows*. To use the service, all you need to do is to set up an account and away you go.

Once online to your friends or colleagues, you are able to have a conversation by text. Often, people will work on their computer and have the program loaded so that if people want to contact them they can do so.

It is possible to have several people in contact at the same time so that a whole group of people can communicate.

This type of system requires that you are online all the time you are using the system. This is not a problem with an 'always on' broadband connection, but if you are using a modem and a dial-up connection you need to connect first.

Chat rooms are special web sites that contain pages (often called 'rooms') where you can 'chat' with other people, often people you do not know. Most people in chat rooms use nicknames and the 'chat' takes place by typing in lines of text, and waiting for a response.

Chat rooms can be fun, but care is needed because you do not know who you are talking to. People in chat rooms can and do hide their true identity.

www.thinkuknow.co.uk/

Newsgroups

A newsgroup is a collection of messages about a particular topic that are posted to a news server by members. These servers then distribute the messages to other participating servers. There are thousands of newsgroups covering a huge range of subjects. People with a common interest often use newsgroups to share ideas or interesting information about the topic. Newsgroups are found primarily on *Usenet*.

Originally set up in 1979–80 by Steve Bellovin, Jim Ellis, Tom Truscott and Steve Daniel at Duke University, it has what is perhaps the largest decentralised information utility in existence.

Anyone can set up a newsgroup. They can choose who joins the group or alternatively go public and open the group up to anyone. Often the person who sets up a group stays in charge of the group and can moderate it. This means that messages considered to be off-topic can be removed or edited.

Newsgroups often consist of a number of *threads*. A new topic starts a new thread and all replies to that message are stored in order under the original message.

The illustration shows how a thread is displayed in a newsgroup, replies to the original posting are indented, each new level is indented further. It can get a bit complicated if you are not used to the way the system works.

Some email packages support the use of newsgroups and allow you to manage the groups that you subscribe to as well as to send and receive messages.

When you subscribe to a newsgroup, you can receive messages as emails or log on to check the group for new messages. You must subscribe to a

USENET: A worldwide bulletin board system that can be accessed using the Internet.

■ Figure 1.29

■ Figure 1.30

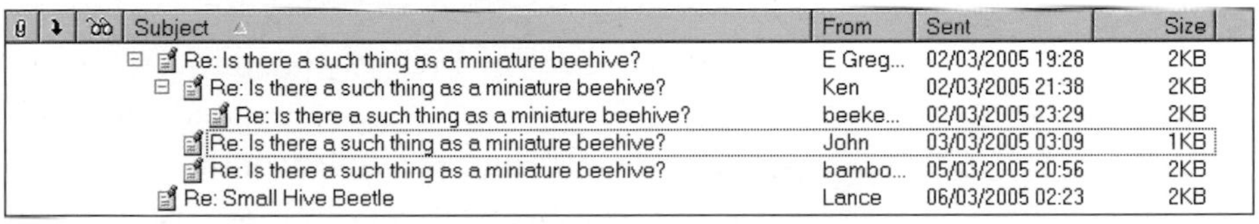

35

newsgroup to participate or to follow the discussions. Joining newsgroups can be a problem if you join too many. If a group is very busy and you choose to receive messages as email, you can end up receiving lots of spam and waste a lot of time cleaning up your inbox.

If you join a newsgroup it is important to follow the rules of that group: users are expected to follow *netiquette* (network etiquette). For example using BLOCK CAPITALS is considered to be shouting. Newsgroups usually have a new user section with rules about what can and cannot be posted. It is a good idea to look at this before joining a newsgroup.

There are also many abbreviations that can be used to make messages shorter, for example:

IME   In My Experience
IMO   In My Opinion
IMHO   In My Humble Opinion
IMNSHO   In My Not So Humble Opinion
IMV   In My View
LOL   Laughing Out Loud
TIA   Thanks In Advance
SFLA   Stupid Four Letter Acronym

Online conferencing

This is a system where groups of people can set up meetings on the Internet. Web meetings can be held with people from anywhere across the world. It is possible to hold a meeting that involves sending text, voice, video or a combination of these. Conferences can be online with participants talking and working together at the same time, but they can also be offline where participants leave messages for each other to read when they want to.

Cameras called webcams can be used to show the people taking part so that you can see who you are linked to. There are many companies offering software and services for online conferencing.

■ Figure 1.31

ACTIVITY
● Search the Internet for online conferences.
● Use your results to prepare a presentation about the benefits of online conferencing.

With a live conference, people log into the conference, sometimes using special software to take part. It is possible to show a presentation on one computer that is connected to the Internet and the presenter can be heard by all the other people who are logged in. The presenter can then receive feedback from people in the conference.

There are many advantages to this type of conference. People do not have to travel to take part and this can save a lot of money if people all over the world are taking part. However, as usual, there is also a downside. To use video or voice over the Internet really needs a broadband connection. There are still some places where broadband is not available. Also time differences throughout the world can cause problems. It may be three o'clock in the afternoon for one person but midnight for another. Nobody wants to get up and go to a conference at that time!

Online telephones

Many people are starting to make phone calls over the Internet. The wider availability of broadband makes this increasingly viable. It uses 'Voice over Internet Protocol' or VoIP. Using a headset and mike connected to the computer, you can call up and talk to someone else who is also connected. There is software available to allow you to do this for no charge.

There are also many services available that will allow you to make a call from your PC to someone who is using a normal telephone. Some services even allow fax messages to be sent from your PC over the Internet to a fax machine. Charges usually apply for these services, but the cost of calling other countries is often less than normal phone rates.

To use this kind of system, again you really do need a broadband connection and even then the quality of the calls is not always as good as normal telephones. The quality is affected by traffic on the Internet. Your connection may be fast, but all the links between you and the other person might not be.

ACTIVITY

● Research the topic of online telephones. Try a search for Web phones or PC phones.

Blogs

The term *Blogs* is a contraction of the words web and logs.

A blog is a kind of online diary of events in a person's life. Blogs can also be someone's thoughts on a topic or just on life in general. People kept blogs long before the term was in common use, but their use became more widespread with the introduction of systems such as *Blogger*. Thousands of people now use these systems to publish their blogs.

There is a need to be careful with the contents of a blog since they are open to anyone with Internet access. In one case someone lost his job because he said something derogatory about the company he worked for in his blog. It was seen by one of the company managers who decided it was so bad that that he should be dismissed.

Blog sites allow others to join in and reply to your comments or the comments of others. The art of blogging is big in the USA and it will presumably spread further afield. Those who think that politicians don't listen can use blogs to make views public and possibly gather a lot of support.

> An online community of bloggers performs the same function as yesteryear's town meetings. Through the tradition of town hall meetings, officials were held to account by local people.
>
> Iain Duncan Smith
> Saturday February 19, 2005
> http://www.guardian.co.uk/comment/story/0,,1417983,00.html

Some blogs are started by organisations.

■ Figure 1.32

You can easily set up your own blog.

■ Figure 1.33

coursework_tip

Try to consider the intended audience for any of the services you are looking at.

It is certain that virtual communities will become more important in the future.

ACTIVITY

- Look for some blog sites that interest you. Are there any that help with your studies? Perhaps you could set one up.
- Think of any disadvantages in the widespread use of blog sites to help students with their studies.

Real-time information

One of the advantages of the web for providing information is that it can be updated quickly and easily. It is possible to update the information automatically from remote locations. With the DHL delivery system (see page 20), when a parcel is delivered, the bar code is scanned and the customer signs on an electronic device. The device then sends this information by radio link to the central DHL system. The fact that the parcel has been delivered is then shown on the tracking system on the web.

It is possible to see the arrival and departure times of trains on a real-time system on the Internet using Network Rail's live departure boards.

Another example for which a real-time system is used for booking theatre tickets (see page 20). When you reach the page to book the seats, the system locks those seats for a short period of time to enable you to complete the booking. That way two people cannot book the same seats. When you complete the booking the seats are then reserved for you.

■ **Figure 1.34**

Birmingham New Street Train Times - Microsoft Internet Explorer

http://www.livedepartureboards.co.uk/ldb/summary.aspx?T=BHM

- Call TrainTracker™ on 0871 200 49 21 for Birmingham New Street or text BHM to TrainTracker™ Text on 484950.
- **Information about Birmingham New Street station.**
- These train times are produced by an automated system. **Our disclaimer** explains its limitations.
- This page does not automatically update. **Click here for a version that automatically updates every 2 minutes.**
- **Click here for details of engineering works and service alterations.**

Station overview

Last updated: 02/03/2005 09:49:22

From	Timetabled Arrival	Expected Arrival	To	Timetabled Departure	Expected Departure	Operator
Wolverhampton	0945	0948	**Terminates**			Central Trains
Birmingham New Street			Manchester Piccadilly via Stoke-on-Trent	0948	Starts here	Virgin Trains
Gloucester	0945	0949	Nottingham	0949	On time	Central Trains
Shrewsbury	0951	On time	**Terminates**			Central Trains
Birmingham New Street			Northampton	0951	Starts here	Central Trains
Birmingham New Street			Lincoln Central	0954	Starts here	Central Trains
Lichfield City	0951	No report	Longbridge	0954	No report	Central Trains
Longbridge	0953	0956	Lichfield City	0955	0956	Central Trains
Walsall	0957	On time	**Terminates**			Central Trains
Birmingham New Street			Shrewsbury	0957	Starts here	Central Trains
Birmingham New Street			Walsall	0957	Starts here	Central Trains
Derby	0954	On time	Hereford	0959	On time	Central Trains
Manchester Piccadilly	1000	0955	**Terminates**			Virgin Trains
Coventry	1000	On time	**Terminates**			Central Trains
Bournemouth	0945	On time	Edinburgh via Warrington Bank Quay	1000	1003	Virgin Trains
Birmingham New Street			London Euston	1000	Starts here	Virgin Trains
Newcastle	0958	1008	Bournemouth via Coventry	1003	1008	Virgin Trains
Plymouth	0956	On time	York via Leeds	1003	On time	Virgin Trains
Lichfield Trent Valley	1001	No report	Longbridge	1004	No report	Central Trains
Redditch	1003	On time	Lichfield Trent Valley	1005	On time	Central Trains
Northampton	1006	0959	**Terminates**			Central Trains
Birmingham New Street			Coventry	1006	Starts here	Central Trains
Birmingham New Street			Wolverhampton	1006	Starts here	Central Trains
Walsall	1009	No report	**Terminates**			Central Trains
Sleaford	1009	1004	**Terminates**			Central Trains
Hereford	1007	On time	Nottingham	1012	On time	Central Trains

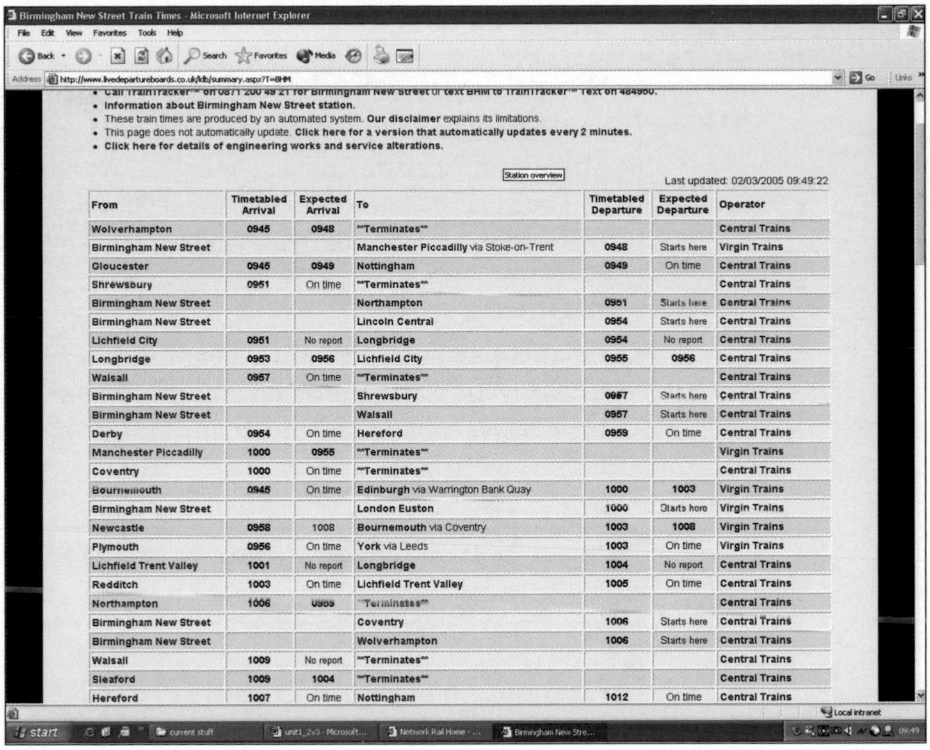

Commerce

Shopping

Online shopping has become a very common activity in the information age, almost anything can now be bought online either through major stores which have web sites or via auction sites. All the big supermarkets in the UK offer an online shopping service. The customer is able to choose almost anything that is sold in the shop and order it for delivery.

Shopping online allows the customer to look around for the best prices. There are some sites that do this for you by comparing prices in a range of stores and listing the best buys for you.

www.pricerunner.co.uk

ACTIVITY

- Carry out a web search for a major household item such as a washing machine or a television.

Shopping online can be good if you cannot get about easily, since you do not have to spend time going in and out shops and looking at prices. It is also possible that you will see a wider choice of goods. You may also save money by buying online (see page 131).

It is not just goods that can are purchased online. There are many other services that can be bought, such as life insurance and car insurance.

Some 'shops' only operate through web sites. There are a number of advantages to the shops themselves by trading this way. For example, they have fewer overheads and they can operate with fewer staff and smaller premises because they do not need a big shop in an expensive location.

There are some things that you do not get when shopping in this way. If you need advice about the item you are buying, very little is available online. In a physical shop, there are sales staff who have knowledge of the product and can offer advice about the suitability of your purchase. Also you have a place of contact if anything goes wrong. With purchases made on the Web, you often need to send things back at your own expense and wait to have them replaced, whereas in a shop goods can often be exchanged on the spot.

Banking

Internet banking has provided one of the biggest changes to the ways people manage money in the information age. Most people are paid directly go to their bank accounts rather than in cash, and increasingly, they use credit or debit cards to buy goods.

ACTIVITY
- Find out the difference between how credit cards and debit cards operate.

Many banks now offer 24/7 services which allow customers to log on and carry out a range of operations at any time. Features include:

- ▶ paying bills;
- ▶ transfering money;
- ▶ checking balances;
- ▶ looking at statements.

Many systems also allow people to apply for loans and overdrafts.

ACTIVITY
For your portfolio research, visit the web sites of some well-known banks and building societies. Make some notes of the kind of services they offer.

Internet banking cannot of course replace physical banks completely. You cannot withdraw any cash from an Internet bank, or obtain personal financial advice.

Auctions

In the last few years, a number of auction sites have appeared on the Web. Perhaps the most well known is *eBay*. They are becoming very popular and many people buy items from them because real bargains may be had. They are a very easy way to get rid of surplus goods as selling them by any other means just might not be worth the time or expense.

It is possible to browse the site and see what people have for sale without taking part in the auction. If you want to buy or sell anything, you need to set up an account to handle the transactions.

The system works like this:

An item is put up for sale by a registered user who places a description on the site. The user can place a minimum bid value below which they will not sell. A date and time is given to indicate when the bidding for that item finishes. No more bids will be accepted after that time. Shoppers see the item, they log in and place bids; the current bid being shown live online. At the end of the auction, the goods are sent to the buyer and the payment is passed through the site. The owners of the site take a percentage of the sale (this is how they make money running the site).

The obvious advantage is that you can save a lot a lot of money, but a disadvantage is that you do not know who you are buying from. Trust is needed on all sides for this system to work.

coursework_tip

Try to comment on what makes a service fit for its purpose.

Government

The British government web site is www.direct.gov.uk

All government departments and services are now available online. Every local council is also online. The domain name suffix.gov.uk is used for all government and local web sites.

CASE STUDY

Inland Revenue

One of the services that can be used online is provided by the Inland Revenue. The Inland Revenue is responsible for collecting tax on people's earnings as well as on their purchases and many other transactions. They offer a range of services that provide both general information and secure access for individuals to manage their tax accounts. A person can track what's happening at any time on any day.

Setting up an account needs to be done in a way that is verified, secure and confidential. You cannot just log on and set up an account. As part of the process of logging on, an ID and activation code are posted to the person's address that is held on the Inland Revenue's records. Only after they have registered fully can they access their individual part of the site.

Once people have set up their accounts, it is possible to see exactly what the position is with their tax affairs. They are able to send online tax returns later than by post. The deadline for paper returns to reach the offices is the end of September. Online returns have until the end of December.

There have been some problems. Recently, some people couldn't make their returns on time because the system crashed: too many people tried to make their returns at the last minute.

coursework_tip

Investigate two or three services provided online by your local council. For example, you could look at rent and council tax collection, but there are plenty more. Include the results in your portfolio.

Another possible way that government can make better use of the information age is evoting. Instead of having to go out and vote at the polling station or use postal voting, voters might be able to log on to the Internet and register their vote. Again, security and confidentiality are very important to maintain the credibility of the voting system.

Although this is a new idea in Britain there are some examples of this in use in Australia.

ACTIVITY

- Use the Internet to research electronic voting in Australia.
- Try to collect some opinions for and against the scheme for your portfolio.

Education

Another big use for online services is in the education sector. Online learning is not just for schools and colleges but is also available to people at all stages of their lives.

The British Government has made many grants available to people to participate in what they call *lifelong learning*, and many companies have been formed to provide online materials for courses.

One example you may have heard of is the European Computer Driving Licence, set up by The British Computer Society and sometimes called the ECDL. There are many providers of this qualification, which trains people in many basic aspects of computer use. At the end of the units of learning, you can choose to take a test and build up towards a qualification that is well recognised.

ACTIVITY

Look at the web site www.ecdl.co.uk and make some notes for your portfolio about the ECDL qualification.

Virtual learning environments (VLE)

Virtual learning environments are being used to provide tuition in a number of different ways, including conventional classroom use, offline distance learning and online learning.

The idea is to provide different ways of learning so that people can progress at their own pace. VLE systems provide a variety of facilities such as:

► breaking down the work into units so it can be assessed and recorded;
► keeping track of the activities and achievements of students;
► providing online tutor support;
► providing other communications, including email and group discussion to help with the work.

coursework_tip

Think about the limitations and benefits of a service and comment on them.

Sometimes sessions are set up where a tutor is online at set times in a chat room type of environment that is only available to those registered on the course. Students can then ask questions, get answers in real time and see the questions and answers of others.

Business

This section looks at how business can be conducted using online technologies. The world of business has a constant need to create opportunities for people to work together. The fact that the Internet spans the globe and is already an established communications system means that it is ideal for providing these opportunities.

The business world uses these communication methods in a variety of ways to help make things easier and more cost effective.

Video conferencing

Video conferencing is a way of connecting two or more locations by a video link using televisions and cameras.

■ Figure 1.35

ISDN (INTEGRATED SERVICES DIGITAL NETWORK): This is a dial-up digital service that provides fairly high-speed data links between devices. It is charged by the time that it is open. This is different from a dedicated link where a line is rented and open all the time.

The locations are often connected directly using an ISDN telephone line to carry the data. The video and audio quality is quite good using a direct link, since the line only carries the video data. The cameras used are special ones that convert the images into a data stream that is sent along the special line linking two machines. One unit calls the other in the same way as a phone call is made.

It is also possible to connect to another location using the Internet as a transmission medium. To do this at an acceptable level of quality, both parties must have a broadband connection to the Internet. Even then, the amount of data on other parts of the link might make the quality unsatisfactory.

The idea is that the use of the video link means that you do not have to be in the same location to meet: travel is avoided. International time differences may cause some problems. Often firms set up expensive video conferencing links but never use them. Sometimes when they are just too much trouble and they can seem to be just a gimmicky add-on to their office facilities. Sometimes a speaker addresses a room full of people over this kind of link it is not the same as having the person in the room talking to you as the immediacy is lost.

Collaborative working

Many businesses need to get people working together to combine ideas and expertise in certain areas to plan and make proposals (see page 18). Many things are better when two or more people work together as ideas can be exchanged, shared and then refined until a consensus is reached.

The Internet provides a ready-made system of communication that makes sharing ideas in this way much easier.

At a very simple level email allows two or more people to share ideas quickly and easily. Using some of the more sophisticated systems that the Internet provides, such as online conferencing, makes collaborative working even more powerful.

ACTIVITY

- Look back at the communication systems already described.
- Choose three of them and for each one describe the advantages they have for collaborative working.

Business networks

Business and professional networking offers the opportunity to share ideas, contacts and most importantly, referrals between businesses.

Groups of companies get together to share ideas and help each other. The idea is that by working as a team they achieve more. To set up a network of this kind requires communication between members. Here again the Internet provides a cheap and ready-made method of exchanging information.

Business networks can be in the form of a web site which provides support for new businesses. Basic information can be provided in this way to help set them up and get going.

www.sustainable.org.nz
www.fbn-i.org

Entertainment

The ability of computers to handle multimedia means that they are ideal for entertainment in many forms. These range from computer games to playing DVDs.

Once you add the Internet a whole new dimension becomes available. One example is multi-user games. Players use the Internet to provide communication between their computers or games consoles and are then able to interact with each other in the game.

Some web sites provide online games. The use of programming languages such as Java to embed applications in web pages has made it easy to run games simply by connecting to the web and going to the site. There are plenty of interactive games available in this way.

Many games consoles now have the ability to connect to the Internet using wireless networking so taking part in an interactive game is easy to set up.

Radio

Radio stations now broadcast on the Internet. This allows people to listen to radio stations even though they may be in another country or out of range of the signals. Local radio is a good use of this as their transmitters only cover a limited area of up to about 50 miles in diameter. Once outside this area the signal is lost. Using the Internet it becomes possible to listen to your local radio station from any Internet connection. Some radio networks also record shows that you can listen to them on the Internet at your convenience.

Video

Video can be played back on computers with suitable software. Video clips can be downloaded and saved on to disk. It is possible to fit TV cards into computers so that they can receive both terrestrial and digital TV. You need a reasonably powerful computer to handle live video action in this way. If your computer has a large enough hard drive, then you can record programmes in the same way as a video recorder. Also because hard drives provide direct access it is possible to pause live TV, for example to answer the phone, and then continue where you left off. The computer will record the program and play back the earlier bit at the same time.

> DIRECT ACCESS: A method of file access where any part of a file can be retrieved without having to read through the rest of it. Direct access is only possible with disk storage, that is not with tape.

Download services

Music

The ability to store files of music in a form such as MP3 has lead to one of the fastest growing sectors of the music industry. There are many legal sites now selling music files. When MP3 files first started to be available online, the sales of millions of music albums were lost. The ease of downloading, and the fact that when you take a digital copy no quality is lost, means that illegal copies were quick and easy to obtain.

This format is capable of a 10:1 compression with no noticeable loss in quality. Previously, a three minute song would take 30 MB when stored as a .war file, but only between 2 and 4 MB when converted to an MP3 file. Typically 1 MB is equal to one minute of music. Cutting down on file size makes it possible to transmit files more easily over the Internet and less storage space is needed on your hard drive as well.

> MP3 is a compression format for audio files. It uses a method called MPeg 1 Audio Layer 3. MPEG stands for Moving Pictures Expert Group.

coursework_tip

To fit your work into the space allowed by the exam board you might have to use compression techniques.

The web site owned by a firm called Napster was closed down by legal action brought about by the music industry. The site quickly set up systems to sell the music and distribute it legally. Legal downloads have now started to outsell CDs.

Upgrades

When you buy software such as virus checkers on CD they are already out of date! The time taken to produce the CD and distribute it to the shops is enough for many new viruses to appear. It is necessary to keep up to date so that fixes for all the latest viruses are regularly installed on your computer.

All software becomes out of date at some time and companies frequently make updates available for download.

PATCH: An addition to an existing computer program in order to fix a problem discovered after release.

Microsoft continually releases updates called *patches*. Computers with the Windows XP operating system check with the Microsoft web site at regular intervals and automatically download any updates. When updates are released, a popup message appears to alert the user that they are ready for download. It is possible to ignore these or even turn them off. However, if you want to keep your data as secure as possible this is not a good idea.

■ **Figure 1.37**

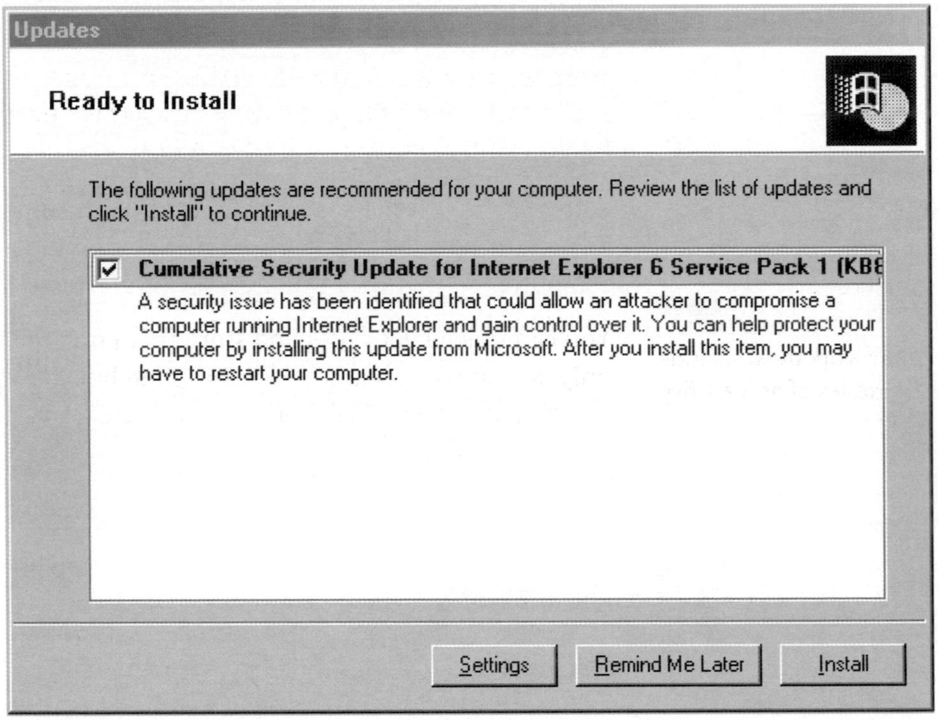

Devices such as printers and scanners need programmes called *drivers* to be loaded onto your computer before they will work. The makers usually have web sites where the latest drivers can be downloaded. People often lose the installation disk that came with a device so when they get a new computer the drivers can be replaced online.

ACTIVITY

You have been asked to set up an HP 1220c printer by a friend who has lost the drivers for the printer. Look at the Hewlett Packard web site and see if you can find the drivers you need.

Software

Software called *shareware* is available from web sites like *Tucows*. This site contains thousands of programs: you can find a program for almost anything. Once downloaded, you can install and use the shareware free of charge for evaluation. The idea is that if you like the software you register it by paying a fee and then continue to use it.

Many of the screenshots in this book were originally made and amended using cheaply available shareware.

ACTIVITY Visit a shareware web site such as Tucows and make a note of the most popular (and common) types of software on offer.

Archiving

X-drives

X-drives are servers on the web that allow people to store files up to a certain size limit. Some require payment, others are free. The safety of online storage can be a concern. If you have files that you want to be sure are confidential, you will probably not save them onto such a site. You do not know who has access to the files. A hacker could get to them without you knowing. They are not a very good idea for storing next year's exam papers!

Keeping back-up copies of files is a recommended way of working. If you do not have access to any other means of back-up then these online storage systems can be a life saver. Yahoo has its 'briefcase' which is a free service. You can upload your files and store them on their web server provided. Not only do you have that important backup but you can access your files from any Internet-connected computer. It is also possible to set these up for sharing by others.

coursework_tip

Your work **must** include examples of at least five online services.

Life in the Information Age

Aims

■ To look at a wide cross-section of human activity.

■ To examine some of the ways in which these have changed in the Information Age.

Most aspects of our lives have been greatly affected by the rapid changes brought about by the Information Age. On the whole, most would probably agree that these changes are for the best. After all, we have access to more information and services than ever before. This increases freedom of choice and in many cases reduces costs. The whole economy of a country can benefit from the widespread use of IT. But there are always costs to go with the benefits. We need to be aware of these costs so that we can take what we need from the Information Age without suffering too many of the ill effects. It is in everybody's interests to be well informed.

This chapter takes a look at some aspects of our lives that have changed and are still changing as a result of the explosion of information. You should bear in mind that the changes are so great that only some examples can be included in this chapter, but you should get some ideas for your own research.

portfolio_tip

You will need to find out a lot about life in the Information Age by yourself, so as you go through this chapter, you will need to undertake your own research and keep a well-organised record of material that may be useful to you, preferably in a directory specially set up for the purpose.

Don't forget that you *must* make use of a variety of information sources. The Internet alone is not enough.

A good plan is to scan the newspapers and magazines for IT-related stories. These can act as useful pointers for follow-up activities such as emailing people for first-hand knowledge.

A further excellent way to find lots of relevant material is to look at the IT trade magazines and newspapers. *Computing* and *Computer Weekly* are always full of useful material such as:

● the latest developments in the IT industry;
● IT horror stories and failed projects;
● job advertisements (these show you what skills are most in demand);
● letters (these give you insider views of what the professionals are thinking);
● reports from professional bodies such as The British Computer Society (look at their web site as well, it is full of interesting and up-to-date material).

Work practices

In Chapter 1.1 we took a brief look at how the Information Age has affected how people work. We saw how there is now a blurring of the distinction between work and home life because it is now so easy to access work-related resources from home as well as when on the move. This has made it easier to become productive, but it can also raise expectations of productivity and increase stress.

Word processors and making mistakes

Computers have liberated us from the fear of making mistakes when we prepare documents. In the past, if you made a mistake when writing or typing a document, you either had to cross out the errors messily or you had to start again. Word processors have transformed the way we write. We can write our thoughts down quickly, without having to be too careful about the order or the way we express ourselves because we know we can refine the work later, whenever we want. Word processors (and other software such as graphics packages) have become *thought processors*. They also make it easier to pass documents to others for editing.

Word processors and other common office software have also resulted in a shift in who does what in an office. There is now less need to pass all document production over to secretaries. Many executives produce their own documents, which removes the delays that were sometimes caused between dictating a document and finally sending it out in a finished form. Often-used documents can be accessed which then only need names or other brief details added. Alternatively, standard paragraphs can be assembled into the order that they are needed. The role of secretaries has changed. It is no longer enough that they can type. They need to be multi-skilled in the use of spreadsheets, email and a variety of other office software. Indeed, the term *secretary* is gradually disappearing from job adverts. You are more likely to see the term *personal assistant/administrative assistant* which covers a much wider range of duties and is better rewarded as well.

> **CASE STUDY**
>
> Dave is a fire prevention officer with the fire service. He needs to produce many legal documents and notices. The wording and even the punctuation of these documents must be totally accurate. Very little changes from one document to the next, only the address and details of the owner of the premises. He uses a computer system where all the standard phrases and paragraphs are saved ready for use. By selecting these from a menu screen, a document is produced: he just adds the necessary custom information. Most documents can be produced in minutes.

Surveillance of employees

IT has not only put lots of powerful productivity tools into the hands of all workers, it has also made it a lot easier for companies to keep a check on their employees. Everything that a computer user does can be tracked. Employers may track:

- emails that are sent;
- web sites visited;
- software used;
- files accessed;
- time spent on the network;
- key strokes pressed;
- number of customers served per hour.

They can also use CCTV to monitor where employees are!

The degree of monitoring varies a lot between employers. A company developing new products that is in fierce competition with another company may be more sensitive about letting information get out than one which is doing less development work. Some companies may be particularly concerned about emails being sent that may damage their reputation.

Employees also have to be careful about the personal emails that they send. A joke that seems funny to two people in the UK may cause offence in other cultures if it accidentally gets sent on. One such case simply involved a worker who intended to send a fairly innocent-looking 'sick' joke to a friend but accidentally sent it to everyone in her address book, including a senior manager in the company in the USA, who did not appreciate the humour at all. The worker lost her job. Other companies are much more relaxed about employees sending private emails. The attitude depends on the company concerned. It is important that workers understand exactly what the culture is in their company.

Companies have to strike a balance between protecting their interests and reputation and allowing their employees a reasonable amount of freedom to act responsibly. If there is doubt, then a sensible company will issue all of its staff with an 'appropriate use' policy so that all employees know where they stand.

Teleworking

Increasingly, people work from home for at least part of their working week. By having a computer and a fast Internet connection, it is possible to free up expensive office space and save commuting time and expense. Working at a location remote from the office and communicating by IT methods is known as teleworking.

Teleworking has brought about a considerable increase in freedom which can greatly enhance the quality of life. People who may find it difficult to travel to work (such as mothers of young children) can remain in profitable employment. It also becomes feasible to live further away from the office which can allow relocation to areas with cheaper housing or a more pleasant environment.

Mobility

Increasingly, people expect to be able to work when they are on the move. We have already looked at how people use their laptops on trains and planes. Not only can they get on with work that otherwise would have been done at the office, they can also often access their company's network. Sometimes, the use of otherwise 'dead time' can liberate more time for leisure when at home.

The technology for doing this is varied. Many hotel rooms are now equipped with network access points where travellers can plug in their laptops and gain access to the Internet. There is usually a charge for this service although it is often a 'per day' fee rather than timed so if there is a lot of work to do, it can be quite economical.

Hotels also often offer WiFi access points so that users can connect to the Internet via a wireless link. The effectiveness of this service is quite varied. Often, wireless access does not work in the hotel bedrooms because the radio waves do not penetrate all the walls very well. The wireless access is therefore often limited to public spaces. It is also important to consider the security of your data when connected to these systems because they are public and no security settings can be used.

Many hotels provide a 'business centre'. This is a room equipped with all the facilities you would expect in a typical office. Again, for a charge, you can use the hotel's computers which are connected to the Internet and you also have access to fax machines and photocopiers. Often, the best thing about these business centres is the help that you can get if you have any particular requirements. The staff will normally be very happy to provide stationery and send letters for you as well as provide copying services.

> **ACTIVITY**
>
> Go to the web sites of a few hotels that you know about (possibly local ones) and find out what they offer in terms of business support services. Find out:
>
> ● what they charge;
> ● whether they have broadband Internet access;
> ● if they have Internet access in the guest rooms.

If you travel on business, or sometimes if you are just a commuter, it may be expected that you can be contactable at all times and that you can continue to do productive work. This is a new approach to working compared with only a few years ago and it takes some adapting to if you are not used to it. It is very reassuring if you can keep on top of things wherever you are; there is much less worry that you are losing valuable time when travelling or that you will be hopelessly behind when you get back to the office. The danger is when you let this work ethic dominate times when you should be relaxing. It can be really hard to switch off, both psychologically as well as literally! Sometimes, the need to break free is apparent when you see a business person on a train tapping madly at a keyboard and when you look more closely you might see Tomb Raider on the screen rather than a spreadsheet!

This trend is continuing very rapidly with the development of many more portable computing and communications devices.

The expansion of work into every part of life can be more than just stressful: the abundance of information can actually be counter-productive. 'Information overload' is a concept that is increasingly recognised and means there is just too much to really understand.

Education

Virtually everyone has to use IT at work, whatever they do. Very few occupations are entirely free of some hands-on IT. Those who cannot cope with basic skills such as word processing and file handling are at a big disadvantage and their prospects for promotion are seriously reduced. For example, all managers use spreadsheets for planning and summarising information.

In the UK, all school pupils receive a basic amount of IT education from their earliest days. In some countries this is not the case and school leavers can be at a disadvantage in the world markets. There is much debate about whether the IT that children learn in schools is the right sort. Years and years of basic word processing and Microsoft PowerPoint presentations can go only so far in equipping pupils for the IT they will need in the workplace. Businesses never cease to complain that they just cannot get enough people with the right sort of skills to help them make the best use of IT. They are not talking about a lack of word-processing skills, but more often the rarer skills of sharp-end IT development. We shall look more at this later in this chapter.

ACTIVITY

Go to your usual search engine and type in 'skills shortage' as a search string. Take a look at what skills businesses are currently worried about.

SEARCH STRING: The words that you enter into a search engine for it to look up web sites, news groups or images.

Retraining and job mobility

Training is more of an issue than it was a few years ago. People often used to get a job and then stay with it throughout their working lives. Often, they did the same thing for their whole career. The Information Age has not only brought about big changes, but also a big increase in the *pace* of that change. No longer is it expected that you will have a job for life, except in some of the traditional professions such as medicine or law. It is normal to change jobs every few years. There are great advantages to this changed approach which can bring about much more freedom than in the past and also much more job satisfaction. During prosperous times of full employment, if you don't like your job, you simply quit and get another one. You may have to move around a bit, but you do not have to put up with, for example, unpleasant working conditions or a bullying boss. More than ever before, you can be completely in charge of your life. In order to have this freedom, you do need to keep your skills up to date. You are more mobile if you have sought-after skills.

The other side of the coin is that there is less job security than there used to be. People who are easily hired can quickly find that after a while, their particular skills become less in demand. It is important not just to have currently usable *skills* but, more importantly, to also have the ability to adapt. You can find that as you get older, it becomes more difficult to get a suitable job, although if you keep up to date, this is not necessarily too much of a problem. Being able to understand the needs of a business and being able to communicate with others can be more important than being totally up to date with the latest fashionable skills.

If you change jobs frequently, you also have to take charge of things like your pension arrangements which previously were looked after by your employer. However, on the whole, this freedom can be very liberating and can lead to a more satisfying life.

Training remains a big issue. A good employer knows that providing training for employees not only helps them to perform better, it also increases motivation and therefore retention. However, you cannot always get the training you want and you might have to organise it yourself. This can be very expensive. Some industry courses can cost hundreds of pounds a day. To make it worse, industry qualifications have to be updated every few years. This is a particular problem for contractors, who have to find time and money to organise all their own training. The good thing is that a lot of skills and knowledge are available free on the Internet and, when it comes down to what matters, most employers are more concerned that you can do the job and have a good CV than that you possess any particular qualification.

Creativity

IT can be a great liberator by allowing things to be done that were not done before. Most workers will find that IT makes them think of ways to do their jobs. Sometimes new technology opens up new prospects.

Teaching has been changing a lot over the last few years: often because of IT. Many teachers regularly use software such as Microsoft PowerPoint to illustrate their lessons. This can be boring if not done well, but if full use is made of its multimedia capabilities, lessons can be much enhanced.

Being organised

Being organised is a much-prized asset. Sometimes, you can be more successful than others in a job because you are well organised. Being organised is often more important than raw ability! Very able people can let themselves down badly by losing important information. It is much easier to be organised when you have IT tools at your disposal. Paper records have to be put back after use. Sorting paper records can be very time consuming. It is a real pain to do this and when you are very busy, it is easy just to put things down anywhere. Later, you can waste hours looking for important documents.

Organising on a computer is much easier. The directory (or folder) structures that all operating systems provide give you a very easy way of grouping things that belong together. This lets you:

▶ find things easily;
▶ back-up a block of related work;
▶ send a group of related files to a colleague in one action;
▶ get rid of out-of-date work.

The ease of reorganising work can actually make it fun. One of life's little pleasures is highlighting lots of old redundant files and hitting 'delete'! If only you could remove real-life annoyances so easily! Fun is a great motivator when taking the trouble to keep organised.

---

portfolio_tip

Your portfolio must use multimedia to show what it can do. This allows you to be more creative in what you present for assessment. Make sure that you are aware of the capabilities of your software and that you use them to enhance what you do rather than just for effect.

DIRECTORY: A division of a storage medium which is used to group together files with something in common. Often directories are called *folders*.

portfolio_tip

Create a folder for all your portfolio work. Keep subfolders for clearly related subtopics such as your ebook. This is part of the section called 'standard ways of working'.

portfolio_tip

Warning! It is easy to reorganise work in folders so unless you are very careful and very awake, you might update a new folder with an old one, wasting hours if not days of work! Take care when backing-up that you replace the correct folder.

CASE STUDY

A sixth-form student called Karl set up a folder for his coursework. He created a subfolder called *ebook* and inside that, he created another two called *multimedia clips* and *text*. He did all of this on his computer at college and set up a similar structure on his PC at home. So that he could work on his coursework at home, he saved all his files into a single folder in a Yahoo! briefcase. That way he could download the work he did at college when he got home.

One day, he saved lots of new files at college and forgot to update his Yahoo! folder. He went home and while listening to his iPod, he downloaded the briefcase files, overwriting his old work. He did a little work and copied the files back to Yahoo!. Next day at college, he updated his files from Yahoo! and found that he no longer had a copy of anything he did at college the previous day.

ACTIVITY

How could Karl prevent problems like this occurring? There is no one right answer but you should be able to come up with a strategy that is more or less proof against forgetfulness.

Decision making

Because it is easy to collect information from all over the world and to process it, the quality of information available to people at work has improved enormously in the Information Age. Business managers used to have occasional informal meetings with their subordinates who could provide them with general trends about how the business was performing (such as how sales were going). The Information Age allows managers to have summaries of information that are completely up to date and much more detailed and accurate. This enables them to make better decisions than in the past. Decision support software allows much greater control to be kept over business activities. It can help to filter information in order to avoid information overload.

Project management software also allows better planning because it is easy to gather together all the information that is required. A complex project can be divided up according to the physical and human resources required and the jobs to be done. This can also take account of which jobs have to be done first and which can be done in parallel with others. You will find that project management software can help you to plan and organise your own coursework because you will always have all the information you require about what you have done and what remains to be done.

If you have access to Microsoft Project, take a look at it and see how it can help you to plan your portfolio. Set up some activities that are relevant to the current state of your portfolio and use the software to make a Gantt Chart.

GANTT CHART: A graphical representation of how resources are to be used in a project over a period of time.

55

Collaboration

We have seen that IT can make collaborative working much easier. Email and Virtual Private Networks (VPNs) mean that it is possible for individuals across the globe, who live in different time zones, to work together without the need for travel. The personal touch is missing from such enterprises, but they can work well if supported by occasional face-to-face contact (see page 18).

VPN (VIRTUAL PRIVATE NETWORK): A private subsection of a larger network or part of the Internet to which only certain individuals have access. A VPN can provide a worldwide private space where individuals can collaborate on a project.

Communication

Email is steadily becoming the preferred method for business communication.

It is better than telephone because:

▶ there is no need to wait for the person to be found;
▶ you can send files as attachments;
▶ delivery is usually more or less instant;
▶ time zones don't matter.

It is better than fax because:

▶ there is no degradation of quality which there is in a fax image;
▶ there is no wastage of paper;
▶ you can send documents that you do not want altered by using PDF files.

It is better than ordinary mail because:

▶ it is quicker;
▶ it is cheaper;
▶ it is more reliable.

Of course, there are drawbacks too, which were looked at in Chapter 1.2. There are issues of privacy, viruses and spam, but as with most IT developments, the advantages outweigh the disadvantages.

PDF (PORTABLE DOCUMENT FORMAT): A file standard for documents where the document is received exactly as in the original. There is no alteration due to different platforms or different software. The document can be protected if necessary so that legal documents, for example, cannot be altered. PDF is a proprietary standard owned by the Adobe Corporation.

Education

The Information Age has, of course, affected education just as it has affected nearly everything else. The effects have been on two main fronts: teaching and learning, and subject matter.

Teaching and learning methods

Teachers have gradually made more use of IT facilities in order to do their job. All subjects and all levels have been affected.

The Internet has provided an easily accessible and massive information source on everybody's desk. Teachers of all subjects can now ask their pupils to look up material on the Internet in the knowledge that there is certainly useful material 'out there'. A good teacher will not leave it totally up to the pupils but will provide links and hints in order to make the best use of the lesson time.

Data projectors have made it very easy to show a group information resources or prepared lesson notes. Software such as Microsoft PowerPoint has made it easy for any teacher to give a very slick presentation without the need to write and rewrite the same notes on a whiteboard every lesson. Notes can be purchased or shared, thereby releasing time that the teacher used to have to spend in laboriously preparing and writing lesson notes. Increasingly, these chores can be shared and adapted rather than started from scratch every time.

Interactive whiteboards are common now and this further liberates the teacher from mice or keyboards. Also, materials developed during a lesson can be downloaded to pupils' computers, thereby making sure that they have accurate materials from the lessons.

■ Figure 1.39

ACTIVITY

Make a log of all your lessons and lectures for a week. Record

- how many made use of IT to any extent;
- how many used IT in their delivery;
- which ones used data projectors;
- which ones used interactive whiteboards;
- which ones used networked demonstrations.

At the end of this, rate them according to whether the IT actually helped you to keep interested and to understand what was being covered.

portfolio_tip

This sort of first-hand evidence will greatly improve the value of your portfolio.

In the UK, the National Curriculum requires all teachers to make use of IT at some stage or another, whatever the subject. Although it can be argued that such central diktats can ignore individual preferences to no good effect, they have helped generally to move forward a more imaginative approach to teaching.

■ Figure 1.40

IT as a subject

The other important change in education is that in many countries, students now study IT as a separate subject; in the UK it is called ICT, but it means the same thing. The separate study of IT has many benefits:

▶ Very few school leavers now have no IT expertise, so they should be more employable.
▶ Pupils can make better use of IT tools in order to study and organise their work. A word-processed essay is more likely to be of good quality because there is the opportunity to edit and revise.
▶ Pupils gain a much better understanding of what is and is not possible if they are taught the underlying principles of IT systems rather than just using them.
▶ Some pupils will be motivated enough by the IT that they learn in order to take it further as a subject and develop an interesting and lucrative career in it.

Entertainment and leisure

In Chapter 1.2, you saw some examples of technologies that have affected the way that entertainment can be provided. Naturally, these new methods are changing the ways that we look at entertainment, but not always as much as you might think.

Music

Music is increasingly being downloaded instead of being bought on CD. Large amounts of music can be stored with perfect quality on the latest digital devices such as Apple's iPod. Listening to music on the move has never been easier or sounded better. But, this has not meant the end of live music. Live concerts are as well attended as ever, so it is possible that the new technology is increasing the appetite for live music of all kinds. Here, IT certainly does not turn us into antisocial zombies!

Films

DVD technology and the development of big plasma screens have made home cinema a much more exciting experience than ever before. The images and sounds are now of a very high quality and these, together with the huge range of films available on DVD, can provide a new dimension to entertainment. In the future, digital quality films will be available on demand on downloadable services.

It is unlikely that these developments will kill off traditional cinema. There is still a big demand for cinema showings, especially at the multi-screen complexes, because they provide a much-wanted social experience as well as the on-screen entertainment.

Games

Not all that long ago computer entertainment consisted of simple crude 'bat and ball' or 'shoot 'em up' games. Games were a lot of fun then, but in a very short time they have become much more sophisticated with the most modern video games being very impressive demonstrations of virtual reality. The very best ones are designed to be played on dedicated games machines with fast graphics processing rather than on ordinary PCs, and these machines can double as DVD players. The time will come when all these technologies will merge so that all the functions of music, films, TV and games will be accessible from the same equipment.

Some video games allow the players to indulge in graphic acts of violence and some people think that these games can encourage violent behaviour in real life. Thankfully, most well-balanced people are able to distinguish between fantasy and reality but it is probable that some violent crimes committed by disturbed individuals have been inspired by the incredible realism of these games.

Banking and shopping

Chapter 1.2 covered some of the services that are now offered by Internet banking. Our whole approach to banking has changed over recent years because of the facilities that are on offer. As in other areas, we generally seem to like the new facilities and eagerly make use of them after an early period of wariness.

Our lives seem to get busier all the time and anything that saves people time from doing chores such as queuing up in a bank is likely to be popular. Many of us make use of online banking now and, apart from saving time, the ease of accessing bank account information makes it a lot easier to manage our finances and avoid debt.

The criminal world keeps up with developments too and almost every week you can read about scams involving banking often perpetrated by sophisticated criminal gangs. The banks are reluctant to publicise how much they lose as a result of this as it could undermine confidence in them.

CASE STUDY

Cash machines sometimes have small scanning devices glued onto the card slot by criminal gangs. The device reads the card details and radios them back to the criminal sitting in a car nearby. A small video camera can also transmit the PIN as it is entered. The criminal can then clone the card and empty the victim's account.

Today, more and more of us are happy to buy things online. At the time of writing, 30 per cent of all adults have purchased items online. Some of the most popular examples of online buying are:

► concert tickets;
► holidays and other travel;
► groceries;
► books and CDs;
► computers and computer accessories.

Many people have been worried about using online services because of credit card fraud or uncertainty that the trader will really deliver what is wanted. Every time we successfully complete an online transaction, we are more likely to do it again as we gain confidence that we will not necessarily be cheated.

ACTIVITY

Suggest some ways that a person can judge whether an online business is likely to be reliable or not.

Employment opportunities

There is no sign of the information revolution slowing down. The 'pull' of business and customer demand ensures that there will be plenty of innovation in the IT world. This provides many opportunities for people with the right skills to have successful and lucrative careers. If a country has a successful IT industry, all its citizens gain from the economic benefits that it brings.

In the UK, there is currently a big demand for people with the right skills and businesses are constantly talking about the 'skills shortage'. Most businesses are now well aware how IT can boost their profits. More managers are IT aware and can see opportunities for increased efficiency or market expansion. What they need is an IT-capable workforce at all levels and also ground-breaking IT professionals who can move the business forward. We have already seen that everyone in a modern business needs good basic IT skills. A company that installs a new computer system should normally be able to expect its workforce to adapt quickly because they have already seen many systems in the past. They expect school and college leavers to be able to handle ordinary office software, the Internet and basic file handling.

Certain areas are in real demand and that is where the best money is. At the time of writing, the skills most in demand are to do with designing and building networks, web development (although this has to include back office applications these days) and programming (notably at the moment in C++, Java and the .Net environment). These premium skills are generally not taught at schools and colleges, often because there is a shortage of teachers who can teach them.

ACTIVITY

Go to any job recruitment web site such as `jobserve.com` or `fish4jobs.co.uk`. Make a small dossier of the jobs that are most in demand. Pay particular attention to the skill sets required, the money being offered and the location of the jobs.

By entering searches into these sites such as 'Cisco routers', you will be able to note the number of jobs currently on offer. You will also notice that the highest paid jobs tend to occur in certain areas of the UK.

The shortage of high-level skills is very bad news for the country as a whole although it is good news for individuals who have the most sought-after skills (until the next skill becomes flavour of the month!). To some extent, individuals can help themselves a lot by tapping into these opportunities. If you have learned how to program in Visual Basic, you will easily be able to transfer your skills to another environment such as Java. Programming will always be the key to getting a level of understanding that will bring rewards in many IT fields.

Despite a recent downturn in the market for IT personnel, the area is now recovering and those who are well informed and enthusiastic about IT will find plenty of well-paid jobs to choose from.

http://www.prospects.ac.uk/cms/ShowPage/Home_page/
Explore_job_sectors/Information_technology/As_it_is/p!empXje

Countries with more awareness of the need for IT skills are fast outpacing the UK in their production of IT graduates. The biggest changes are happening in Asia. More and more software work is now being outsourced to India, and China is producing far more IT graduates than the UK. They will be able to find work anywhere or, with global communications, there will be less need for them to travel physically to supply services worldwide. China is now one of the most dynamic economies in the world and its IT awareness is playing a big part in its success.

Possibly in the future, countries such as China will outsource the menial and low-paid jobs to the UK and other Western countries, keeping the lucrative development work for themselves!

ACTIVITY

Use a search engine to explore how China is dealing with its need for IT staff. This could provide some useful material for your portfolio.

Crime and Crime Prevention

The criminal records bureau (CRB)

Many countries now have central databases of offenders, which hold details of their crimes. This has taken a long time to come in the UK, but it is now possible to check on the records of anyone to see if there is a history of convictions that might be of interest in the solving or prevention of crime. One example of this is a mandatory CRB check that all teachers and others who work with young people have to agree to. This is to prevent previous child sex offenders taking jobs that bring them close to children.

In some countries anybody can check up on criminal records. This is yet another privacy issue that we need to make decisions on.

CCTV

The UK has the greatest density of CCTV (closed-circuit television) cameras in the world. If you take a walk through any city street and visit banks and shops, you will be photographed many times. The stored images can be used by the police, sometimes in conjunction with public appeals on TV programmes such as *Crimewatch UK* to track down criminals or witnesses. There are obviously many ethical issues here, but it seems, certainly in the UK, that the public is prepared to put up with such surveillance in order to provide some reassurance about crime prevention and detection. There are plenty of reasons why citizens might not take kindly to such widespread tracking of their movements. It could cause all sorts of problems if someone were featured on *Crimewatch*, possibly as a bystander, who had told people that he was in a different town on that day!

Development work is currently going on in which individuals caught on CCTV cameras can be automatically identified by facial features.

ID cards and passports

Many countries insist that their citizens carry identity cards. These often carry biometric data along with the usual details of name and address. Biometric details are unique characteristics of the holder's body such as a

■ **Figure 1.43**

retinal image or fingerprints. Biometric cards are likely to be particularly welcomed by airline operators because they will be able to perform checks on passengers as they check-in, and they hope that this will allow them to detect suspicious characters.

The trouble with introducing technology of any sort as a way of outwitting terrorists or other criminals is that it is easy to get hold of the relevant technology so you can be sure that the criminals will develop their IT capabilities just as the law enforcement agencies do.

Machine-readable passports

Most countries issue machine-readable passports. These contain lines of data that can be read by scanners. Information about the individual can be looked up immediately. The UK has been issuing machine-readable passports since 1997.

Identity theft

The Information Age has provided criminals with a host of new opportunities. One of the fastest growing criminal activities is where criminals gather people's personal details from a variety of locations and use them to access bank accounts or create new credit card accounts on which they run up huge debts. The bills then get sent to the person whose details have been stolen.

The criminals can do this because there are Internet sites where birth details and other information can be found. There are also many documents sent by post that carry personal details such as names and addresses as well as banking details. Particularly useful are items of information such as:

- ▶ bank sort code number;
- ▶ account number;
- ▶ card expiry dates;
- ▶ card credit limits;
- ▶ telephone number.

These documents can be retrieved from bins where careless people have thrown away bank and credit card statements that they have finished with. One recent survey showed that 80 per cent of householders' bins contained documents that could be used to forge an identity. It is a good idea to shred or burn all documents that include personal details when they are finished with.

Spam emails sometimes contain viruses or Trojan horses that transmit the user's keystrokes back to the criminal who created the virus.

Phishing

Many people are concerned about Internet banking. Many have been caught out by scams. One of the most well known is called *phishing*. This is a scam that uses email or pop-up messages to deceive you into disclosing your credit card numbers, bank account information, passwords, or other sensitive information which can then be used to access accounts.

Banks *never* ask for details by email, so you should never respond to scams like this. You can send on phishing emails to a web site so that evidence can be built up against the perpetrators.

www.antiphishing.org/report_phishing.htm

VIRUS: A computer program that is designed to copy itself. It may attach itself to other programs or it may be a stand-alone program, when it is then called a worm. Viruses often cause harm to a computer system.

TROJAN HORSE: Malicious software that is disguised as something else, possibly a program that you want.

On the CD is a copy of an email received by one of the authors (phishing.txt). Load it up and read it. It sounds very convincing. Some people have been taken in by emails like this but anybody who sends information is likely to lose a lot of money!

Here is some advice suggested by the consumer magazine *Which?* in order to avoid identity theft:

- Never use your mother's maiden name or place of birth as security passwords.
- Check your credit file annually for suspect applications.
- Shred all post before throwing it in the bin.
- Never use the same password on more than one account.
- Never carry details of your address along with bank cards.

Comment on the rationale behind these suggestions and add some more that would help to avoid identity theft.

Check through one week's mail that arrives in your home. Make a list of the items that contain information that could form part of a successful identity theft.

Civil Rights

Huge databases

We have taken a brief look at how organisations, including governments, are keeping more and more data about us on their computer systems. This process is likely to continue indefinitely because it is easy to do. Computers make the collection, copying and transmission of data very convenient. Governments in particular will always say that there is a need to do this so that it can better understand the needs of the population or because it will help fight terrorism or some other evil that happens to be in the news that week. Often, they don't even admit to what they have stored about people because the security services are not subject to the restrictions of the Data Protection Act (see the next section).

There is some justification for this attitude. There have been some impressive cases where potential terrorists or other criminals have been detected before they committed their crimes. However, many people are deeply concerned that personal data is being kept for more sinister reasons or that the data may not be accurate. One thing we can be sure of is that the process will continue. The readers of a time capsule about life in the Information Age may be surprised about how paranoid we were in the early twenty-first century. Or maybe they will think we weren't careful enough!

Government departments exchanging data

As well as holding a great deal of data about us, government in the UK has grown enormously over the recent years. There are more Government agencies employing more and more people. They unsurprisingly, share their data in order to make life easier for themselves.

Errors

Our dependence on IT systems makes it increasingly important that they are reliable and that they contain accurate data. If data is inaccurate, it can be a matter of life and death in medical or air traffic situations, but it can often be just very annoying and inconvenient.

Life is a lot easier for people with good credit ratings. If you have a history of defaulting on debts, you can sometimes be refused credit for further purchases or accounts. There are several agencies that keep credit records and most of us do not know who they are and what details they have on us.

It is possible to look at your own credit rating at one of a number of credit reference agencies.

https://www.econsumer.equifax.co.uk/consumer/uk/ forward.ehtml?forward=cr_online_sample

It is perfectly possible that a single missed payment on a loan such as a mortgage (possibly caused innocently or by a failure by a bank in paying a direct debit) can result in a bad credit record which can be very difficult to put right.

Legislation

As you will have seen as you have read this chapter and done research for your portfolio, changes in information gathering and processing have been so rapid that society has hardly had the chance to react sensibly to events. New opportunities and new problems arise almost daily, so trying to keep up is more or less impossible. Nonetheless, certain dangers of the Information Age have become clear and governments have passed laws in order to counter known threats. In the UK these include the Data Protection Act of the Computer Misuse Act.

The Data Protection Act

Many countries have passed laws to protect individuals against wrong data being held about them or data being passed around too freely. The need for laws of this nature arose because of the ease with which data can be transmitted and processed. When data was all paper-based, it was much less of an issue because it was far more laborious and time consuming to share data.

In the UK, the first Data Protection Act was passed by Parliament in 1982. It was updated in 1998. It established the concept of:

▶ data controllers (those who hold personal data)
▶ data processors (those who process data on behalf of a data controller)
▶ data subjects (those about whom personal data is held)
▶ the information commissioner (a Government-controlled office that keeps details of and regulates data controllers).

■ Figure 1.45

Data Protection Act 1998

1998 Chapter 29

Personal data is defined as any data about a living person who can be identified from the data.

The Data Protection Act has the following underlying principles:

▶ Personal data shall be processed fairly and lawfully.
▶ Personal data shall be obtained only for one or more specified and lawful purposes, and shall not be further processed in any manner incompatible with that purpose or those purposes.
▶ Personal data shall be adequate, relevant and not excessive in relation to the purpose or purposes for which they are processed.
▶ Personal data shall be accurate and, where necessary, kept up to date.
▶ Personal data processed for any purpose or purposes shall not be kept for longer than is necessary for that purpose or those purposes.
▶ Personal data shall be processed in accordance with the rights of data subjects under this Act.
▶ Appropriate technical and organisational measures shall be taken against unauthorised or unlawful processing of personal data and against accidental loss or destruction of, or damage to, personal data.
▶ Personal data shall not be transferred to a country or territory outside the European Economic Area unless that country or territory ensures an adequate level of protection for the rights and freedoms of data subjects in relation to the processing of personal data.

There are exceptions to these principles. For example, the Act may not apply when data is required for medical or state security purposes.

The Computer Misuse Act

This is basically legislation against hacking. It was passed in 1990 in the UK and defined three offences:

▶ **Unauthorised access to computer material**: This covers offences such as guessing passwords and having a look at confidential files. A term of three month's imprisonment can be imposed for this offence.
▶ **Unauthorised access with intent to commit further offences**: This includes situations where someone transfers money from one account to another unauthorised account. This carries a sentence of up to five year's imprisonment.
▶ **Unauthorised modification of computer material**: This includes deleting files and introducing viruses. It, too can carry a prison term of up to five years.

Many changes have occurred in the world of data processing since this Act was passed. Many new ways have been devised to carry out unethical or potentially criminal acts using IT resources.

ACTIVITY

Make a list of ways in which crimes can be committed by means of computers.

The Digital Divide

Aims

- To define the digital divide.
- To examine the existence of the digital divide.
- To examine the factors that have created it.
- To consider measures that have been taken to reduce the gap between those who have access to the Information Age and those who do not.

Introduction

portfolio_tip

You need to comment on aspects of the digital divide in your portfolio. What you say can be your own opinion. Collect a range of views and formulate your own. You may decide that the digital divide is nothing much to worry about. If so, start collecting reasons to justify your opinion.

Access to digital technology is now an essential part of life for much of the world's population who depend on computer technology both at home and at work. However for some, access to the technology is either limited or non-existent. The difference this makes is known as the 'digital divide'.

Those who have full access to IT resources generally:

- live in industrialised countries;
- are reasonably well educated;
- are reasonably prosperous;
- are able to take control of their lives;
- are young enough (at least in outlook) to embrace change.

Those who do not have full access may be:

- located too far from Internet points of access;
- uneducated;
- set in their ways;
- living in a country that discourages outside contacts.

ACTIVITY

Type 'digital divide' as a search string into any search engine. Take a brief look around some of the top 'hits' in order to see the varying views on what this is and how it affects people. Remember, this is a very subjective area so the issues are not clear cut.

The extent of this lack of access varies according to where and how people live. This chapter looks at the impact of this divide on people from a range of backgrounds and areas. The extent of the digital divide and its impact is constantly changing, so you will need to do some research in order to include the most recent aspects in your portfolio.

What is the digital divide?

The digital divide is the differences between people, families, businesses and geographical areas created by different levels of access to Information and Communication Technologies. This is particularly concerned with access to the Internet but it also refers to other computing and communication technologies.

The divide varies greatly in its extent as do the reasons for it. It has economic as well as social consequences. The extent to which these consequences matter is debatable. A large part of the world's population simply lacks any form of access to digital technologies. But it goes much further than that. People living in some parts of the world lack basic essentials such as food and clean water and access to digital technologies may seem to be a rather unimportant detail to them. Sometimes, the basic essentials are in short supply but access to the Internet *is* available. All sorts of different situations exist and this provides you with a good opportunity to undertake research and to formulate opinions and possible solutions.

Factors which create the digital divide

The digital divide is such a debatable issue that it is difficult to pin down just how much of a problem it is in a particular area or for particular people. However, there are some generally identifiable reasons why it exists.

Technological factors

One reason for differences in access to the Internet is the communications structure available. In the UK, all areas of the country have access to fixed line telephones and about 90 per cent have access to mobile communications. Access to broadband communications depends on where you live. Broadband connection is more or less essential if you want to get the most out of Internet-based services. British Telecom has set a target that 99.6 per cent of UK households should be connected to broadband exchanges by August 2005. When this happens, the country will have the best DSL broadband availability within the G7 group of countries, but when finished, about 100 000 customers still will not have access to broadband. It all depends on where you live.

At the time of writing, broadband signals have a distance limitation so that customers over 6 km from the exchange cannot have access. That gives access problems for some remote buildings.

In some parts of the world, the prospect of installing landline-based broadband is a long way off and, in these cases, wireless connections will play a more important role.

DSL (DIGITAL SUBSCRIBER LINE): A means of providing digital broadband connectivity by adding additional channels to existing telephone lines.

Economic factors

Being connected costs money. There are costs involved both for the communications company as well as for the user. Users of digital resources must have computer equipment which includes suitable software as well as a connection to the Internet. In the UK, it is necessary to pay a regular charge to your ISP and there may be an additional cost for the physical line that you use.

These costs are not excessive for people in industrialised countries such as the UK. Individuals who want an Internet connection can usually afford one. Household income to some extent plays a part in the use of digital technology although prices of hardware and connections are reducing all the time. Some people have other priorities than owning a computer or accessing the Internet. If a family is on a low income, Internet shopping may not be a priority.

Costs sometimes become an issue when you think about corporate access. For instance, schools and colleges have to pay a lot more for broadband access that is fast enough to serve a big network. For state schools, this has implications for tax levels. Not all voters see the need to spend huge amounts of their money on a resource that may be of questionable value.

In the UK and other economically developed countries, communication companies target areas of high population where the higher uptake of services will produce better returns for the money invested in the infrastructure. Government policy can affect the roll-out of connections because some areas benefit from development grants.

In the UK, all state, and most independent schools, are connected to the Internet, but only 20 per cent of *classrooms* have access. Different education authorities receive different amounts of Government grants and so the provision of computer equipment varies across the country. Rural areas tend to receive less in grants from central Government and this can make a big difference to the level of provision in different areas.

> **ACTIVITY**
>
> Think of reasons why a government might allocate more resources per pupil in a big city than in the country.

A visitor to a typical school in Birmingham will see a vastly greater supply of IT equipment than in neighbouring rural Worcestershire. Many schools there are still making do with old and obsolete equipment. This picture is repeated across the UK.

> **ACTIVITY**
>
> Look at this Internet link; www.bt.com/broadband/
> What advantages does BT think that having broadband access has?

The economic issues can have more impact in non-industrialised countries. The distances involved are often vast and the population density is often low, especially in rural areas. This makes the installation of the infrastructure particularly expensive.

It should be remembered that there are big economic benefits in introducing a digital economy, so once an infrastructure is in place, the country often benefits as it is able to trade more widely and develop the IT skills of its population.

At a global level, if food is short, a computer is not going to be a priority at all. Similarly, Internet providers are not likely to invest in an area if returns are going to be low as will be the case in many remote regions. This may change with developing technologies. Clearly, cable links are going to be more expensive to set up than radio and satellite links.

Many villages in Less Economically Developed Countries (LEDCs) do not even have access to electricity, so a computer would be of no use until some provision is made to provide power.

In most parts of Africa, there are only three computers for every 1000 people and the priority for many people is simply to feed their families.

Mobile phone coverage is more widespread and gives access to a range of services in some very remote areas. The use of satellite dishes is common in some remote areas of the world.

Generators and solar power are used to provide a limited supply of electricity in many very poor areas. A number of UK charities now recycle old mobile phones for use in other countries.

Only half the world's population has access to a fixed-line telephone. Broadband is not an issue when there is no IT infrastructure or power at all!

ACTIVITY

Make a list of some of the countries with the least access to the Internet. Can you also find out the GDP (Gross Domestic Product) of these countries?

Social factors

People differ greatly in the extent that they take advantage of the digital age. We have seen that most users of modern technology tend to be economically active and reasonably well educated. They also tend to be fairly young. Groups that use the facilities less include:

▶ pensioners;
▶ the disabled;
▶ those who are not 'plugged into' the world of credit cards and bank accounts.

ACTIVITY

Consider some groups who do not take advantage of IT. List some of the disadvantages that they face by not being actively involved in the modern digital age. Are there perhaps some advantages as well?

Younger people have a greater level of exposure to IT in school than previous generations and find the technologies much easier to use than some of their older counterparts. However there are many of the older generation who have adapted their skills and have taken onboard the Information Age: there are plenty of silver surfers!

One factor that is often neglected is that the Internet consists largely of pages that have to be read: IT requires literacy skills. Whilst illiteracy rules out a lot of things, not just the Internet, the lack of literacy skills greatly limits the benefits that can be had from using the Internet technologies. In the UK, we now have the strange situation of having unparalleled IT provision and Internet access in schools, but 15 per cent of 11-year-olds were not meeting the Government's own literacy targets in 2004! Some young people are using the Internet with quite poor literacy skills to play games, to follow sport, and to download games and MP3 files.

Culture

In some societies, there is differential access to digital communications imposed by local customs. Some countries limit the availability of access to the outside world to women. Perhaps this will change over a period of time just as other restrictions have.

Geographical factors

In the UK, small villages are less likely to be provided with cable TV because of the cost of providing the system in relation to the number of people likely to take up the service. Some telephone exchanges in the UK are still not broadband-enabled but dial-up connections are available from all fixed lines. Access is also available in one form or another via suitable mobile phones, although the service provided is not the same as that to a computer.

As explained earlier, at a global level, the distances in many countries are much greater than in the UK and the population density much less. This makes the cost of providing access greater than the income likely to be generated. We have seen that the introduction of wireless services could make this less of a problem in the future.

Fear

For some people, a lack of understanding of the benefits of the system can inhibit their use of the Internet. This can include not being aware of the financial and other benefits open to them. They simply do not see the need to use the services. In some cases this could be due to a lack of skills, confidence, or access to training, but in the UK it more likely to be legitimate fears such as privacy / fraud problems or sheer lack of interest that puts people off using the Internet services.

The number of people who are scared of using computers (the so called 'technophobes') is reducing fast, partly because of the widespread adoption of IT in all aspects of life and also because of the constant improvements made to user interfaces which make computers much easier to use. There are still quite a few (mostly older) people who are aware that there are good reasons to get involved in the Information Age, but don't know where to start. Often they don't even know what questions to ask.

> **ACTIVITY**
>
> Make a list of reasons why you find it easy to use a new piece of software.
>
> Look in your local paper or library to see what courses there are in basic computer literacy and who offers them. Do you think they look useful to non-specialist members of the public?

Lack of motivation

In some cases, people simply do not want to use the technologies, either because they remain to be convinced of the benefits or they simply see no reason to be part of the system. There may be very good reasons for this.

> **ACTIVITY**
>
> Interview a person who has not used the Internet. Try to find out why they have not done so and what their views are.
>
> Do you think you could persuade an Internet 'non-believer' to make the effort to take a look? What arguments would you use?

The impact of the digital divide

Economic

The digital divide has economic effects both personally and commercially. At a personal level they could include missing bargains, issues to do with employment and business opportunities, and as a means of making a living.

At a commercial level, plugging into the world boosts the amount of trade available to a business and also that of the countries where they are located. Opening up access to world markets boosts other local industries too, such as the businesses that supply the world trader. However, some countries cannot afford the investment. Others such as North Korea don't want to open up their economies to the outside. In some countries, businesses are not interested because the people there are so poor that there is no profit for them in return for the investment.

Social

In the UK, there are some who cannot afford new equipment, therefore they cannot keep up with the increasing speed of development. Although it could be argued that this is not an issue in the UK, everybody has enough money for quite a high standard of living, so connecting up is usually a matter of personal priorities. Studies have been carried out on the impact of connection on education, which looked at the development of children with home access and those without. However, with the provision of access in schools and the availability of access in the community, any impact has been difficult to measure.

There is little doubt that digital communications have made differences to our social lives. It is too early to make more than a few observations. Young people in particular use chat rooms and messenger services a great deal in order to keep in touch with friends, and sometimes make new ones. The use of language has altered greatly as well to accommodate rapid typing by saving letters.

Those with a broadband connection can communicate with others cheaply and fast so this becomes an important issue for the housebound and ill. This is particularly useful as once you have a broadband connection, you often do not have to pay any extra however much you use it.

Educational

In the UK, there is a lot of Government-provided IT access at school. Every school is expected to teach ICT and all UK schools are connected to the Internet. As we have already seen, the nature of the provision varies a lot. Even at a local level, there are different degrees of provision in different areas. Some as these provide added educational material as well as just access to the Internet. Many educational authorities have what they call a 'grid for learning' where all sorts of local services can be made available to their schools.

ACTIVITY

Many local education authorities have some kind of online education content.
There is also a National Grid for Learning: www.ngfl.gov.uk.

- Go to the National Grid for Learning and investigate what is available in your area of the country.
- Write a short article for your school magazine about one useful educational site in your region.

Some independent schools have much less to spend on IT than local authority schools and may in some cases not be able to provide as much access across their classrooms or provide newer and faster computers. They may also not be able to expose their pupils to IT in a range of subjects as much as in state funded schools.

ACTIVITY

Visit a range of school web sites, both in the UK and in other countries. Try to include state schools, independent schools, urban and rural schools. See if you can find out how much emphasis they give to IT / ICT both as a specialist subject and as a support to other subjects.

At a global level, schools can use Internet communications to increase awareness of other cultures. This can be particularly powerful if schools from different countries work together on common projects. These can help to improve education at all levels. However there are some areas in the world where access to even a basic education is limited and many children are forced into work at an early age to help provide food for their families. In these circumstances the provision of computer equipment will be of little concern. Lack of penetration by Internet communications can restrict the outlook not only of the pupils in such countries, but also of the rest of the world which will miss opportunities to see their points of view.

Cultural

The patchy nature of Internet connections across the world has affected and has also been affected by local customs and attitudes. In particular, there are some countries which severely restrict the degree to which their citizens can access the Internet. China places restrictions on certain web sites in order to reduce the exposure of its people to external ideas.

North Korea is a more or less totally closed community and its people are not able to communicate with the outside world.

Apart from curtailing business opportunities, such restrictions are intended to reduce the possibility of the country concerned being influenced by foreign ideas.

ACTIVITY

Enter a suitable search string into a search engine in order to find out which countries enforce restrictions on digital communications for their people.

www.freedomhouse.org/pfs2000/sussman.html
www.al-bab.com/media/articles/saudi000511.htm

Internet access is tightly controlled in the UAE (United Arab Emirates). All Internet access is via the ISP's proxy server and access to sites that go against Islamic beliefs are barred, for example pornography, gambling and dating sites.

The extent of the divide

In the UK, a digital divide between the haves and the have-nots is largely a matter of choice. We have seen that by global standards, there is no serious poverty in the UK and Internet access is relatively inexpensive. There is therefore less of a problem in the growth of ebusiness in the UK and other developed countries since there is a ready market for countless services. People want access to shopping and email so the other benefits such as access to knowledge come too. Many forms you fill in ask for your email address and it is common to provide online forms for many things. These trends show how the Internet is fast becoming a normal part of life for all of us, just as the telephone did.

ACTIVITY

Identify any group of people for whom the digital divide remains a reality in the UK and the rest of the industrialised world. To what extent do they suffer disadvantages because of it? This could be a useful point to make in your portfolio.

At a global level, the gap is slowly narrowing. More and more 'developing' countries make money by being connected. Places such as Bangalore in India have found new prosperity in setting up call centres for companies in the UK. These would not be possible without the widespread adoption of the technology. India seems likely to greatly improve its economic performance with the reduction in the price of computer and communication technology and the adoption of widespread connectivity. This in turn is likely to feed on itself and attract more investment, leading to yet more commerce.

Measures to narrow the gap

In the UK, pilot projects are being developed by the DfES (Department for Education and Skills).

portfolio_tip

You need to include some idea of measures, both global and local, that are addressing the closing of the gap.

A project costing £10 million in Kensington, Liverpool, regarded as one of England's most disadvantaged inner-city areas has provided 400 homes with connections to the Internet. About 2000 PCs are to be installed as part of this project. Whether this has a significant impact on the wealth of the community will take some years to determine.

In Brampton upon Dearne, South Yorkshire, all 1500 houses in the community are to be wired up and all the children at the local primary school will be provided with laptops.

In most parts of the country, libraries are providing free Internet access. Some schools are loaning equipment to pupils, particularly to those with special needs.

Increased competition in the telecom market has meant that broadband access has been made available more quickly, as companies race to cash in on the desire to connect at high speed.

It is debatable whether much needs to be done at Government level to increase the uptake of connections and reduce what there is of the digital divide. A hands-off approach generally allows free enterprise to provide what people want. Tax incentives to the communications providers would help them to increase the provision of the sort of fast access that businesses require if they are to locate in areas where there is currently little penetration. That would allow more employment opportunities outside the big cities.

The benefits of being connected are apparent to most people and demand will ensure that the supply is eventually provided. Affordability is less of an issue as prices come down. People will afford it if they want it. There has been no need for any Government initiatives to promote the widespread use of mobile phones: these have become an essential part of modern life for virtually everybody because people *want* them! When there is a demand for something, businesses will respond and if they compete with each other, prices inevitably come down.

The most effective way for a government such as that in the UK to reduce what is left of the digital divide is to keep the economy buoyant by creating a low tax environment which will help the business community to improve the availability of IT resources.

At a global level, more economically developed countries are being encouraged to recycle older technology by making it available to charities which send computers to countries were the technology is not as advanced. This can help a lot in the short term, but in the end there is a final disposal problem. The machines will soon be outdated and the cost of environmentally safe disposal may be too much for those countries and eventually lead to serious local pollution problems.

 www.computers4africa.org/

In February 2005, The World Summit for the Information Society (WSIS) in Geneva agreed to the creation of a Digital Solidarity Fund. It was agreed that a voluntary contribution of 1 per cent on the contracts signed by private service providers could be made to the Digital Solidarity Fund.

The fund is intended to help finance local community-based projects in areas where the development of digital technologies is slowed down by a lack of funding.

Benefits gained by narrowing the gap

In the UK, computer skills can help people avoid poverty and greatly improve their standard of living. For example many people use the web when looking for jobs (see page 59). There is also freely available information about how to apply for jobs.

- Look at the web site
  www.direct.gov.uk/Topics/Employment/Jobseekers/
- Make a list of ways this site could help someone to seek employment.
- What IT skills would someone need to access this site?
- What further skills would be handy to follow the advice given?

ICT skills and access to equipment can also help with acquiring knowledge that can itself improve work and promotion prospects. There are lots of online courses, some of them charged for, that can make a difference to someone's employability.

www.ecdl.com

Word processors can help students to develop confidence and self-esteem by aiding the production of better looking work. Increased access also helps in pursuing leisure interests and opportunities (see page 57).

By making it easier to publish and broadcast opinions and ideas (see page 38) increased access to the technology leads to more freedom of speech and a healthier degree of democracy. If more people feel empowered to participate in the democratic process then democracy becomes strengthened. Governments could claim greater legitimacy if they made use of the technology to access public opinion concerning their debates and decisions (see page 37).

At a global level there are benefits in providing increased business investment in some countries but this could be at the expense of others less fortunate.

Any increase in trade could mean more prosperity for all with international understanding and communication being useful gains as well.

Drawbacks to narrowing the gap

It is hard to argue in favour of maintaining a digital divide. We all benefit more than we suffer from improved communications. It is worth considering how far intervention is required in something which is expanding anyway. It is worth asking 'once connected to the Internet, what use will it be?' Research indicates that one of the most common reasons to access the Internet is to play online computer games. Should governments or companies really provide widespread access to games and similar material on the Internet?

However, any attempt to deny access to certain forms of content will be resisted. The freedom of speech in some countries is already restricted. Would the ease of online monitoring and censorship simply increase the ability of some governments to control access to information?

portfolio_tip

The foregoing has been largely a discussion chapter. The issue of the digital divide is very much a debatable one. You can take this approach in your portfolio. You do not necessarily have to come up with definite answers.

Ebook

Aims

■ To introduce the concept of an ebook.

■ To examine some of the components of a ebook.

The assessment for this unit is coursework based. For this piece of work, you need to develop an ebook. Before you set out to do so, you need to understand some of the principles behind ebooks.

What is an ebook?

An ebook is an 'electronic book'. It can contain a variety of information from a digital copy of a paper book such as a novel to a more sophisticated set of pages with which a user can interact. The content can include hyperlinks and multimedia, such as video, audio or animations.

Although the definition of an 'electronic book' varies, in its basic form it is a book in digital format that you can download to your computer or PDA and read using suitable software. The book can be available in a portable format such as PDF (Portable Document Format) which is a standard owned by the Adobe software company. PDF documents are read using Adobe's Acrobat reader program.

There are various commercial pieces of software available that enable books in electronic format to be read. One example is Microsoft's free *Reader* application, which can be downloaded as an extension to Microsoft Word. There are also book-sized computers that are used solely to read electronic books, for example Nuvomedia's Rocket ebook.

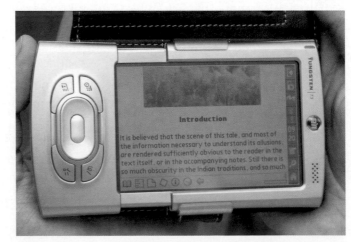

■ Figure 1.46

The idea of replacing a conventional book with an ebook has some drawbacks. A normal book is often light, very tough, (it does not break if you drop it) and is portable. It can be used almost anywhere (assuming there's enough light available for the reader to be able to see the pages). Many traditional paper-based books that are several hundred years old are still in existence. Books have been around for a long time and most people know how to use one.

Even with recent advances in portable electronics and computer technologies we cannot come close to the durability and convenience of a book.

The paper book has a familiar format. It is a collection of pages bound in a fixed order into a volume. However, the electronic book changes the way a book is formed and presented so the focus shifts from form (i.e. the type of paper, the cover, binding, etc.) to content and the way it is presented and made interactive. An electronic book is digital, so its contents can include anything that can be stored digitally: video, audio, images and / or animations.

Users can buy ebooks on CD, or as a downloadable ebook file from a web site.

ACTIVITY

- Use the Internet to search for information on ebooks.
  Do you think they are aimed at children or adults?
  What kind of topics do they cover?
  Can you find examples of any well-known novels or authors in ebook format?
- Use the following links and look at how one firm sees the idea of an ebook: www.franklin.com
  Who do you think this type of ebook is aimed at?

Examples of ebooks

Just as there are many purposes for conventional paper-based books, ebooks are also produced for many different reasons. You need to examine how ebooks fulfil the purposes for which they are intended.

▶ How do they meet the needs of the intended audience?
▶ What techniques have been used in them to help them meet these needs?

Children's books

For several years, ebooks have been primarily targeted at the children's market. Most very young children cannot cope with large amounts of text or longer words. There are electronic books that the child can listen to as the words are 'read out' and highlighted simultaneously. After all, children learn to speak and listen long before they can read.

To make an ebook as interesting as possible, the children are able to interact with the book by pointing (using the mouse pointer) to pictures, words and symbols in order to make things happen. Sounds can be attached to these objects on the page and the child can be engaged in the process of the telling of the story.

Creative writing

Most well-known authors have become popular because of the quality of their creative writing. They have an ability to convey their thoughts and ideas using the written word. There is nothing new about this; it has been the case for many hundreds of years. Good authors can build up a picture in the reader's mind without the need for pictures as books are, traditionally, largely based on text.

Reference materials

Some books are written for the purpose of providing information; they are used by readers for looking up specific references. This category of books includes works such as encyclopaedias, historical manuscripts and dictionaries.

This is an area where ebooks can provide more than simple plain text. For example, if you are looking for information about a particular musical instrument, it might be useful to listen to a sample of the sound it makes. Similarly, references to modern historical events could feature a text-based outline of what happened and an accompanying video clip. These added functions are all possible in a digital book.

Collaborative projects

Computer technology means that ebooks can be developed or used interactively by more than one person. The way in which they are stored electronically means that they are easy to edit, add to and link together, just as with any digital information. An ebook can be developed in sections, which can then be linked together when all of the sections are finished.

ACTIVITY

- Using the web sites below as sources of information, carry out some research on different types of ebook:
  www.bbc.co.uk/cult/doctorwho/ebooks/index.shtml
  http://ebooks.whsmith.co.uk/
  www.globusz.com/children.asp
- Choose one ebook from each site and write a review on that book.
- For each book,
  – state its purpose;
  – name its intended audience;
  – describe how the author has used the medium of an ebook to meet that purpose;
  – what features (if any) are used that cannot be found in a conventional book?

Aspects of an ebook

Content

As mentioned on page 77, one of the most important features of an ebook is that is not limited to containing text alone. The medium of ebook opens up a huge range of possibilities that cannot be accommodated within traditional books. The content of an ebook can be much enhanced, providing an alternative experience for the reader. Additional helpful features can also be built in. One useful add-on is the ability to search the contents for a particular word or phrase. This can greatly improve the usability of a reference book in particular.

Ebooks are very easy to copy. This makes the information they contain portable and allows for quick and easy distribution. The contents of ebooks can be downloaded from a web site or a network server, or sent to friends and colleagues by email. It is important to remember that just like paper-based books ebooks are copyright.

Structure and layout

Traditional books are linear. You normally start at the beginning and work your way through. Reference books are also arranged this way, even though you will probably use the index to find the exact place that you need. With ebooks, this process of finding particular references can be taken much further. The reader can move around the ebook by following links between pages. To make an ebook work well in this way is not easy. It needs careful planning so that the reader can gain the maximum benefit from the links that are included in the content.

The layout of an ebook also needs careful thought. The book must fit the computer screen. Some ebooks are designed for PDAs. For these, the layout should take into consideration the smaller and differently shaped screen.

Format and style

If an ebook requires special software to enable it to be read, that might mean the format of the book is restricted to way the software works. For example, you may need special programs to read some file formats, such as Microsoft Reader to read *.lit* files and Adobe Acrobat ebook Reader to read *.ebx* files.

Style is about the way an author expresses ideas. It involves the choice of words and suitable sentence structures to target the needs and expectations of the intended audience, and to fulfil the purpose of the ebook.

Multimedia components

Multimedia is the combination of some of the following:

▶ Pictures
▶ Sound
▶ Movies
▶ Text
▶ Animations

A good ebook will make effective and creative use of multimedia in association with the text-based content.

Multimedia should be used in such a way that really helps the reader of the book and enhances the information provided. Multimedia effects can be very irritating if they are used just because they are possible. A good ebook author uses multimedia sparingly and only in order to achieve a particular effect, or reinforce an idea or concept.

PDA (PERSONAL DIGITAL ASSISTANT): A small hand-held computer that has much of the functionality of a PC but is easier to carry around when travelling.

coursework_tip

A good ebook will take into consideration the amount of material that fits onto a screen, so that the reader does not have to scroll up and down the pages but can see each page in one go. Scrolling can be annoying, especially if you have a small and difficult to use mouse controller device.

Technical considerations of multimedia

The more that multimedia are used in an ebook, the greater is the need for the author to consider the equipment that is required to view the ebook.

Multimedia are a very memory-hungry additions to any form of electronic communication. Each image may require at least 1 MB of storage and a moving image may require up to 25 frames (images) per second. This would mean that a one-minute movie clip could require $60 \times 25 = 1500$ MB of storage.

Compression technologies can allow large files to be stored using much less space but when they are displayed there can be a delay while the file is decompressed.

ACTIVITY

- An ebook includes 20 full screen colour images and five one minute movie clips. Calculate the amount of storage required for the visual parts of this ebook, based on the example given.
- Suggest, with reasons, the most suitable storage media that should be used to store and deliver such an ebook.

Movies and sound need fast processors and fast displays. Without a screen display that refreshes itself very quickly, a moving image will appear jerky. The author of an ebook must take into consideration the fact that some readers may have less sophisticated hardware than others, and understand the implications this has for the development of the content.

Navigation

■ Figure 1.47

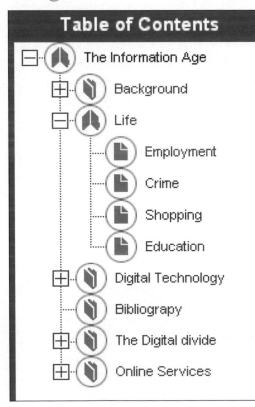

One of the main features of an ebook is the ability to navigate through the book in a variety of different ways. This will allow readers to move though the book in a way which they find best suits their interests. It should be possible to follow links easily and not get lost in the depths of the text.

portfolio_tip

Making the book easy to navigate is an important part of the planning.

Navigation is normally done using hyperlinks. By clicking on a link, the reader can move to a different part of the ebook. Links are used in a number of ways. Normally you will find a contents page, which links to the chapters in the book. A reader can then move to any chapter quickly. Sometimes the contents list is shown in a separate section of the screen, called a frame. Using this method cuts down on the amount of viewing space for the current page but it makes navigation easier.

Individual words on a page can be made into links. If this book were an ebook, you would be able to click on the glossary words and a window would be opened showing the definition.

■ **Figure 1.48**

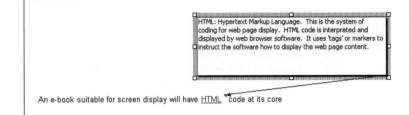

> HTML: Hypertext Markup Language. This is the system of coding for web page display. HTML code is interpreted and displayed by web browser software. It uses 'tags' or markers to instruct the software how to display the web page content.

An e-book suitable for screen display will have HTML code at its core

Ease of use / accessibility

If an ebook is not easy to use, people will not get the best out of it and they may not choose to buy that type of ebook again. It is important to consider the intended audience and their abilities.

Multimedia can be used to help make an ebook both easy to use and improve its accessibility. One way might be to provide buttons for some functions, such going to the index. These are often placed at the top or bottom of the page so that they are easy to see.

The illustration shows some simple icons for moving forward a page, back a page and going to the index (home).

■ **Figure 1.49**

> The Information Age

An ebook that reads the text out or is able to increase the size of the text may help people with visual difficulties to read the book more easily.

Some ebooks need special software or equipment in order to be read. This can reduce the accessibility of the ebook since people might have to buy the equipment or the software to be able to use them. They will also need to be familiar with the software before they can use the book. For the widest audience, it is best to work with a standard PC and software such as a normal web browser or Acrobat Reader.

portfolio_tip

In your planning, consider how you will address the issue of accessibility.

Fitness for purpose

Some ebooks are for entertainment, some are for information. The way they are written needs to match the purpose for which they were produced.

Adults will prefer more words and fewer pictures, however if the intended audience is a younger person, then fewer, shorter words, more pictures, sounds and music will be better.

Just as in conventional books, the way the book looks is important. The reader must be persuaded that it is worth reading. It must also conform to the standards set out for it to be loaded into the machine to be used. If the book does not conform to the standards required then it is not fit for its purpose

Developing your ebook

1.6

Aims

■ To understand the requirements of the ebook.

■ To produce the ebook according to the specifications.

Introduction

By now, you have had a good look at many ebooks that are available on the Internet. You should have seen a variety of approaches. Many are simply text-based reproductions of printed books, often these are free of copyright because they were written a long time ago. There are lots of examples on the Project Gutenberg web site. You will also have looked at many examples of ebooks that make use of multimedia techniques.

www.promo.net/pg/

There is nothing wrong with plain text-based ebooks for certain purposes. They won't do for your portfolio, but they are just the job when someone just wants to read an ordinary book but wants the convenience and versatility of an ebook reader of some sort. You could ask yourself whether many novelists of the past and present would write their books differently if they had modern multimedia techniques available. In most cases, the answer is probably 'no' because they would value leaving most of the impact of their work to their words alone.

Because the concept of ebooks is a new one in the history of books, we are still only just discovering where they are best used and what techniques are the most successful. Your own ebook gives you a chance to make some original decisions based on the research that you have now done. Your ideas may be as good as anyone else's because there is no great tradition established as yet.

However, there are certain principles that it makes sense to follow when you are putting your work together and this chapter looks at the issues.

> **portfolio_tip**
>
> You should make sure that you have evidence in your portfolio that shows you have considered the factors in this chapter so that whoever marks your work can see immediately that you have been thorough in your approach.

Remember, your ebook is about life in the Information Age. It must include:

(a) A description and evaluation of at least FIVE different types of online service, drawn together to give a picture of the current scope and limitations of the Internet as a whole.

(b) A description of how ICT is affecting at least FIVE different aspects of people's lives, considering the benefits and drawbacks, drawn together to give a picture of life overall in the Information Age. ☞

(c) A description of at least THREE factors contributing to the digital divide and some of the measures being taken to bridge the gap, with an evaluation of the impact/extent of the digital divide, drawn together to give a picture of the current situation.

(d) & (e) The ebook should:
- ▶ contain your work for (a), (b) and (c);
- ▶ demonstrate your understanding of multimedia design principles and your ability to use software tools appropriately;
- ▶ include some ready-made and some original multimedia components.

(f) An evaluation of your ebook and your own performance on this unit.

> **portfolio_tip**
> Keep a record of new skills you have developed as you create your ebook.

Audience

It is always vital to take your audience into consideration when you are writing *anything*. You only have to look at a range of newspapers to see different approaches to writing. In an ebook, you have even more choices to make in order to communicate effectively with your readers.

Here are some tips to bear in mind. You may well be able to make up some more.

Sentence length

It is usually good to keep sentences short, whoever you are writing for. Short sentences allow the reader to pick up information in easily digested chunks. Short sentences should certainly be used when addressing children, people in a hurry or when you are trying to get a point across with the greatest clarity possible. Longer sentences are more suitable for narrative passages, where you are trying to convey an atmosphere.

There may be a case for varying this at different points within your ebook depending upon the audience of the ebook.

Fonts

Fonts make a big difference to the impression you make. Many books have been written about the importance of fonts, but bear in mind that serif fonts are generally easier to read where there is a lot of text and sans-serif is better for short passages and headlines. The size of font that you choose will depend upon the impact you want to make at any point and also, on the screen that you envisage will display your ebook. You have the freedom to use colour as well. Consider foreground and background colours. Careful choice in this will also affect the impact that you make. Some colour combinations 'shout' at the reader. You will probably want to keep that to a minimum.

Links

You have the freedom in an ebook to include as many links as you like. These links will probably be within the document because Internet links are unlikely to be the same in 100 years! You need to consider whether the number of links you use is helpful in providing cross-references or merely a distraction from the narrative. Different readers will have different requirements.

Multimedia elements

Multimedia can make a big difference to the impact of an ebook, as you have seen in your research. A movie or sound clip is great for grabbing attention and communicating quickly, but these features are less good at providing lots of detail that can be studied later. You need to think about whether your target audience is likely to want a quick impression or something that can be useful later. For example, if an historian, a researcher for some media production or a research student wants to use your ebook in the future to gain insight into life in the present age, you will need to provide quite a lot of reference material that can be studied over a period of time.

Illustrations

These, too, are useful for impact. Readers in our own age have become used to seeing quite a lot of images in order to speed up the process of information gathering when reading any medium. You only have to compare the amount of illustration in present day newspapers with that included in the past. This is partly due to improvements in technology, but few newspaper readers would now be happy with a totally text-based newspaper. However, the reader of a novel expects few, if any, illustrations.

You will notice that different newspapers vary in the amount of illustration compared with the amount of text that they provide. Compare the 'red tops' such as the *Sun* and the *Mirror* with the 'qualities' such as the *Times* and the *Telegraph*. Just think about the different ways in which these papers try to communicate. Some give a quick impact that takes only a few minutes to read, others provide more information. You need to make very deliberate choices about this when designing your ebook. You may want to mix and match. E-book technology lets you have high-impact fast-absorption sections, with links to more detail for those who want them. This is the approach adopted by many web sites.

Possible target audiences

Historian

If you are primarily addressing a future historian, you will want to include as much factual data as possible as well as some less formal 'impressions'. Ask yourself, 'What will a historian need such a first-hand resource for?' The answer will probably be in order to compile his or her own reference work, maybe another ebook or futuristic equivalent. You will need to consider how to lay out the material to make it easy to research and it will be best if you include many cross-references to other sources so that the historian can check your accuracy.

School group

Pupils of the future will also find original source material useful. They will probably have totally different technology for accessing and reading your material, but you cannot guess what that will be. You can, however, organise and present your material in such a way that pupils will find it accessible and interesting. It is unlikely that children of the future will be very much different from today's in terms of wanting a variety of approaches and plenty of visual stimulus. That is biological, not just cultural.

Children of the future will probably like to see plenty of movie images and sound so that they can get as immediate an impact as possible. Just think how the grainy film images of the First World War still have enormous impact even today. The contrast between present day filming techniques and whatever happens in 100 years will probably increase the interest of your ebook rather than diminish it.

Adult in a library

Imagine someone in the future who is simply interested in our life today, maybe as a family tree research project or working for a degree at home. You will probably adopt similar approaches as you would for the historian, possibly with more personal references. Careful organisation of your material will make it easier for your future reader to copy whole folders that relate to a particular field of interest.

IT specialist

IT specialists in the future may be interested to see how material was put together in the early days of the digital age. To help people like these, you need to include some technical notes and a clear description of file and folder structures. You will describe the hardware and software resources that you used. It is unlikely that anyone except specialists will understand what you mean by a specific brand names so it will be useful if you provide some reference material taken from hardware and software suppliers.

It is likely that future authors of such material will have far more automated tools at their disposal, so the IT people of the future will probably be interested as an historical exercise just as we are interested in how computers and data processing have developed in the last 50 years. Make sure you provide plenty of technical information, possibly as 'out-takes' or links to glossary references.

> **portfolio_tip**
>
> Make sure the intended audience is clearly stated in your planning.

> **ACTIVITY**
>
> Make a detailed list of the hardware resources that you are working on at the moment. Include details such as the processor, the processor speed, the amount of RAM, the hard disk size, the screen and printer. List all the software that you are using at the moment. Don't forget to give full details of the operating system.

Purpose of the ebook

You never write anything without a purpose, but you may not always think very hard about what that purpose is. You might write an answer to an assignment and try to address what your teacher has asked for, but you will normally concentrate on answering the question. In real life you have to think much more carefully about what a particular piece of writing is for. What is it supposed to achieve?

Often people do not consider this very much. Just take a look at the letters page in a newspaper. If you look at a local paper, you will see all sorts of weird and rambling moans and groans about bad bus services, broken pavements and people riding bikes on the pavement. It is unlikely that the writers of these letters ever gave much thought about what they hoped to achieve by writing them. In many cases it is an outlet for frustration and achieves nothing apart from making the writer feel better.

Take a look at some personal web sites too. Many are random collections of thoughts and images that appeal to the author. This is fine as long as it's just for fun, but most people who set up personal sites do not have any particular ambitions for them except to communicate with friends.

You, on the other hand, *must* give some serious thought to the purpose of the ebook. It isn't good enough just to do it for the sake of it. A few clear purposes are essential. If you have already decided upon an audience you are halfway there. Here are some possible reasons for leaving an ebook for posterity, but don't forget you might have better ideas yourself. The ideas will probably be altruistic or a way of making a mark for the future as you are not likely to get any income from a book that is opened 100 years on!

Providing a source of information

You may want to provide an accurate source of facts that those in the future can refer to. This approach is most likely to be useful if you are concentrating on facts that you have special knowledge about, rather than publicly available facts that will probably be recorded by many 'official' agencies.

The special focus you may want to handle could well be

▶ your family;
▶ your friends;
▶ your school or college;
▶ your neighbourhood;
▶ a particular interest or hobby that you know a lot about.

portfolio_tip

Don't forget to include information under ALL the criteria that are required.

The advantage of focusing on a small aspect of contemporary life is that (a) you will have knowledge that others do not have and (b) it is likely that you will have a keen interest in it and will be able to make a more interesting product.

If providing information is your focus, you should keep that in mind throughout and start with a list of headings that you will use to categorise this information.

portfolio_tip

Let's say you have some views about freedom of expression. If this is the case, then when you are setting out your FIVE online services, your FIVE aspects of people's lives and THREE factors contributing to the digital divide, make sure that each example carries your argument forward and illustrates your points.

Putting forward a viewpoint

You may simply want to help future generations to understand the present age by explaining a point of view that you think they might not get from other sources. Possibly you think that many of the more 'official' records are likely to give a wrong viewpoint to people in the future and you want to give your own slant to current events. If you have a strong set of views about some aspects of life in the digital age, you should keep a clear focus on that and design it into your presentation. It would be helpful if you make a list of viewpoints that you want to emphasise. This way you can avoid getting sidetracked. The best examples of written communication (other than literature) take a viewpoint, have a clear objective then achieve it as effectively and economically as possible.

Illustrating the uses of information

You may wish to make your focus the ways in which information is used at the moment. You can include many examples such as the information that businesses need in order to communicate with each other and to make money. You can go into detail about the information that banks, schools, hospitals or any other organisation store. You can distinguish between personal information and that needed for the running of the organisation. You can distinguish between facts that are needed in a formal organised way and the information which is of a more free-form nature such as makes up the stories in a newspaper.

This approach will work well because there are many examples to choose from.

portfolio_tip

Keep the assessment requirements very much in mind and make sure that the examples you give are varied.

Aims

You could start your planning with a series of clear aims, for example, when finished, my ebook will:

▶ give an historian details about the technologies used in the information age;
▶ be structured to provide easy navigation through my ebook.

You can then refer back to these in your evaluation and write about how you met the aims or not.

Prescribed content

Whatever angle you decide to take, you will benefit greatly if you set out your aims clearly right from the start. You should make a clear plan that builds in the prescribed content as laid down in the specifications. To remind you, the basic requirements are that you must include:

▶ FIVE online services;
▶ FIVE aspects of people's lives;
▶ THREE factors contributing to the digital divide and measures being taken to remedy it.

If you make these into section headings and tick them off as you do them, you can be sure that you have covered everything. You may like to use the spreadsheet that is provided on the CD to help you.

As well as covering the main headings as given here, there are other requirements that you need to keep to if you are to get the highest marks that are available. These are prepared for you on the CD spreadsheet.

ACTIVITY
List five online services that you may decide to cover in your ebook.

portfolio_tip

It is not enough just to produce an ebook with lots of impressive features. Even if your ebook is easy to follow, looks good and covers what you intend, you will not get full credit unless you adhere rigorously to the specifications.

Check carefully that you have done *everything* that you are supposed to.

Outline of ebook requirements

Make sure that you have included everything in the table.

What must be included	Comments
Five different online services.	These should be completely different from each other and they should cover a good range of services. (You must choose online services from five different bullet points.)
A summary of these services that gives an overall picture of Internet services.	Comments and summary that gives a flavour of how these services affect life in the Information Age. You must have some comments about the Internet as a whole.
Five different ways that ICT affects people's lives, giving benefits and drawbacks in order to give an overall picture of life in the Information Age.	Choose aspects that are different from the online services already covered. Again, comment on some widely different ways that IT can affect the lives of people. You can be inventive here.
Three factors contributing to the digital divide plus measures being taken to reduce this and an evaluation of the impact of the digital divide.	<ul><li>Choose some examples that are local and some that are global in their effect.</li><li>Include measures that are being taken to reduce the gap between those who have access to online services and those who do not. These could include various business expansion plans by providers as well as government plans.</li><li>You should include a good summary of the current state of access both locally and globally.</li></ul>
As well as your work, you should check that you have made use of multimedia techniques including ready-made and original multimedia elements.	<ul><li>Your work should not be just text-based. You should include a good range of multimedia elements. These elements should be chosen because they *help* the purpose of the ebook, not just obvious add-ons to meet the specifications.</li><li>Your ebook should match its intended audience.</li><li>There should be evidence that you have adhered to standard proper working practices such as choosing sensible filenames and producing an effective directory structure.</li><li>You should provide evidence that you have thought about appropriate hardware and software.</li><li>You should test your ebook *thoroughly* and show that the links all work.</li></ul>
An evaluation of your ebook.	<ul><li>You should obtain feedback from others.</li><li>You should include at least one sensible improvement that could be made.</li><li>It is a good idea to refer back to your aims and say to what extent they have been met.</li></ul>
An evaluation of your own performance.	<ul><li>You could compare your performance with others' by discussing it with them.</li><li>You could describe how your IT skills have improved as you have developed the ebook.</li></ul>

Message

We have already looked at the possibility that you may want to convey a 'message' as well as or instead of just presenting facts to your future audience.

What message do you want to put across? We live in an age of 'spin'. We have learned that most information we receive is much more than just the obvious content. There is usually an additional sub-text that the provider of the information wants us to absorb.

Spin has become very much a dirty word in recent years in the UK because of the obviously dishonest ways that some people 'massage' their words in order to get a particular 'message' or attitude across in a devious way. Sometimes this is achieved by the careful choice of words. For example, a high-taxation and high-spending government might speak of 'investing'

Disgraced MP Quits!

money when they really mean just 'spending' it. 'Investing' sounds so much more responsible.

Sometimes spin is achieved by repeating a slogan or word again and again until people accept it as an undeniable truth. Call someone an 'opportunist' enough times and people might think badly of that person whether or not he actually is an opportunist or indeed whether we care if he is or not. Be aware that there are 'hooray' words and 'boo' words that provoke a reaction as well as or instead of conveying information. Look at any 'red top' newspaper and notice how often they decide for the reader what the appropriate reaction should be to a story.

These are crude examples of the dishonest use of language and you should be acutely aware of the tricks involved. However, you may decide to play this game yourself. Just be aware of what you are doing. It is perfectly normal and legitimate to compose your presentation or piece of writing in order to get across a point of view. There is no obligation on the part of someone arguing against fox hunting to put the opposition's point of view. That is not dishonest, it is arguing a case. Beware of libellous statements!

Decide on the 'take' that you want for your ebook. Are you going to paint a picture of life in the Information Age that:

► is optimistic;
► is pessimistic;
► simply gives the facts;
► is technically based;
► gives a flavour for how people react to change?

Technical specification

There is a huge range of software that you can use to create your ebook. It is entirely up to you what you choose. You will probably make use of a variety of software. Just a few examples might include:

► a word processor for the text;
► a graphics package to generate your own designs;
► a screen grab utility to make image files of screens or parts of screens
► an upload facility for digital camera cards (or possibly you will simply use Windows Explorer);
► Microsoft PowerPoint or similar to make a multimedia presentation;
► Microsoft Excel or a similar spreadsheet package to make tables and graphs;
► a multimedia creation package;
► a programming language such as Java to make an interactive display or applet;
► a web authoring package such as Microsoft FrontPage or Macromedia Dreamweaver to create and edit HTML files.

You may well have access to software that few other people have heard of.

Whatever software you use to create your ebook, you must make sure that it can be read by anyone. Ebooks *can* be designed to work on a variety of devices but in your case, you must make your ebook conform to certain technical standards. This is so that the greatest number of people can read it (in particular, the moderators who will check your work will not necessarily have access to the software that you used to make your ebook).

Remember your ebook *must* be designed to work on-screen. A static paper book will not do. To make sure of this, you must make your finished product such that it can be read by a standard web browser such as Microsoft Internet Explorer v5.0 or later, Netscape Navigator v5.0 or Mozilla Firefox. It should be designed to work well at a resolution of 1024 × 768 pixels.

Your ebook must be no bigger than 15 MB. Your basic files must be in one of these formats:

▶ pdf
▶ html
▶ swf

although they may reference others such as jpegs and mpegs.

There should also be an index page containing links so that all the files in your portfolio can be found easily by anyone marking it.

An ebook suitable for screen display will have HTML code at its core.

Your ebook, just like a web site, will probably consist of much more than just HTML code. It will call upon a variety of other resources, at the very least image files. Image files should be saved, preferably in their own directory, in JPEG format. This (a) reduces the amount of file space that they take up and (b) ensures that as many browsers as possible will be able to display them.

You will need to set up a sensible folder (directory) structure to hold all your ebook resources and to keep them organised. A basic plan could start like that shown in Figure 5.6.

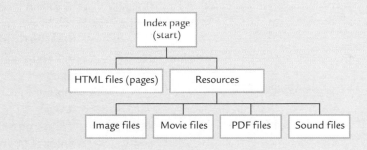

Many ebooks and web sites need to display documents in exactly the same format as in the original. If you need to do this, you can make a PDF file, using Adobe Acrobat Professional or suitable shareware. Your HTML code can be set up to access PDF files.

You can assume that your reader has access to software that can display flash movies.

The technical specifications that underlie the reading of ebooks and web pages will certainly evolve over time, so it is a good idea if you check on Edexcel's web site to see what the latest rules are.

The user of your ebook may have a PC running a version of Windows, Linux or may have an Apple Mac. If you produce your work in the required format, this will not matter since any of these platforms will be able to display your work.

HTML (HYPERTEXT MARKUP LANGUAGE): This is the system of coding for web page display. HTML code is interpreted and displayed by web browser software. It uses 'tags' or markers to instruct the software how to display the web page content.

JPEG: (Joint Photographic Expert Group): A standard for compressing and storing still images. It is the most common image storage standard used for web pages

portfolio_tip
It will help you a lot if all your work is organised in folders contained in one root folder and the files all have sensible names.

Deadlines

portfolio_tip

As well as being helpful to your planning, you may find it appropriate to include some coverage of IT-based planning as one of the ways that the Information Age has affected people. You must include some of your planning as part of your ebook report.

It is important that you complete all the work on your ebook in time to present it for assessment. Although it is up to you how you keep on top of things, it may be helpful to you if you work to some plan. Planning work can be done quite effectively on paper, but paper-based work has all the usual disadvantages of getting lost or not being available when you need it.

It can be a lot easier to plan if you use IT methods.

Planning with a spreadsheet

One easy way to plan a project of this sort is to use a spreadsheet. The great thing about using spreadsheets is that you can alter things very easily, insert new rows and columns, add notes and sort things into order. You can fill in target dates and set it up so that you can easily see what you have done and what is the next milestone to reach. You can add columns to keep track of what you have done or you may find it more helpful and flexible to add comments to some of the cells.

	A	B	C	D	E	F
1	**E-Book Schedule**					
2						
3	**Week**	**Information Gathering**	**Report Writing**	**E-book activities**		
4	1	Internet research	Keep notes on computer	Proc dire stru	*Half done - need to finish by 10 Oct*	
5	2	Collect magazines	5 online services decided on and rough notes taken	Decide on style for e-book		
6	3	Interview users	Notes on impact of IT.	Create pages for online services		
7	4					

ACTIVITY

Make sure that you know how to add comments to spreadsheet cells and how to display them all.

There is an example spreadsheet template on the CD that you can adapt to suit your own circumstances (ebook checklist.xls).

Planning with diaries

There are lots of examples of diary software that can be customised to help you keep on top of a project. Microsoft Outlook has a useful diary, but ideally you will need to have it installed on your school or college network to get the best out of it, especially the online capability.

Alternatively, you may find it handy to use one of the online diaries provided by the search engine companies. Yahoo!, for example, not only gives you a search engine, it also is a web-based email provider which gives you a host of useful extras. It provides online storage in a feature called the briefcase. It also gives you a useful diary. You can use this to plan your portfolio work. The diary can be set up to send you an email automatically when a certain date or time is reached. The nice thing about this system is that you can access it anywhere and check your progress.

Planning with project software

Project management software such as Microsoft Project is specifically designed to help you organise the resources, milestones and cut-off dates for projects large and small. It not only helps you to make sure that everything is done at the right time and in the right order, it also can produce visual representations such as Gantt charts (see below) and PERT charts to make it obvious when each job needs to be done.

<u>B</u>eing organised

We have seen before how important it is to be well organised. Not only is it important in most jobs, it will help you greatly in making your ebook. It can be a real bore setting up structures to organise a job such as this and it is often tempting just to get on with it and think about organising things later. That approach is always a mistake as the time spent in organising your work at the beginning repays itself many times over. You can find things when you need them and you also know where you are at all times.

Paperwork

Your ebook development will involve a fair amount of paperwork: or at least it should. You will find unlimited sources of information about contemporary IT issues in magazines and newspapers. You should try to see some of the specialist trade computer magazines such as *Computing* or *Computer Weekly*. They also have their own web sites, but you can often get a better 'feel' for current issues from a printed publication; it is easier to see the bigger picture if you are not constantly following links. Another great help that these trade magazines can give you is found in their letter pages. IT practitioners express comments and concerns about the technology of the moment and you can gain a lot of very sharp insight from these.

portfolio_tip

portfolio_tip

For the section on life in the Information Age you must include sources other than the Internet.

portfolio_tip

Decide for yourself whether you are going to store computer file resources in separate folders according to their subject matter or according to their file format. A separate folder for jpegs and movie files makes sense, but so does keeping everything together about, say, online shopping. Try to find a system that works for you. The good thing about computer resources is that it is always easy to reorganise if the system doesn't work for you any more.

coursework_tip

It may be helpful if you can keep details of your storage and filing system to include in your portfolio.

The jobs section in a trade magazine is another goldmine for getting a good impression of what skills are in demand and for what businesses. You will also get a good idea about the relative value of different IT-based jobs. Don't neglect the adverts either. You will learn a lot from seeing what hardware and software, and what solutions are currently being pushed.

The ordinary newspapers also carry a lot of IT-based stories. There is seldom a week without another exposé about a public sector IT disaster that won't work or has passed its deadlines and will end up costing the taxpayer more.

Keep cuttings or photocopies of any stories that may come in handy. Make sure you date them and write on them the name of the paper that they came from.

You might interview some people in order to get a more personal view of some IT-related topic. If you do, you might want to record it or produce a transcript. Keep physical records in a separate file from the cuttings. You might find it convenient to put all these paper resources into a large box file.

Another excellent way of finding things out is to use email. You might want to make a questionnaire and mail it to a number of people. You can try this out on the representatives of organisations and some of them might respond. If you do approach people that you do not know, you will be more likely to get a response if you are 'super-polite' and choose your email subject line carefully. A line such as 'please help with A-level IT project' (don't say 'ICT' as most IT professionals won't know what you are talking about!) is more likely to survive the 'delete' button than something like 'help' or 'in response to your communication' or worse still 'please open this'. If your message looks like spam, it won't get read.

Keep copies of helpful replies that you get by email. They will help in your evaluation as well as provide useful quotes in your ebook.

If you find useful material on television, you may find it useful to video record it and transfer the clips to a multimedia display.

Research – the correct way to record sources

It is very bad practice as well as being unethical to use quotes from sources without acknowledging them. Nobody appreciates having his or her work plundered without getting some of the credit for all the effort. People who plagiarise rightly come in for a lot of criticism and lose their reputation. If you enter unacknowledged work for your exam assignments, you can be disqualified from the award.

In print, there are standard formats for recording sources. They make sure that the author is given credit and also include the name of the publication or web site involved and the date of publication (if known). This allows others to check your sources or follow up their own research.

A typical entry about an article in a periodical might be:

Guy, Chris. 'Why bee stings are good for you'. *Annals of Bee-keeping*, Vol. 10, No. 3, Mar. 1995.

A reference to a book might be:

Guy, Chris. My Favourite Brood Parasites. London: Hodder, 2005.

Or if it were taken from a web site:

Guy, Chris. 'Queen spotting.' 13 May 2004 <http://
www.thehappyapiarist.co.uk/>.

Developing the ebook

How you finally do this will depend on your own preferences. Possibly you already know how to develop a web site with Microsoft FrontPage or maybe you are happier using Microsoft PowerPoint. Maybe you have some other favoured software that will allow you to produce a multimedia display that will run in a web browser.

On the other hand, maybe you haven't yet decided. If not, there are plenty of issues to consider.

If you contemplate 'getting your hands dirty' by editing the HTML code, this will give you a much greater degree of control over the product. However, if you decide to get started by using software that is not primarily designed for making web pages, beware! You could make the whole ebook from start to finish with a word processor such as Microsoft Word. It will allow you to put in links and you can even insert various multimedia elements. If you select View | Toolbars | Web Tools, you will get lots of easy to use ways of inserting active elements into what was otherwise a plain word-processed document.

You may decide that this is the way you want to go. It is, after all, very easy to use Microsoft Word to do a lot of impressive things.

If you select *Save As Web Page,* Word will generate all the HTML and other code that you need to run your ebook in a web browser. However, it will add in **lots** of unnecessary stuff as well that will make editing the HTML a nightmare. It will also use up more storage space, and remember you must stay within the limits set.

Here is the HTML code that Microsoft Word produced for a document containing nothing but the one word 'hello'. It defines almost everything you could ever imagine. You could achieve the same thing with much less: and possibly understand what is going on!

```
<html xmlns:o="urn:schemas-microsoft-com:office:office"
xmlns:w="urn:schemas-microsoft-com:office:word"
xmlns="http://www.w3.org/TR/REC-html40">

<head>
<meta http-equiv=Content-Type content="text/html;
charset=windows-1252">
<meta name=ProgId content=Word.Document>
<meta name=Generator content="Microsoft Word 9">
<meta name=Originator content="Microsoft Word 9">
<link rel=File-List href=" /hello_files/filelist.xml">
<title>hello</title>
<!--[if gte mso 9]><xml>
 <o:DocumentProperties>
  <o:Author>Sean O'Byrne</o:Author>
  <o:Template>Normal</o:Template>
  <o:LastAuthor>Sean O'Byrne</o:LastAuthor>
  <o:Revision>1</o:Revision>
  <o:TotalTime>1</o:TotalTime>
  <o:Created>2005-03-10T19:06:00Z</o:Created>
  <o:LastSaved>2005-03-10T19:07:00Z</o:LastSaved>
  <o:Pages>1</o:Pages>
  <o:Company>Sean O'Byrne</o:Company>
  <o:Lines>1</o:Lines>
  <o:Paragraphs>1</o:Paragraphs>
  <o:Version>9.3821</o:Version>
 </o:DocumentProperties>
</xml><![endif]-->
<style>
<!--
 /* Style Definitions */
p.MsoNormal, li.MsoNormal, div.MsoNormal
     {mso-style-parent:"";
     margin:0cm;
     margin-bottom:.0001pt;
     mso-pagination:widow-orphan;
     font-size:12.0pt;
     font-family:"Times New Roman";
     mso-fareast-font-family:"Times New Roman";}
@page Section1
     {size:595.3pt 841.9pt;
     margin:72.0pt 90.0pt 72.0pt 90.0pt;
     mso-header-margin:35.4pt;
     mso-footer-margin:35.4pt;
     mso-paper-source:0;}
div.Section1
    {page:Section1;}
-->
</style>
</head>

<body lang=EN-GB style='tab-interval:36.0pt'>

<div class=Section1>

<p class=MsoNormal>hello</p>

</div>

</body>

</html>
```

Testing

You need to test the ebook. This need not be difficult because an ebook is not a complicated thing. Unlike a piece of software, which requires testing with all sorts of input data in all sorts of circumstances, an ebook is read-only. You do not need to test inputs, only outputs. But, you do need to test that it works under all reasonable circumstances. You need to test your ebook in two main ways. You need to check that it works and you need to check that it achieves what it is supposed to do.

Functional testing

You have to test that the ebook physically does what it is supposed to do. Your ebook may be read on an ordinary PC or a hand-held device. You need to be sure that it looks good on the target for which it is intended.

Your functional testing is rather like the testing that you may have done before in earlier ICT classes and coursework. You should bear in mind that testing the functionality of a software product is more than just 'checking that it works'. To do the job properly, you should actively try to break it! This job is often done better by someone else who might be more motivated to find faults.

The functional testing should include at least testing:

- ▶ that it runs in a browser (possibly more than one browser);
- ▶ all the links;
- ▶ the correct functioning of multimedia elements;
- ▶ the correct functioning of animations;
- ▶ that the pages fit as intended on the screen;
- ▶ that it can exit cleanly.

Fitness for purpose

You need to go further than just functional testing. This, strictly speaking, is not conventional testing. It is nearer to an evaluation and again it will help if you get someone else to give a second opinion. This is a somewhat subjective approach. You will ask such questions as:

- ▶ Does the ebook convey the impression you intended?
- ▶ Is it easy to read?
- ▶ Is it easy to navigate?
- ▶ Do the special effects work well in conveying the right impression?

You may find that the grid on the CD will help you to remember to cover everything.

Iterative testing

Iterative means repeating. Here, it means testing, then going back and changing things because of the results of the tests. You should build testing into your development process. In other words, you should carry out tests as you go along and record what happened. Then, you make adjustments in the light of the test results.

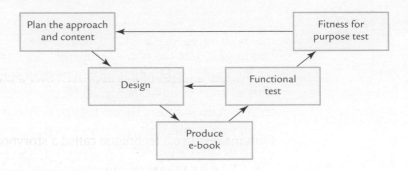

A useful approach is to follow a project management practice called the V-model. This reminds you to keep testing as you go and to make changes to your planning and designs if the test results suggest improvements.

You can build in the stages of testing into your plans if you use project management software. When testing you need to include spell checking, proofreading and testing on users. These form part of the functional and fitness for purpose tests in the chart.

Techniques

There are many ways to plan a project such as your ebook. Most of the best ways involve using a computer.

We have already looked at how you can use software to help plan the project. You can use it to plan the contents of the ebook as well. One basic approach is to rough out your major headings using a word processor or a spreadsheet. As we have seen when planning the timescale of the project, a spreadsheet is particularly helpful because it has many built-in features that help in ordering and reorganisation.

However, you do not want to be too restricted by this approach. A spreadsheet is an excellent tool for planning an ordinary book. The authors of this book used one in order to plan the contents. It works well because an ordinary physical book has to follow a sequence: the pages go from lower to higher numbers. You may use a textbook in a more random way, dipping in where you need, rather than reading it right through, but it cannot be made in a non-sequential way.

An ebook can be different. *Your* ebook will *have* to be different. It should not be sequential. It should make use of the non-linear approach used by web sites. It will need to use hypertext so that the reader can jump about and look at the contents in any order.

You can adopt an alternative approach when planning something non-linear.

> **portfolio_tip**
>
> Using project planning as an example of how people are affected by the Information Age could be a good idea. You will be able to add a lot of personal experience to your account.

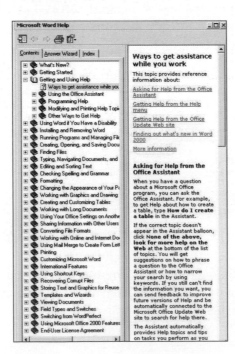

In most common software such as your word processor, press F1 to access the help pages (see above). These will be written in hypertext so that you can follow links to related topics or explanations. Make a list of advantages and disadvantages of this approach over a paper-based instruction manual.

Storyboarding

Film makers use a technique called a storyboard to help them plan a movie. The main scenes are sketched out with references to the images that will be displayed, the part of the story dealt with and how the parts link together. This can be a very useful way to plan an ebook.

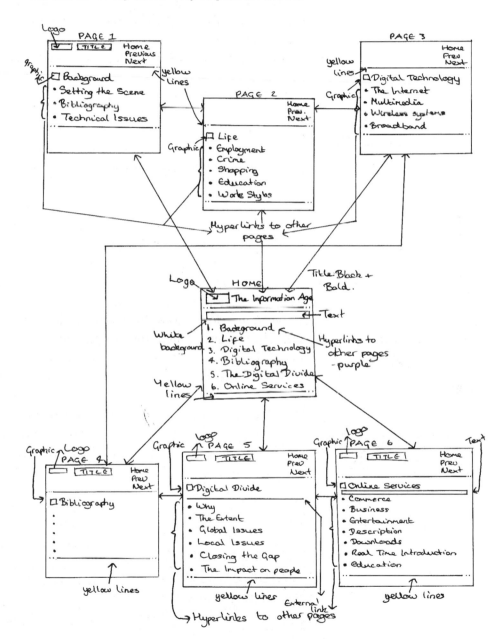

Create a storyboard for your own ideas.

You can then start thinking about overall subject headings and how they might be linked together. During this process, you may change your mind about what goes in. At the end of the process, you should have a fairly good idea about the basic structure and will be able to formalise it with other diagrams.

Structure charts

Further development can be planned in exactly the same way as you would plan a web site. You need to think about how the material will be organised on pages and how the pages can link together.

Some basic rules to follow here are:

► don't make the pages too big;
► don't make the writing too dense;
► if in doubt, start a new page;
► don't put too many links on a page.

You may think up other rules that suit you.

An important diagram that can help a lot in your planning is the equivalent of a site map for a web site. You should try to keep it fairly simple or the links will cross over and make it difficult to understand. In this example, there would probably be a link from each page back to the start, but you don't need to draw that in.

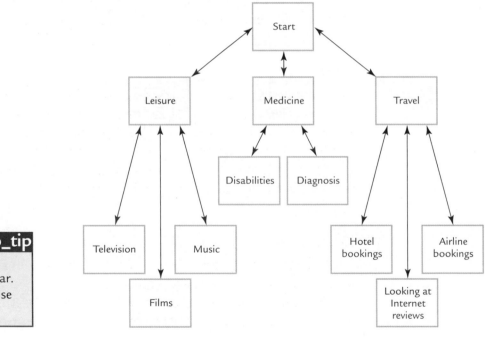

Folder structures

As you start work on your ebook, you will accumulate files that may be useful to you. Set up working files for:

► images
► web references
► sound files
► movie files
► text fragments

portfolio_tip

Some browsers have problems with hyperlinks. If you put spaces in the names of files and folders, use the underscore e.g. my_first_page.

coursework_tip

The first page on a web site is normally called index.htm.

Once you actually get to work, you need to set up a working directory structure as shown on page 00 which you will not want to change later. It is important to have such a working structure because the links will expect the resources to be in a certain location. If you move them later, they won't work. Similarly, you may have problems with linked images not showing up if you move them around.

Create and save the pages first

You will find it a lot easier if you start by creating dummy pages for all the pages that you have planned. Save them in their final locations and, very importantly, give them meaningful names. Even if there is nothing on these pages to start with, apart form a label, you will not be able to make the links from other pages until they exist. It is very frustrating to be working on a page and attempting to add a link and finding that there is nowhere for it to go.

Checking

We have already summarised the testing process. We shall now look at it in more detail. You want to have an ebook that works well and is professionally constructed. With computer technology there is no need to let any mistakes get through to the end product. You should make a number of checks periodically as you go through the work. Apart from ensuring a good final product, you will find it easier to keep to deadlines if you do a lot of the checking as you go.

Spelling and grammar

There is no excuse for producing a product that contains spelling errors. Use a spell checker and you should fix any errors that are flagged up as you go. You can then do a full spell check when you have finished a page.

It is worth running the grammar check, but don't follow its advice unless you know it is good advice. If it picks up that you have missed a verb from a sentence, then that is useful to you. If it points out that you have used a passive form of a verb, you may have meant to (and what's wrong with that?).

Proofreading

The text part of your ebook should be read after it has been typed or pasted in to check that it reads well and contains no errors. This is called proofreading. Proofreading is not easy. There are courses that people go on in order to become professional proofreaders. It is very easy to miss even big mistakes when the general sense looks all right.

> Aoccdrnig to rseearch at Cmabrigde Uinervtisy, wehn yuo're wirting in the Enlgish lagnauge, it deosn't mttaer in waht oredr the ltteers in a wrod are, the olny iprmotant tihng is taht the frist and lsat ltteer be at the rghit pclae.
> *London Evening Standard* 10 March 2005 – Victor Lewis-Smith

It is easier to proofread someone else's work. If you made a mistake when you wrote something, you might miss it when you re-read it because you are familiar with it. If you can get help to proofread, then do so. Otherwise, look out very carefully for typos that might escape the spell checker. It is easy to miss silly little errors such as typing 'fro' instead of 'for' or 'ion' instead of 'in'. The spell checker won't pick them up.

Layout

Your ebook should end up looking rather more visually appealing than lots of plain text. You will want to use all sorts of tricks to make things attractive and work well at communicating your ideas. But you can overdo these things. You will have seen web sites and Microsoft PowerPoint presentations where there are so many special effects that you miss the sense of what is there.

A few rules to bear in mind are

▶ **Be consistent**. A basic style carried through an ebook helps the reader to see the coherence of your material. This consistency can range from choices of colours and fonts (not too many of either) to a design feature that appears on each page or each page in a group. Above all, know what you are doing and do everything deliberately and for a reason, not just from a whim. You can use the software to help you. Most of the software that you are likely to be using will provide templates or style sheets that can automate your consistency. Use master pages to hold any design features that you want to appear throughout.

▶ **Don't put a lot on the start page**. Just as with a web site's home page, this should function in a similar way as the cover on a book: it gets you interested and gives you a clue about what follows, but that's all. A button labelled 'Proceed' or 'Enter' takes the reader in.

Links and pathways

You should have taken care to get all the pages and resources well organised so that the links are to the expected locations. Once you are sure of this, you should copy the entire structure to another location and test it again. The simple way to do this is to click on the directory that holds *all* your work and copy and paste it into a subdirectory or onto a USB flash drive. Then, test it again. If all the directories are in the same relative positions, it should work well.

Trying on test users

We have seen that it is useful to test the basic functionality and accuracy with other people. You also need the opinions of others in assessing the sense and impact of your work. You should try to get several people to look at your ebook, not just in the sense of 'testing' it but you could regard it as an exercise in market research. You could even give your 'evaluators' a questionnaire to fill in. A possible questionnaire might be based on the following:

If you use a questionnaire of the type in the example, you can convert your findings to usable statistics. You can say, for example that 80 per cent of testers found that the ebook was easy to use. As it is important that you can quote the opinions of others, a standard way of responding makes your job a lot easier.

portfolio_tip

Once you have created a link to a page, do not change its filename. The link will not work if you do. If you really must make a change, then remember to change the links as well.

portfolio_tip

Testing is often done very badly by pupils. Remember that collecting opinions is *not* testing. Complete testing *must* include a planned set of objective tests that attempts to find technical errors in a product.

Ebook Questionnaire

Rate the ebook on a scale of 1–5 on the following criteria:

1. agree strongly
2. agree
3. neither agree nor disagree
4. disagree
5. disagree strongly

Please tick the appropriate box

The ebook is easy
to understand.

1	2	3	4	5

The images are well chosen.

1	2	3	4	5

The ebook is easy
to navigate.

1	2	3	4	5

The font sizes are
appropriate and easy to read.

1	2	3	4	5

The material is
attractively presented.

1	2	3	4	5

The pages are not cluttered.

1	2	3	4	5

There is a sense of unity
about the ebook.

1	2	3	4	5

The colours are well chosen.

1	2	3	4	5

The movies help to
convey the message.

1	2	3	4	5

The overall layout was good.

1	2	3	4	5

The sound is well used.

1	2	3	4	5

The display was fast.

1	2	3	4	5

A copy of this questionnaire is available on the CD under the file name questionnaire.doc.

It is important for you to realise that a questionnaire like this can only be a *part* of your evaluation. If you are collecting opinions from others, you should also allow them to make free-form comments *in addition* to filling in boxes.

Questionnaire .doc

Evaluation

The example questionnaire gives you some ideas about how you can evaluate your ebook. One way or another, you need to include a number of aspects of your ebook in the evaluation. You may want to adapt the questionnaire or you may want to ask people in a more informal way.

Your evaluation needs to include your own reactions as well as those of others. Check under the following headings. A good evaluation will include reference to you aims and it will comment on how you fulfilled them.

portfolio_tip

Your evaluation should be separate from your ebook, not part of it.

Structure

Can you get back to the start quickly? A well-designed ebook will have links to the start throughout. You will probably not have put these explicitly into planning diagrams because they would make it too cluttered.

Can you follow a theme? There should be some logical routes through your ebook. For example, a theme about Internet banking might contain links to other forms of online service, banking fraud, encryption and statistics about numbers of transactions over a period. It should be easy and natural to progress along such a thematic pathway.

Was there any thematic planning? This is a question you ask yourself. If you are reading ahead perhaps you should incorporate some plans for routes through your ebook and implement them when you make your final product.

Back references. If you follow a theme, is it relatively straightforward to find your way back again? There should be some logic built in rather than just depending upon the user clicking the 'back' button.

Layout

Pages should have a common look. Ask yourself and your testers whether there is a satisfying common look and feel throughout the ebook. If this is missing, the effect will be disjointed and difficult for the reader.

The pages do not have to be all different. It is probably a good thing if related pages are very similar in terms of layout, colour schemes, fonts and general design. Is there evidence of this?

How could the ebook be improved? Think this over yourself and be honest about it. There is no need to 'design-in' some obvious faults for the benefit of the moderator! There are bound to be ways that you think that the ebook could be improved. Think back to the start if necessary. Are the themes well chosen? Does the whole product cover a solid and unified theme? Ask others the same questions. You don't have to action this now, just record these as ideas.

Multimedia components

File types. Review the file types that you used. Record the reasons why they are appropriate. Perhaps you used JPEGs to speed up loading and to reduce the file space required. Were the file types chosen suitable? Did they give an acceptable compromise between usability and screen quality?

Space. It would be beneficial if you could record some details of the file sizes that your final product required. Give a table of file sizes for all the resources that it uses. How much disk space is needed for the software that runs the ebook?

Compression. You almost certainly used compressed file types such as JPEGs or MPEGs. These need re-expansion at run-time. Does this expansion slow it down to any noticeable extent?

Check the specifications. Don't just rely on what you have seen in this book, although it tries to cover all the things that you need. As a final check, look at the exam awarding body's specifications to make totally sure that you have covered everything. Remember, it is not enough just to produce a good product. You have to conform to each and every one of the specification's requirements or you could lose marks heavily.

Presentation techniques

You will have checked all this as you went along. Just as for final reassurance check once again:

Are the pages appropriate? Is each page a suitable 'bite-sized' chunk of information that is coherent and easily absorbed?

Not too much text. People are less inclined to read lots of text than they used to be. They are accustomed to 'sound bites' and quickly absorbed web pages. Although many people still enjoy reading novels, the likelihood is that they do not expect a text-heavy approach in an ebook. It may even be painful to the eyes to read a lot of text on a screen. Are the pages concise and brief?

Are the images put to good use? The images should add value and not just be a distracting addition. Are they well chosen and spaced out sufficiently to act as a focal point without interrupting the reading process?

Remember, in order to achieve a good layout of images you should make use of tables, and not just drag and drop them which doesn't work well in browsers!

Are the images a suitable size? You can quote your HTML code if necessary to show the actual figures.

ACTIVITY

There are three images on the CD: image1.tif, image2.gif and image3.jpg. These are all the same photograph taken on the same digital camera. The only difference is the format used when they were saved.

Right click on the images and look at the file size.
Which is the largest?
Which would be best to include in your portfolio?
Load the images. Can you see any difference in the quality when viewed on screen?

image1.tif
image2.gif
image3.jpeg

Ease of navigation

Do you always know where you are? Is it always easy to find your way 'home' or back to the last main theme that you followed? Some use of icons may help to make it easy for the users.

Some users may not be able to display all your images or they may be slow to load. Have you provided text-based equivalents of your navigation aids?

Frames. You can use frames to provide a constant navigation panel at the side or bottom of your page. Some designers find this a reassuring way of showing the users a way to the main parts of the ebook, but constantly occupying the screen, no matter what is being looked at can be an irritating waste of space and detract from concentration on the current page.

Position of links. Does the provision of links follow a pattern? Is it consistent so that the user does not have to exert mental effort to find a way around?

Consistency

A thematic approach. Is there a consistent 'look and feel' throughout (a) the whole ebook and (b) throughout subsections? Did you use master pages or other aids to make this easy?

Accessibility

Can anyone use it? Don't forget, your users will have different computer platforms. Have you checked that it works as well under a variety of browsers and operating systems? Are there likely to be difficulties for people with disabilities such as colour blindness?

Aims

Take a look back at your original plans. Have you fulfilled them all, some of them or did you end up somewhere else entirely?

Enhancements

How could you improve the ebook? What extra features would be good? How could you group the material better? Would other choices have been more suitable as a way of telling people in the future what life in the Information Age is like? Remember, you must refer to the opinions of others.

Are there any additions that you would like to add if you spent more time on the ebook?

Skills

Aims

■ To examine some of the skills needed to build an ebook.

■ To examine some of the techniques needed to create an effective ebook.

Browsers

The browser is client software that allows you view material on the World Wide Web. Microsoft Internet Explorer is the most well known example and is very commonly found on PCs. This is because it is installed with Microsoft Windows. However, it is not the only one available. Netscape Navigator is another popular browser. The purpose of the browser is to display documents created in Hypertext Markup Language (HTML). It can also interpret scripts and programs that are downloaded with the HTML pages.

The illustration shows the most common buttons on Microsoft Internet Explorer. Some of them are described below.

■ Figure 1.57

Home

Back/Forward: These buttons allow you to move through pages that you have already visited, in reverse or forward order.

Stop: This button stops the loading of the current web page.

Refresh: Reloads the current page from the Internet or, in the case of your ebook, from disk. If you make changes to the HTML code from a page and save them, the page will need to be reloaded by the browser before you see the changes.

Home: Displays your home page. You can set this to any page you want, using the Tools menu, however on your college or school network this feature may be disabled.

Favorites: This is a list of pages you want to remember and often return to. When looking at the results of a search it is often a good idea to mark sites that seem useful and then when you have more time go back over them.

Adding sites to the favourites list is easy, but the list can quickly become unmanageable. Look at the illustration. This is only part of a list. Notice the range of sites and topics. They are in alphabetical order but it might be better to organise them in some other way.

■ **Figure 1.58**

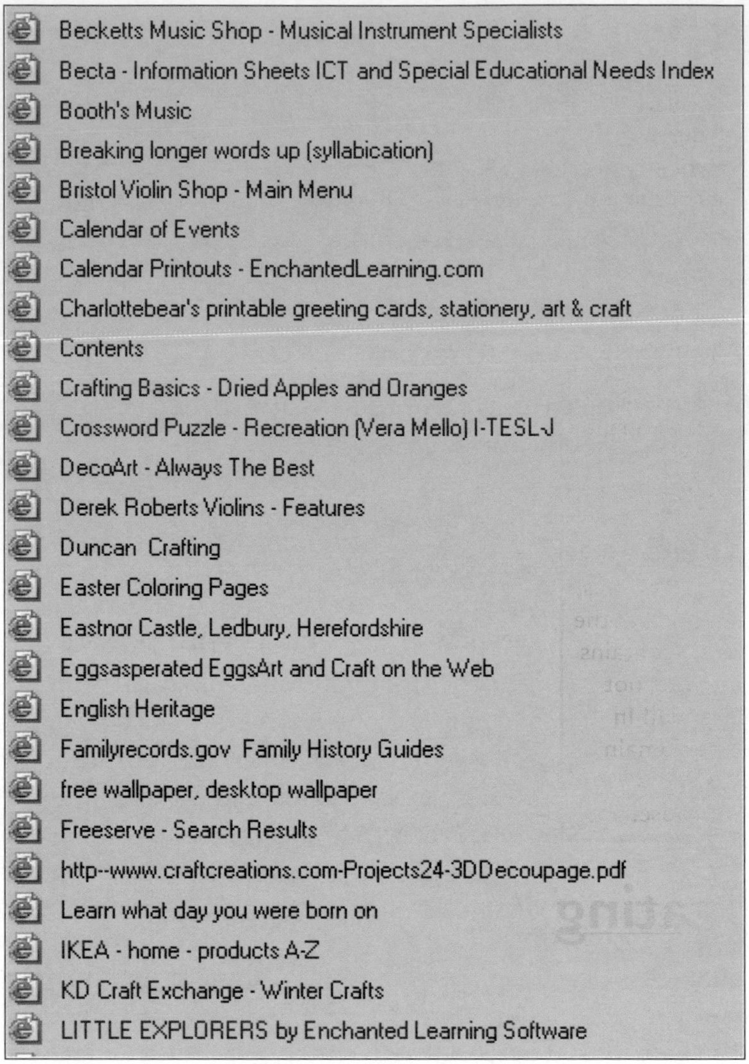

📄	Becketts Music Shop - Musical Instrument Specialists
📄	Becta - Information Sheets ICT and Special Educational Needs Index
📄	Booth's Music
📄	Breaking longer words up (syllabication)
📄	Bristol Violin Shop - Main Menu
📄	Calendar of Events
📄	Calendar Printouts - EnchantedLearning.com
📄	Charlottebear's printable greeting cards, stationery, art & craft
📄	Contents
📄	Crafting Basics - Dried Apples and Oranges
📄	Crossword Puzzle - Recreation (Vera Mello) I-TESL-J
📄	DecoArt - Always The Best
📄	Derek Roberts Violins - Features
📄	Duncan Crafting
📄	Easter Coloring Pages
📄	Eastnor Castle, Ledbury, Herefordshire
📄	Eggsasperated EggsArt and Craft on the Web
📄	English Heritage
📄	Familyrecords.gov Family History Guides
📄	free wallpaper, desktop wallpaper
📄	Freeserve - Search Results
📄	http--www.craftcreations.com-Projects24-3DDecoupage.pdf
📄	Learn what day you were born on
📄	IKEA - home - products A-Z
📄	KD Craft Exchange - Winter Crafts
📄	LITTLE EXPLORERS by Enchanted Learning Software

portfolio_tip

Set up some folders to keep sites sorted according to the topics in your ebook. For example, create folders for:
- online services;
- life in the Information Age;
- the digital divide.

Organising favourites is quite easy. Folders can be added for topics and favourites can be sorted by topic.

■ **Figure 1.59**

portfolio_tip

When researching sites for your ebook, put any useful sites into your favourites list; that way you can easily go back to them if you need more information later.

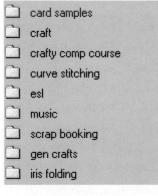

📁 card samples
📁 craft
📁 crafty comp course
📁 curve stitching
📁 esl
📁 music
📁 scrap booking
📁 gen crafts
📁 iris folding

History: This keeps a record of the pages you have visited. You can normally set a time limit for how long to keep the records.

ACTIVITY

Figure 1.55 shows some buttons not covered in the text.

Find out what each of these does and write a short description.

Search engines

portfolio_tip
Use several different engines for your research, the result are not always the same.

portfolio_tip
Since your ebook is mainly a factual one, you could try narrowing down your search to domains from academic institutions. To do this, you can specify that the domain name contains .ac. But beware, not all .acs are equal! In the USA, the domain name suffix .edu serves the same purpose.

A search engine is a service provided on a web site which produces indexes of web pages. Given a list of keywords, the engine searches the indexes and produces a list of sites that fit the criteria entered by the user. The suggested sites are called hits. Major search engines include Google, MSN, Infoseek, AltaVista, HotBot, Excite, Lycos, and WebCrawler.

When using a search engine, you often receive lists containing many thousands of sites. You will not have the time to look at them all so you need to be selective with your results. The search engine gives you a brief extract from the site and looking at this sometimes gives you a feel for what is contained on the site.

It is possible to be more selective in a search than simply using a list of words. It is possible to narrow down a search using AND (some engines use the & symbol). Doing this will cause the search engine to look for sites that contain both the words you are looking for and this will reduce the number of hits. You can search for a phrase by enclosing words in speech marks for example "digital divide" will look for the exact phrase "digital divide" rather then the two words used anywhere in the site.

Most sites have an advanced search option which gives you a range of tools to improve the search you carry out. It is possible to be much more specific in you searches using this method and this increases your chances of finding exactly what you want.

Navigating large web sites

Large sites can be difficult to navigate. A single home page can sometimes not hold enough information and once you move off that page it can be confusing to find your way around. Some sites use frames which split the screen into a number of independent areas. This makes it easier to find your way around the site because the menu in a frame is always in view.

ACTIVITY
Look at the BBC news site http://news.bbc.co.uk/. Look at the way frames are used to help navigate the site.

It is important on any web site to track your position. The bigger the site the more important this is. Another method used by some sites is called a crumb trail. This is a line of links normally at the top or bottom of the page that tracks your position and allows you to see at a glance where you are. Each section of the trail also acts as a hyperlink to that section.

For example: `Ebook_home > section_one > services > banking > advantages`

In the example above the user has moved from through the following section in order.

1. Ebook home
2. Section one
3. Services
4. Banking
5. Advantages

Hyperlinks

A hyperlink is a piece of text or an image in a document or web site that when clicked takes you to another document or to a different page on the web site.

Links are normally represented by words or images that are highlighted. Sometimes, due to poor design, it is not obvious where the links are. It is easy to tell if you are on a link by hovering the mass pointer over a word or image. If it is a link, then the cursor will change to a hand shape. You will also see the destination of the hyperlink displayed on the status bar at the bottom of the screen.

When you are designing a page, it is important to position links carefully. A good idea is to have the link to the home page in the same place on each page. This is one way to make the site easier to navigate.

Your ebook will be a series of linked pages so you will need to be able to create hyperlinks between your pages. Before you can link to a page, you need to have first created the page. This is an important planning issue. You need to have a plan of your ebook before you start, (see Chapter 1.6). It will also help if you follow standard ways of working by naming your files carefully and keeping a record of them. For hyperlinks to work correctly, it is normally necessary to have no spaces in the filenames or the folder names. Look at the file names used for the ebook on the CD.

Judging the content of sites

One of the problems of using the web for any kind of information is the reliability of the data. Anyone can put information on the web. Sometimes the information may not have been updated for a long time so adding dates can help users to assess the relevance of your material. As a user, you should look for clues on the site to see when it was created.

Reliability can often be a big problem. You should try to compare the information from several sites. In this way you can be more confident that the facts are true. Bias is a common problem with web sites; often people create a web site to put forward their own views and they are hardly likely to give much prominence to opposing views. This need not be too much of a problem as long as you know what to expect. The web site of a political party is not likely to contain much in praise of its opponents! You need to look carefully at any information before you use it.

Acknowledging sources

portfolio_tip

You must use some ready-made components in you ebook.

When using web sites as a source of information it is easy to copy and paste information. This might seem like a quick way to produce your ebook but remember while it is acceptable to use quotes you must acknowledge your sources.

There are standard ways of doing this described in Chapter 1.6.

Incorporating ready-made components

Ready-made components are things like clip art, sound clips, movies and pictures that have come from a library of some kind.

To use images in a web page you need first to save the image in a folder and link to them using your development software. Don't forget that sound files can be used to provide music in the background.

Using a digital camera

Digital cameras are a good way to collect images for your ebook. Most cameras have settings for image size and resolution. Since your ebook is going to be viewed on a screen, the resolution need not be very high, also try to use an image size as near as possible to one you need.

Once you have your images in the camera you will need to connect the camera and download your images onto the PC hard disk. Put the image files in a folder so that you can find them when you want them. Images can also be downloaded using card readers which means you do not need to connect the camera itself.

Your camera will save its images as numbered files. These numbers will be the same each time you fill your memory card. It can sometimes save effort to save the current batch to a dated folder. That way you don't have to rename them.

Using scanners

Scanners are another way to capture images. Make sure that you keep a close watch on the file size. Since you ebook is viewed on a screen, 72 DPI is good enough. Any higher will use too much space. The image resolution is normally something you can set before scanning.

The best way to scale an image is to set the output size when you scan. The software will then produce the best output for that size.

Scanners can also capture text. You can use Optical Character Recognition (OCR) software to create a file suitable for your word processor to read so that you can then edit it. When using OCR you need to proofread your text very carefully since OCR is not 100 per cent accurate.

It is also possible to use greyscale to reduce file sizes. This produces a black and white image and could be useful if you need to save space.

Capturing screenshots

Screenshots are very useful as illustrations in any publication. This book contains many screenshots. On a PC, you can press the print screen button and then use the paste function to add the captured screen to your work. This produces a large file and contains the whole screen. Even if you crop the image, it still takes up a lot of file space. A better way is to use other software to capture the image and crop it before you take the shot to only store what you need. This has the advantages of saving file space and producing better images.

Producing word-processed documents

A word processor will be an essential tool in producing your ebook. The text can be edited much more easily. Remember to think of a word processor as a 'thought processor' as well. You should, of course, use the spelling and grammar checkers that are available. However, you will need to proofread the text as well.

Using appropriate file formats

portfolio_tip

Look carefully at the requirements for the finished ebook. You must include a wide range of images both ready-made and some that you have made yourself in order to gain high marks.

You will need to convert many of the files for the finished portfolio. It is important to follow the requirements of the examination awarding body here, or your work may not be assessed correctly. If you word process your evaluation, you will need to convert your files into portable document format (pdf). See Chapter 1.1.

You can tell the format of a file by looking at its extension, that is the three letters after the dot in the filename. Here are a few common ones you might need:

- ▶ .pdf   Portable Document Format
- ▶ .jpg   Jpeg file
- ▶ .doc   Document file
- ▶ .htm   HTML file
- ▶ .tif   Tagged Image File format

Combining and presenting information

The design of the pages in your ebook is a very important factor. You need to have a balance between images and text. You should also record sounds and add them to the final ebook. You can use any common utility software to record sounds, and then place them into your ebook.

Combining information from different types of software

Most software used on PCs is capable of using data from other software packages simply by using 'cut and paste'. If you need to move data from one computer to another using a different platform, then you need to use a standard type of file for information exchange. There are lots of different file types to choose from but some of the common ones you might need are:

- ▶ **Comma Separated Variables (CSV):** This is used to transfer information between databases and spreadsheets, or tables in a word processor. See chapter 1.1.
- ▶ **American Standard Code for Information Interchange (ASCII):** This is a very basic way of moving plain text. It does not contain any information about formatting, just the text, so an ASCII file cannot make use of bold, italic and other presentation effects.
- ▶ **Rich Text Format (RTF):** This is used to pass text between word processors so that some of the formatting information such as fonts, bold and underline are retained.

UNIT 2
The digital economy

The digital economy

Aims

- To examine the needs for information in the Information Age.

- To examine ways in which data is collected.

- To examine ways in which information can be processed in order to find out more about customers and offer them a personalised service.

- To understand some of the ways that organisations use IT.

Introduction

This unit looks at how the Information Age has caused widespread changes in the way we do business. The main changes to be examined in this unit are

- ► the reduced dependence on paper transactions;
- ► improved ease of communications (both between businesses and between businesses and customers);
- ► the increase in the use of cashless transactions.

The unit also looks extensively at online transactions. We look at how they work and how they have affected the attitudes of consumers. We now expect to be able to source goods from a much wider range of suppliers than before. We expect to make more of our own decisions as IT resources let us interact with suppliers' data directly, cutting out those who used to advise us. In short, modern ways of doing business have made us more autonomous. For example, many more people put together their own holidays rather than buy a pre-prepared package.

> **ACTIVITY**
>
> Go to expedia.co.uk and see how it is now easy to check flights, hotels and car hire for any destination and book it. Customers can now have control over every aspect of their holidays.

This unit covers how IT has made it easier for organisations to understand their customers in order to maximise their business opportunities. It also looks in detail at the processes that must take place when online business takes place.

Transaction web sites

There has been a great expansion in recent years of businesses providing their services on the Internet. You can now buy nearly anything on the Web. A purchase is a *transaction* carried out between the customer and the company providing the goods or services, so web sites that allow such activity to happen are called transaction web sites. They all have to:

▶ collect details from the customer;
▶ collect payment.

At the heart of online commerce there are always databases. You cannot begin to understand the importance and the functioning of online business unless you understand something about how databases work. This unit requires you to study how databases can be used to underpin an online business. As part of this, you have to produce a database of your own, to store a particular set of data, relating its structure and processing to the jobs that are required of it. You will be at an advantage if you already have experience of setting up reasonably complex relational databases.

Information needs of organisations

Organisations have always needed to store and communicate information in order to function. This has ranged from informal verbal communications to large amounts of paper-based information. The Information Age has made it much easier to gather, store and process information. Because we no longer have to struggle just to handle information, we are freed up to think of ever more inventive ways of using it. Organisations have learned just how vital information is and how it can give them a competitive edge. Information is now seen as one of the most valuable assets possessed by any organisation.

Businesses can succeed or fail depending on how effective they are in information handling. They have never had so much information at their disposal. The winners are the ones that make the best use of it. We need to examine some of the most important ways that businesses now use information.

Capturing and processing data

We sometimes tend to treat the words 'information' and 'data' as meaning the same. It can often help to understand the difference but be aware that these definitions are often blurred in everyday useage.

Data is a collection of facts. It is what we input into computers and what computers manipulate. It can be a set of numbers from a bar code or a list of items stocked by a factory. To the computer, it is all just 0s and 1s. The computer works with these according to its current instructions.

Information is what humans want. It is generally the output from a computer system. It is data in *context*. It has a *meaning* to us.

Knowledge goes even further. It is a coherent understanding based on information. It includes understanding links between different items of information and how actions can be decided on because of the information.

Computers need data: they have no use for information. Computers need to receive data in such a way that their software can process it to make it useful to us. In most cases, this means that they need to be fed with data in a structured and methodical form. Unfortunately, the real world is not like that, it is full of messy information. Much of what we want to know is 'out there' but mixed up with a lot of other stuff that we need to ignore. Imagine a business meeting in a bar at a railway station. The participants have to ignore the other conversations all around, the train announcements, the adverts on the bar and the menu on the table. Humans are good at that. Computers are less so. We have to sift through real-world *information* so that we can give computers useful *data*. Collecting the data that we are going to feed into the computer system is called *data capture*.

The trouble with data capture is that if we make mistakes in gathering the data, the mistakes will get processed along with the good data and our results will be unreliable. Assuming we know what data we need to collect for a particular purpose, we need to be careful not to make technical errors. This means that we should avoid using humans to collect and input data as much as possible. However, a lot of data *has* to be captured by humans in order to extract it from all the noise around it.

Paper forms

Human data collection usually means filling in forms. Forms are useful because they can force a structure on the data being collected. For example, if someone is filling in a form in order to provide a name and address, there will be separate spaces for each item of information. Tick boxes can be used to restrict the information being entered. An example of a form with fields for personal data is shown in Figure 2.1.

> Forms help to convert information into data. They break information up into *fields*.

When forms are given out to many people, they will collect the same *fields* of data from each person. This makes the data easy to process. Often data from forms can be subjected to a batch process.

■ **Figure 2.1**

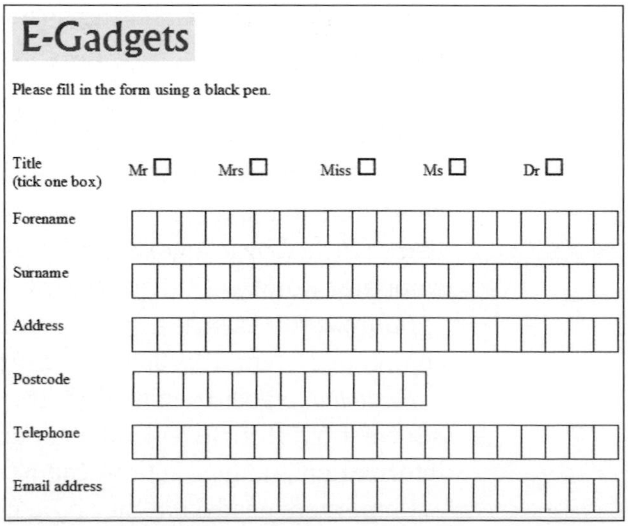
E-Gadgets

Please fill in the form using a black pen.

Title (tick one box) Mr ☐ Mrs ☐ Miss ☐ Ms ☐ Dr ☐

Forename

Surname

Address

Postcode

Telephone

Email address

Screen forms and validation

VALIDATION: the checking of data by the software **as it is being input**, to prevent the entry of unreasonable data.

Data from forms is often typed into a computer system by copying the data into a screen form that has the same fields as the original paper document. Screen forms are structured so that only the desired data is entered. A screen form has the additional advantage that it can be *validated*. Validation rules can be used by the software to trap certain types of mistake as the data is being entered. This makes it less likely that incorrect data will be input. Examples of validation rules might be:

► no surname is longer than 15 letters;
► no name has numbers in it;
► a postcode must start with one or two letters;
► a date of birth must be between 21 and 65 years ago (e.g. this could be used for job applications);
► a price must be between the lowest and the highest possible (e.g. this could prevent entering negative values).

portfolio_tip

Your database should include some validation checks. If you use Microsoft Access, these checks can be applied very easily at the time of table design.

ACTIVITY

Imagine you are applying for a web-based email account. What fields are required? Which of these can be validated? Check your answers against a real web-based sign-up form.

Are there examples where validation can lead to problems in data entry? Hint: think of US zip codes and UK postcodes.

Validation cannot stop all mistakes. In a table that holds stock items, validation can check that you do not enter a letter for the number of items in stock, or a number less than zero. But, if the number in stock is 25 and you enter 35, validation checks are unlikely to spot the error.

ACTIVITY

Think up some more validation rules that could reduce the number of input errors in a file for customer details.

Drop-down boxes and other screen controls

You can reduce the likelihood of errors by putting controls on the screen that only accept certain entries. A combo box is a good example of this.

■ Figure 2.2

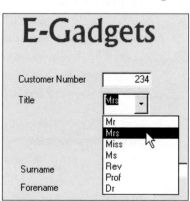

ACTIVITY

List some other screen controls that can reduce the number of mistakes when data is entered.

Automated data capture

To avoid errors, it is best to minimise the amount of human involvement. Wherever possible, you should use hardware devices to collect the data that is needed. There are lots of methods for collecting data automatically.

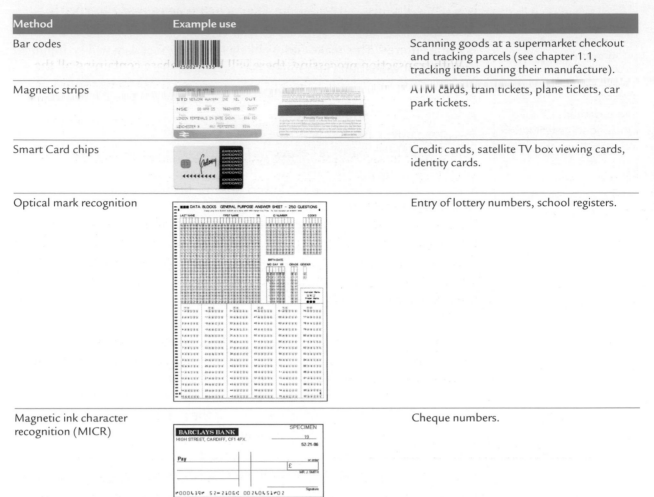

Method	Example use
Bar codes	Scanning goods at a supermarket checkout and tracking parcels (see chapter 1.1, tracking items during their manufacture).
Magnetic strips	ATM cards, train tickets, plane tickets, car park tickets.
Smart Card chips	Credit cards, satellite TV box viewing cards, identity cards.
Optical mark recognition	Entry of lottery numbers, school registers.
Magnetic ink character recognition (MICR)	Cheque numbers.

Data processing

Batch processing

A batch process is a process where a set of similar data is first collected together, then fed into the computer system for it to process. Each record is processed in the same way and there is no further human intervention.

Batch processes are used in many business activities. Examples where computers are used to do the same processing on numerous records are:

▶ preparing electricity bills;
▶ processing cheques;
▶ processing exam results.

> **ACTIVITY**
> List three other business activities that could use batch processing.

Transaction processing

We have seen that when a deal is done between a company and a customer, it is called a transaction. Transactions do not have to be just about buying and selling, for example when your teacher sets you an assignment and you hand it in, it is also a transaction. Transactions can be easily handled by computer systems. Computers make sure that the details are always up to date and as accurate as possible. Full records are kept.

With transaction processing, there will be a database containing all the fundamental information that is needed, such as a list of stock or a list of students. Each transaction will be stored as a new record. The record can be linked to the basic data tables so that the user can have access to all the details about any transaction.

In some transaction processing systems, the database is updated according to the day's transactions at the end of the day.

Real-time processing

With some transactions, it is important that the database behind them is updated immediately. This is called real-time processing. It means that the data is as accurate as possible. This is especially important when bookings are being made. It is crucial that if a flight or concert seat is booked, then the next customer cannot book the same thing.

> **ACTIVITY**
>
> Make a list of transactions where immediate database updating is necessary. How can the system stop a double booking when two people are online to the same database at the same time?

Types of information required by businesses

Businesses need information in order to fulfil a number of basic purposes. A large company has many departments that all need information. Often the information can be shared between departments and IT systems make it easier for all to have access to the same up-to-date information.

Most companies have at least the following departments:

Sales: The people in sales have to make sure that customers get the goods or services they require when they want them. Sales managers have teams of sales staff who try to persuade customers to buy the products and they also have to look after them so that they get a good service. It is important that the sales department knows what has been ordered and when it was ordered so that it can keep track of delivery. It also needs to check that enough is being sold to provide the company's income.

> **ACTIVITY**
>
> Imagine your school or college is thinking of buying some new IT equipment. What information will sales staff need from the school or college and what information will they need to give back in order to complete a transaction?

Marketing: It is no use having products for sale if nobody knows about them. The marketing department has to come up with ways to advertise the products in an effective way. This involves them in having enough information about what people are likely to buy. This usually involves some market research.

Imagine that a publisher wants to sell a new textbook. Who needs to be contacted in order to find out what is needed in the book? How is it best to advertise such a book? What alternative ways are there?

Finance: A company needs to keep a very close eye on its income and expenditure. If it spends more than it earns, it will eventually go out of business. The finance department has to control all financial activities. It has to deal with payment of taxes, salaries and purchases. It needs lots of up-to-date and very accurate information.

Even non-profit making organisations, such as state-funded schools and hospitals, should work within financial limits. They have set budgets and cannot always look for more money if they overspend.

What are the main categories of expenditure in your school or college?

Production: Most businesses sell a product. It may be something obvious such as a car or a pen. It may be a service such as a tax advisory service or an investment product. Someone in the company has to put the product, whatever it is, together. This is called production. They have a great need for information too. A car manufacturer cannot afford to run out of components or the production line will come to a standstill. The workers will still want to be paid, but nothing is being produced. A good IT system will keep the supply under control.

Make a list of the information that is needed by the production department of a large bakery company.

Human resources (HR): Large organisations have a whole department that looks after recruiting new staff and looking after existing workers. They have to make sure that promotions are dealt with, applicants have the right qualifications and that interviews are conducted according to set rules. They need information about the applications and about the staff who are already working at the company. IT systems are vital here.

A PC retail outlet wants to hire some sales staff. What information will they need before they call an applicant to an interview? What extra information will they need if they appoint someone?

Is this the same when your school or college appoints a new teacher? Hint: look up CRB on the Internet.

Other departments: Most large companies have many other departments as well as the ones listed here. Often they have found that their own special activities require a new type of department.

Go to the web site of any large company such as Sainsbury's. Follow the links to the pages about the company structure. Compare this structure with another company from a different trading area (possibly you could compare a big grocery retailer with a bank).

Planning for the future

Most businesses need to consider:

- ▶ possible expansion;
- ▶ new areas of business;
- ▶ new ways of doing business;
- ▶ keeping costs down.

Most of the staff in an organisation are concerned with what can be called operational tasks. These are the things they have to do each day in order to keep things running. A class teacher has to plan and deliver lessons, a sales person has to visit customers, a production line worker has to put doors on cars, for example. Things change in the real world and doing the same thing for ever is not an option. Someone has to look ahead and plan.

The people who do the planning are the directors, helped by their senior managers. Planning where the company is going is a vital activity. If they get this wrong, everybody suffers and may lose their jobs. This is called a strategic activity. The directors are deciding strategy about how to use staff and resources just as a wartime commander has a strategy about how to use troops.

Management needs the big picture and wants processed data that illustrates trends. They do not need all the details. The data that they need to look at will normally be considerably processed and have its origin at lower levels.

The raw data from middle managers is often summarised by decision supporting software which can include everyday office software to make charts and presentations.

Presenting and exchanging information

Presenting information

Most of the feedback that customers get from organisations is now computer generated. It is still largely delivered in paper form, although with the rapid increase in ebusiness, screen-based data is becoming more common. There are hundreds of different examples of the presentation of data to customers. Some examples are listed in the following table.

Information example	Possible means of presentation
Items bought at supermarket	Itemised bill
Hotel booking confirmation	email notification
Concert tickets	Printed and personalised tickets
Tax demand	Paper form
Bank statement	Paper or screen-based
Credit card balance enquiry	Voice output over telephone
Announcement of next station on a train	Voice output and visual matrix display

Many utility companies are offering a discount to customers who choose to receive their bills electronically. This saves them the costs of printing and postage. However, utility bills are often used to provide proof of a person's identity and bills printed on a home printer are not accepted.

You will have experience of the presentation of information from your previous work in ICT classes and will have plenty of knowledge about how IT methods can enhance the presentation of information by means of DTP, presentation software, web sites, word processing, spreadsheets and database reports.

Exchanging information

For years, businesses have exchanged data with each other by electronic methods. For this to work well, the data has to conform to certain standards. The set of bytes sent to a computer must be such that the software that reads and processes it can produce meaningful results. Your word-processed files written in Microsoft Word conform to a standard so that most other word processors can read them. Microsoft Word has become what is known as a *de facto* file standard and most organisations have either Microsoft Word itself or other software that can read Microsoft Word files. The same is true for Microsoft Excel spreadsheet files.

However, not all data can be usefully stored in the format imposed by everyday office software. Certain simple standards have arisen to make it easy for data to be prepared using one computer system and then read and further processed by another. This allows data to be moved easily between systems running on various platforms such as Microsoft Windows, Unix and Linux and Apple. A single organisation can insist on consistent file standards throughout its departments, but when interacting with other organisations, the data must be in a commonly recognised standard.

One of the most common file standards for data exchange is CSV (comma separated values). With this, each data item is separated from the next by a marker (usually a comma). There is an example of such a file in Chapter 1.1 on page 16.

Large amounts of data have to be exchanged between many organisations these days, some examples are

► Schools make examination entries and send in coursework marks online.
► Exam results are passed from the exam board mainframes to the universities.
► Orders for goods are passed from a supermarket to a supply company.
► Bank statements can be downloaded to a PC in a variety of different file formats such as MS Excel, Intuit Quicken or CSV.

Conducting transactions

Business to business (B2B) dealings have long been carried out electronically, but nowadays, the ordinary consumer also has more opportunities to benefit from conducting business online.

Increasingly, business transactions are conducted by the transfer of electronic data. There are many advantages to doing business this way. They include

▶ ease of record keeping;
▶ speed of transaction;
▶ automatic audit trails;
▶ less reliance on possibly unreliable postal services.

The more we use the Internet to transact business, the closer we get to a cashless society; although it is unlikely that this will ever become a total reality.

ACTIVITY

> Make a list of reasons why it is unlikely that we will ever have a cashless society, (e.g. young children cannot have credit card).

One of the most familiar examples of a cashless transaction that involves electronic transfer of data is the widespread availability of EFT and EFTPOS.

The benefits of electronic transfer of business data become even greater when the customer can interact directly with the organisation's database. For example, hotel, travel, concert and holiday bookings allow customers to see availabilities as they are now, that is in real time. A customer knows immediately if a ticket has been purchased and gets an emailed confirmation almost immediately.

Likewise, real-time interaction with bank account details allows bank customers to keep much tighter control on their finances.

Marketing goods and services

Businesses have always been quick to take advantage of any technological developments that can help them market their goods and services better. For example, they make good use of electronic type setting to produce quality copy for newspapers and magazines.

The Internet has provided more opportunities to place their goods and services in front of their audience.

Web advertising

Many web sites contain advertisements for companies other than the one that owns the site. Many useful services such as web-based email are offered free to the user, but the service is paid for by sponsorship and the placing of advertisements on the site.

Some web-based advertising is intrusive. Pop-up screens can appear that have to be closed, thereby wasting the user's time. Sometimes floating advertisements wander over the screen and they can be difficult to close because of their movement. It may be that advertising like this becomes counter productive by annoying potential customers. Free software can be obtained to block pop-up screens.

Web sites

The whole culture of doing business has evolved to the point where a web presence is expected. You just assume that every company or organisation has a web site where you can find out what they sell, what they do or how to contact them. It can be damaging to a business *not* to have a web site. Small businesses often don't have the time or expertise to run their own sites, so there is a constant need for others to do this for them.

If you look at newspaper, magazine, television or poster advertising, you often see the web address of the company included.

Visit www.checketts.co.uk to see how a small local business makes use of a website.

ACTIVITY

Run a search engine check on the businesses that have shops near to you. See how many do not have a web presence.

email

You can subscribe to receive regular emails in order to keep up to date with new marketing initiatives. If you register a piece of software, you will get regular updates about improvements to the product. If you subscribe to *Friends Reunited*, you will get a notification when new contacts have registered.

Spam is a very irritating form of email advertising. Spam is unsolicited email used by unscrupulous individuals to bombard users with advertising material. Although most sensible people bin it without opening it, enough gets acted upon for it to be worthwhile for the spammers.

Distributing goods

Today, distributing goods usually involves IT. Customer orders are processed to produce picking lists in warehouses. This prevents mistakes being made in copying the customer requirements to those who make up the orders.

■ Figure 2.9

Many goods and parcels are given a bar code that makes sure they get sent to the correct destination, for example, bar-coded labels are put on new cars before they are shipped to distribution on all continents. In Chapter 1.1, we saw that courier companies put bar codes on packages in order to route and track parcels across the world.

Managing customer relations

Call centres

When you call a company with an enquiry or to discuss new business, you will often be put through to a call centre. This centre can be anywhere in the world. The operators at the call centre have extensive access to IT-based systems so that they can see your previous business history. This enables them to advise you better on the basis of your needs.

Call centres can save the customer time and prevent errors. All you have to do to identify your address is to quote your postcode and house number. A postcode database fills in the rest.

Car insurance

If you want a car insurance quote, you no longer have to go through all the details about your car. If you quote the car's registration number, the insurance company can instantly look up the make, model, colour, engine size and all the other details that it needs to make a quotation. Your postcode also indicates the sort of risk that insuring your car will be.

Banks

A bank sometimes makes 'courtesy calls' in order to alert customers to special new accounts or services that they may not be aware of. This can be personalised because of the details that they keep on their databases.

Loyalty cards

Some supermarkets and other stores operate loyalty card schemes where points are awarded for your purchases. The points can be exchanged for money off more goods or special offers. The stores can build up an incredibly detailed picture of someone's purchasing habits and overall lifestyle. This allows them to tailor 'cold calls' to match the customer's interests or to send specially selected discount coupons.

Tesco sends discount vouchers to loyalty card holders. Apart from the basic vouchers, there are always some which apply to specific products. These will normally be products that are likely to be of interest to that customer.

CASE STUDY

A well-known supermarket scans its customer database to see which customers have not used the fresh fish counter. They send all of them a coupon offering 20 per cent off their next purchase of fresh fish. This encourages people to buy something they have not bought before, and improves sales. The number of coupons returned then acts as a measure of how successful the promotion was.

ACTIVITY

Make a list of the calls that you or your family have received over a two-week period. What databases are possibly involved? Where did the data come from?

Is this problem getting worse? Can you think of any advantages to the consumer of getting 'cold calls'?

'Just-in-time' purchasing

Most modern retail outlets operate what is called 'just in time' purchasing. This means that they do not order large amounts of stock in advance. They order what they need from their suppliers and expect it to be delivered quickly. This has big advantages for the store.

▶ The store's cash flow improves. It does not need to spend until it knows it has a need for the goods. Its money can therefore stay in its accounts for longer, earning interest.
▶ Perishable goods can be fresher. By ordering goods soon just they need them, they avoid the risk of having fresh foods deteriorating on the shelves. If there is a hot spell of weather, they can order extra salad foods just a day or so in advance.
▶ They can reduce the need for storage space. The goods spend more of their time either with the supplier or on lorries.
▶ The shelves are always stocked. Empty shelves look bad to shoppers.

This gives very fast turnover and looks like good news, but in fact, there are big disadvantages to 'just-in-time' purchasing, although not for the supermarkets. The risk of holding unwanted stock is transferred from the supermarket to the supplier. Suppliers have to be ready to provide (often perishable) goods at a moment's notice. If the supermarket decides it doesn't need, say, several lorry loads of lettuces, the supplier will be left with acres of wasted crops and has to bear the cost. The transference of risk to others that IT-based ordering systems make possible is just one of many reasons why certain supermarkets can make such staggering profits.

From 'brick' to 'click'

Aims

■ To examine the background to Internet shopping.

■ To consider the benefits of eshopping for the consumer and the business.

Introduction

The phrase 'from brick to click' strictly refers to companies who change from conventional methods of selling based in physical premises (bricks) to online methods of selling (click). Another similar term 'brick and click' is more appropriate when referring to companies who have sales premises combined with online selling. Most big companies now trade in this way.

Using the Internet as a method of selling goods and services has many benefits for companies, but also carries some risk. This section examines some of these.

Access to a worldwide customer base

Once a company is set up on the Internet its site can be viewed from any Internet-connected computer in the world. This, in theory, gives the company the ability to trade worldwide. Although smaller companies might not be in a position to handle such trade immediately, they might have to grow so as to be in a position to do so. Larger companies with a worldwide presence find it easier to take advantage of the increased exposure to such a large market.

Trading worldwide on the Internet provides an enormous market with potentially millions of customers with access to the 'store'. After all, they do not need to travel anywhere to reach the shop!

Delivering goods worldwide is not a great problem with many delivery companies competing for trade in this sector. The main difficulty facing a business is the complicated nature of import and export laws in different countries.

ACTIVITY

Perform a web search for companies offering worldwide delivery.
Write a brief comparison of the services offered by any two companies.

Low start-up and running costs

Setting up a business online costs much less than setting up a business in retail premises or offices.

At a basic level, all that is needed is a computer, with access to the Internet and suitable software. There are also many companies that can set up an interactive web site, and host it on appropriate servers. Other companies such as PayPal and WorldPay can handle the credit card transactions as required. This leaves the new business free to concentrate on its goods and services. Obviously these services cost money but not as much as it costs to build or rent premises in a town or city centre.

CASE STUDY

Shopcreator is a company that provides ebusiness solutions to small companies with as few as ten products, giving them an ecommerce facility. For less than £200 set-up costs and £10 per month, Shopcreator will host the web site, and receive and process transactions using their own secure payment servers. They also sell a larger system that allows for over 10 000 products, with more facilities as would be expected in a system of this size.

www http://www.shopcreator.com

For someone with the right IT skills, the start-up costs are much less than setting up a conventional shop. It is also possible to use freely available software to set up and manage a web site.

'Comersus' software

CASE STUDY

On the CD in a folder called 'Comersus' is some open source software called 'Comersus ASP Cart'. This is a free set of web pages linked to a database which will set up a web store. Some IT skills are required, but the hard bit is done already. The software will manage all aspects of running an online store. Because it is 'open source' software it is completely free to download and use. This software will be used later in this book.

Many Internet sales companies operate from warehouses based on industrial estates, where they pay lower rates than in a good position in a town centre. They do not need space for customers to walk round and look at goods and as there is no need for display space, smaller buildings can be used. Sales staff are not required to look after customers, so the business can exist with fewer staff. Duties will mainly involve packing and preparing goods for dispatch. Another cost saving is that no cash is handled on the premises, since all transactions are electronic. A large shop needs to make arrangements for the safe transfer of cash from the shop to a bank, as well as needing to make sure the cash is kept secure whilst on the premises.

High street buildings are expensive to maintain because they need to look good, rates are high because the shops are expected to have high turnovers and have the potential to make a lot of profit. It is possible to build a web site in days. Buildings take months to construct.

The Internet makes it possible for companies to operate from countries with lower employment costs and lower taxation (see Chapter 1). Many banks and insurance companies already operate from India.

Extension of product range

Some businesses have been able to use ecommerce much more easily than others. Airline tickets are one of the Internet's big success stories; buying tickets online is now commonplace. Ryanair, one of the most profitable European airlines, sells over 60 per cent of its tickets online. Other airlines also report that a high proportion of tickets are sold by this method.

Retail grocers such as Tesco and Sainsbury's are now seeing the potential of ecommerce. Tesco created 7000 jobs as part of its Internet home-shopping service. It has almost 300000 registered customers and Internet sales of £2.5m a week.

For some businesses, the expansion of the Internet into people's homes has provided an alternative way of marketing existing goods and services. Tesco already sold groceries, airlines already sold tickets. The Internet brought with it a demand for new services. Many companies see this as an opportunity to expand and provide new Internet-related services and goods.

A large number of high street retailers have expanded into new areas as a result. Dixons, who sell computers and other electrical goods, set up one of the country's first free ISPs called *Freeserve* (now called *Wanadoo*) and others including Sainsbury's and Tesco followed with their own competitive products.

 https://register.tesco.net/online/

Site hosting is a big growth area. Most ISPs offer free web space. There are also many online companies offering web hosting services either free, but paid for by pop-up adverts on your pages, or in the form of subscription services.

Broadband connections are now offered by many companies in the telecom sector in addition to their traditional telephone services.

24/7 presence

Perhaps the biggest advantage to having a business online is that customers can shop 24/7; there are no opening hours, no restrictions such as there are on Sunday trading, Christmas Day, or Easter Sunday. People can shop from home whenever they like and look round many stores in a short time.

This 24/7 presence does not cost extra; the web servers are online all the time, and unlike staff in shops they do not need to be paid overtime for working extra hours, or holidays.

In the case of an online store, orders can be placed at any time of the day or night. The system stores the orders in a database until the staff arrive again to deal with them. In the case of goods such as downloads, the system can email passwords or access codes immediately and the goods can be downloaded with no need to wait!

Stores do not even need to trade online to take advantage of this, a web site can advertise goods that can be bought from a high street store, enabling the customer to look around even though the store is shut.

Faster response times

The advantage of electronic shopping is the instant online purchase. A few clicks of a mouse button is all that it takes. However it is pointless if it takes 'up to 28 days' for delivery. Customers expect a faster response when an order is placed. In many cases an order placed one day is delivered the next. This is because an order is placed direct with the warehouse with no need to wait for stock to move to the shop. Most web sites offer a choice of delivery, with next day delivery often costing more.

Faster response times are possible for a number of reasons:

▶ Credit card transactions can be validated online automatically, so the risk of not being paid for goods is low.
▶ Much of the clerical work required can be automated.
▶ Invoices and delivery notes can be printed at the time the order is placed.
▶ The system can analyse sales patterns to make stock control easier.

Real-time sales information

Real-time information is provided by linking the sales web pages to the stock database. This provides the customer with true online information if the goods are in stock. It is also possible to provide estimated delivery dates if the goods are not in stock.

If goods are not available, the site can collect a customer's details and then send an email when the goods are in stock. Many sites offer a way of tracking an order that has been placed so that the customer can log in and see the progress of the order.

Customer expectation

People expect that a big company in the Information Age will have an online presence. Marketing goods on the Internet is not a choice anymore; few companies can ignore the fact that online marketing is now big business. With a professionally designed web site, a small business on the Internet can have the appearance of a large business.

Drawbacks associated with operating online

On a web site, customers are not embarrassed when they leave their shopping cart without buying anything; many will come in and leave having just looked prices. There are no sales staff to help persuade a customer. Surfers can use search tools and other facilities on a site without any intention of buying anything.

Because it is easy to set up a web site, online shoppers are often overwhelmed by choice. This can make it difficult to make a business stand out from the crowd. Where technical problems arise, customers can be put off quickly. Complete crashes, are still common online and even large web sites are not immune from these. All sites rely on connections belonging to others to transfer the pages from server to customer. Poor navigation systems and poor design will encourage customers to click off a site very quickly.

The fact that the Internet provides some degree of anonymity means that checking and payment procedures need to be quite complex compared with shop premises.

A web site is still limited by the dimensions of a screen. Bricks-and-mortar stores have the advantage of the physical experience. In a shop all senses are used: goods can be seen and physically handled by potential customers, music can calm and influence, the smell of bread freshly baked in the bakery can entice.

Security of a web site to prevent unauthorised access (hacking) is a major task and needs expert help and good robust systems.

Advantages and drawbacks to customers

The growth in Internet shopping sites has brought with it many advantages for the consumer. Some have already been mentioned such as 24-hour shopping.

It is very easy to shop around on the Internet. A quick search and a few clicks are all it needs to move from one shop to another. Goods are often cheaper and order tracking helps to keep the customer in touch with an order.

As with anything in life there are drawbacks. Sometimes there no other methods of contacting a company and this can make it difficult if a customer has problems. Emails are much easier to ignore than a customer banging on the counter demanding to see the manager in a shop full of people. Terms and conditions listed on sites are often difficult to understand and can make it more of a problem if anything goes wrong.

Transactional web sites

2.3

Aims

■ To give guidance on the study of transactional web sites

■ To investigate the nature of transactional web sites.

> **portfolio_tip**
>
> Set up a folder in your browser favourites to hold the bookmarks for the web sites you visit. That way you can easily go back to them if you need to.

For your portfolio, you need to investigate the design of a commercial transactional web site. This section examines some of the topics that you might like to include in an investigation. Before deciding on the web site for your portfolio, you should investigate a number of web sites considering the headings below. You can then decide which web site will provide you with the best evidence for your portfolio.

When choosing a case study, you need to look at a web site which is transactional, that is it accepts orders or other data from customers and collects it in some way. A web site that simply provides information will not fulfil the criteria for this unit.

A good idea might be to look at some commercial web sites and some public sector sites.

You will need to consider the following sections.

The purpose of the site and how successfully it meets this objective

> **portfolio_tip**
>
> Make sure you name the web site you have studied and give its URL.

Start by asking yourself, "What is the purpose of the web site? Is its objective to sell goods or services?"

It will be necessary to spend time looking at the web site to get a feel for the range of goods or services it sells. Try to imagine yourself as a customer on the web site and make a note of your first impressions, these are very important, since a real customer might be put off in a few seconds if the first impression is not a good one.

CASE STUDY

Dell is a very large computer company. The objective of its web site is the online sales of computers. The web site allows a customer to buy a range of products starting with small home computers and going up to a very large file server suitable for a big business. There is also a range of other products on the web site.

Now spend some time on the site considering how well the site meets its objective.

Dell only operates online and telephone sales. Their computers are not sold in any retail stores. The web site allows you to chose options for your PC. You can complete the purchase of your computer online without speaking to a sales assistant. The web site guides you through the process and has all the necessary pages to read about the options and an order page which summaries your final specification.

How it is structured

The structure of a web site is very important. Customers need to become familiar with the web site very quickly. All parts of the web site need to be accessible in a quick and easy to find way. The customer should experience no problems dipping in and out of various parts of the web site.

Frames are often used to ensure that a customer does not get lost inside the depths of the web site. Designers often keep the pages simple and uncluttered to make sure they are easy on the eye.

A search facility is essential on a big web site. This enables customers to locate and look at an item without going through many menus and layers to find something.

portfolio_tip

If possible use screen shots in your work to illustrate the points you make.

ebuyer.co.uk sells many thousands of computer-related items. The home page contains large panels with special offer items. These change on a regular basis. There are many ways to find items on the web site, for example tabs across the top of the page separate major headings. A menu in a frame at the side provides further divisions of these headings. Clicking on a subheading in the frame expands that heading and changes the main area of the screen to show items in that category. There is a search facility at the top of the main page.

The goods and/or services it offers

It should be easy to see what type of goods or services a web site offers. If it isn't, then the web site is failing in its objectives. After all what use is it if a web site sells something when it is difficult to see what it is selling?

Spend some time on the web site and make a list on the kind of items it sells. If you are looking at a large web site, then listing categories of items will be enough; you are not going to be able list everything.

■ Figure 2.11

> **Extra**
> ▸ Books
> ▸ CDs
> ▸ DVDs to buy
> ▸ DVDs to rent
> ▸ Electricals & DIY
> ▸ Flowers
> ▸ Games
> ▸ Gas & electricity
> ▸ Holidays & flights
> ▸ Music downloads
> ▸ Legal store
> ▸ Tesco Jersey - DVDs & CDs
> ▸ Videos
> ▸ Wine by the case

> **Groceries**
> ▸ How to shop
> ▸ Start shopping
> ▸ Tesco eDiets

> **Healthy Living**
> ▸ Healthyliving club
> ▸ Wellbeing @ The Nutri Centre

> **Finance**
> ▸ Credit cards
> ▸ Loans
> ▸ Mortgages
> ▸ Savings

> **Insurance**
> ▸ Breakdown
> ▸ Car
> ▸ Home
> ▸ Life
> ▸ Pet
> ▸ Travel

> **Telecoms**
> ▸ Home phone
> ▸ 118 321 Directory enquiries
> ▸ Broadband
> ▸ Tesco mobile

> **About Us**
> ▸ Careers
> ▸ Clubcard
> ▸ Computers for schools
> ▸ Corporate responsibility

portfolio_tip

Describe the types of goods or services available on the web site you have chosen for your portfolio.

CASE STUDY

Figure 2.11 is a screenshot of the category menu at Tesco.com. The web site offers a vast range of services and goods, some of which may not be expected of a supermarket. The goods and services sold are broken down into sections on this part of the screen. Other areas of the page relate to different goods and services. The groceries section contains many thousands of items for sale.

The product information provided

A web site can use multimedia techniques to provide information about a product. It is important for a web site to provide as much information as possible since the customer cannot see or handle the goods before they are delivered. By law the information provided must be honest and not make false claims.

Pictures are often used. Clicking on them can enlarge small images, and short versions of the item description can be expanded to give detailed specifications. The idea is to provide a brief overview for the person in a hurry but allow the more discerning shopper to obtain further details.

CASE STUDY

The ebuyer web site (Figure 2.12) shows how a series of images are provided in a gallery for an item. The shopper can click on an image and view the object from a variety of angles, almost like being able to look at it in a shop.

IMAGE GALLERY

■ Figure 2.12

Types of transactions that can be made

A transaction is a where interaction takes place with a database management system. In your study you need to look at how the shopper interacts with the web site and the methods used to collect the data.

On a shopping web site you are interacting with a complex stock and customer database. Transactions can be as simple as clicking on an image of an item to see if any are in stock. They may be more complex in the case of the order form for a first time customer where all new details need to be captured.

Figure 2.13 shows some of the typical data required by a transactional web site to complete an order. The system needs to collect the payment information, in this case a credit card number and other details used to validate the card and the name and address of the person paying the bill and the delivery (or shipping address). The main way of interacting with this page is to use text boxes that require information typing into them. The payment method shows another method, called a drop-down menu, where a choice is given and the user selects one of the choices.

EXAMINERS INC

Please enter your personal details and submit the order for processing.

Product	Description	Cost	Quantity	Total Cost
1	Course work writer.jpg	£50	1	£50.00
			Total Cost:	£50.00

Payment Method

Payment Method	Visa ▾	
Credit Card Number		
Expiration Date	(mm/yyyy)	Credit Card Security Code

The Credit Card Security code is on the back of the MasterCard, Sears MasterCard, Visa, and Discover cards. The Security code is on the front of the American Express cards.

Billing Information

Name					
Company					
Street					
Town		County		Post Code	
Phone		Fax			
email					

Shipping Information

☐ Same as Billing Address

Name					
Address					
Town		County		Post Code	
Phone		Fax			

portfolio_tip

Describe the types of transaction possible on the web site you will use in your portfolio.

Many web sites also allow the customer to track orders and see if an item is in stock. On most web sites you will register as a user by entering your details, which will be stored in a database. Other transactions might include being able to edit your customer details.

The methods used to capture customer information

Web sites use many methods to capture customer information. Some of them are open and obvious, called *overt* methods. With these methods, the customer knows that the information is being taken. By using the form in Figure 2.13, the customer can see what is being collected.

In other cases, the information is collected without the customer realising. Methods that do this are called *covert* methods. The amount of information that is collected in this way is quite considerable. Some web sites, when taking credit card details, will log the IP address of the computer making the transaction. Since IP addresses are allocated to a computer by the ISP, they can easily be traced back to a particular computer. (Of course, as most home computers are assigned a dynamic IP address, this information is only useful to a company at the time the user is connected to the Internet.)

Other methods of collecting data involve putting code on web site that leaves *cookies* on the user's computer. The cookie contains code that identifies a computer when it returns to a web site. Using cookies, a company can see how often you visit a web site, what pages you look at, how long you stay on the site (see Chapter 2.5).

Figure 2.14 shows some basic statistics about the activity on small web site.

[Daily Statistics] [Hourly Statistics] [URLs] [Entry] [Exit] [Sites] [Referrers] [Search] [Users] [Agents] [Countries]

Monthly Statistics for March 2005		
Total Hits		1038
Total Files		987
Total Pages		37
Total Visits		2
Total KBytes		1266
Total Unique Sites		1
Total Unique URLs		8
Total Unique Referrers		2
Total Unique Usernames		1
Total Unique User Agents		6
	Avg	Max
Hits per Hour	43	1020
Hits per Day	1038	1038
Files per Day	987	987
Pages per Day	37	37
Visits per Day	2	2
KBytes per Day	1266	1266

Code on a web page can also log statistics such as which search engine referred you to the web site, and the words you put into the search. This enables the company to see what methods bring people to a web site. They can even tell which browser you are using and the computer's operating system.

> **ACTIVITY**
>
> Look at the link www.statcounter.com/. This is a system for collecting data from visitors to a web site. Browsing the site will show you the range of data that can be covertly collected.
>
> Make a list of items that this system collects.

The techniques used to engage, retain and entice customers

With a web site, there is no sales person to persuade a customer to buy goods or for a customer to build up a relationship with the vendor helping to ensure that the customer comes back. The web site needs to use special techniques to help retain customers.

For a web site to be successful, people must be know that it exists. They need to be encouraged to visit it. Customers go to web sites for many reasons, so a web site needs to reflect as many of these reasons as possible. Once a potential customer is there, several techniques can be used to hold visitors. Banner advertisements can show off special offers to the visitor and these need to be as eye-catching as possible.

Advertisements in newspapers and on TV can inform potential consumers about the web site. Even putting the web site address on carrier bags given away in supermarkets makes more people aware that it exists. The use of a well-chosen URL can draw people to the web site through simple trial and error: how many times have you tried putting the name of the company and adding .co.uk?

When customers find the web site, it is very important that they become engaged in the pages as quickly as possible. If they are not, they will leave. If the web site is too slow they even go before the page has finished loading. If they do leave quickly then the chances of them coming back are low.

The web site's content should engage people. Presentation and clear design principles will do this. Poor content, slow loading pages and complex interaction methods will not.

Once a visitor is engaged, then it is important to retain his or her attention. To do this, the content of the web site should be updated frequently. The content should be relevant and carry up-to-date prices. Any images should show the latest products, not something that is well out of date. If at all possible, the users should find their visit to the site enjoyable.

> **portfolio_tip**
>
> Describe how the web site for your portfolio holds and retains your attention and what techniques it has used. Some screen shots will help here.

The site's usability and accessibility

Web sites must be easy to use. It is often easy for IT experts to forget how difficult some people find using a computer. If a web site is too complex then many users simply cannot access the information they need. This needs to be taken into account at the design stages.

It is also important to make the web site accessible to people who might not be able to read small text on a screen. Many web sites now make changing the text size a feature. Look at the bottom of the Dell web page shown in Figure 2.10. There is a button at the bottom of the page to display larger text.

> **portfolio_tip**
>
> How is the web site you have chosen made easy to use? Describe some features that are used, such as searches.

The 'customer experience' offered

> **CASE STUDY**
>
> It's the sum total of the interactions that a customer has with a company's products, people, and processes. It goes from the moment when customers see an ad to the moment when they accept delivery of a product – and beyond. Sure, we want people to think that our computers are great. But what matters is the totality of customers' experiences with us: talking with our call-center representatives, visiting our web site, buying a PC, owning a PC. The customer experience reflects all of those interactions.
>
> Richard Owen, former Vice President of Dell Online
>
> As is stated here the experience goes well beyond the web site. A good web site will be part of an integrated system that supports the customers from the moment they load the web site to the aftercare they can expect following delivery.

> **portfolio_tip**
>
> Look for signs of customer care on your chosen web site. Are clear contact details available, can you phone the company? Is there a way to provide feedback on the web site?

Conditions of purchase

All web sites have conditions of service displayed somewhere on them. They are sometimes difficult to find, but a good web site from a reputable company will make them not only easy to find but also easy to understand. Companies are often criticised for making them long and difficult to read. You need to look at these for a range of web sites. Do they have things in common? Typically they will cover:

► conditions of sale;
► how to return goods.

You should be careful if a company makes it difficult to return goods.

Security of customers' personal and credit card information is also important and likely to be covered in the terms and conditions. What provision does the web site make for this? A good company will make its position clear and have a statement about how it complies with good practice.

Portfolio evidence

You must choose your website very carefully, remember it must be a transactional web site, so look for one that users interact with. Shopping web sites are a good idea but they are not the only possibility.

Your portfolio should contain an evaluation of the web site as a whole as well as descriptions and evaluations under each of the headings above. Try to discuss what makes the web site good for customers, for example what are its strengths and weaknesses?

You should also make some suggestions of how the web site might be improved to improve the experience of shopping on it.

To gain high marks you will need to work independently and use the Internet to find a suitable transactional web site. You description needs to be detailed and clear, and illustrated with appropriate screenshots. If it is a big web site you might not cover absolutely everything but select good examples of the main features that illustrate the design features.

You evaluation needs to be well balanced. There are no right or wrong answers but the examiner will need your opinions on the web site effectiveness and to be able to see what improvements you suggest.

Back office processes

Aims

- To define the term 'back office processes'.
- To investigate back office processes.
- To illustrate some of the back office processes using diagrams.

Introduction

- Figure 2.15

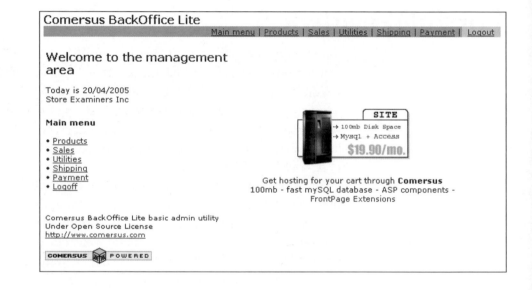

portfolio_tip

Most of your evidence for this section will be in the form of diagrams.

The purpose of back office processes is to ensure the smooth ordering, payment and reporting of transactions on the web site. The processes are not accessible or visible to the general public. Some back office functions include accounting, record keeping of clients' orders, stock control and the management of the public facing web site.

■ Figure 2.16

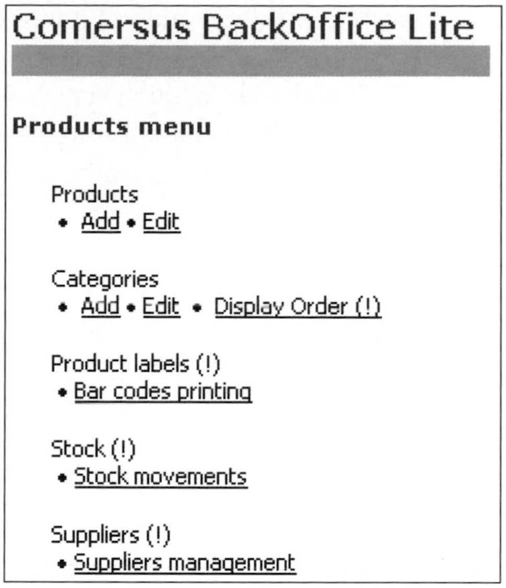

Comersus BackOffice Lite

Products menu

Products
- Add • Edit

Categories
- Add • Edit • Display Order (!)

Product labels (!)
- Bar codes printing

Stock (!)
- Stock movements

Suppliers (!)
- Suppliers management

> **portfolio_tip**
>
> Some of the activities in this screenshot are stock control activities. When making your diagrams think about what happens to the stock when items are sold.

Stock control

One of the major back office processes involves keeping track of items for sale. This is called stock control. It is simply making sure there is always enough stock to meet demand and at the same time not having too many items on a shelf because that ties up money. When a customer wants to order an item, the database is checked to see how many of that item are available. If the customer orders an item then the number in stock needs to be reduced so that the same item is not sold twice.

The back office processes involve a large amount of information processing before, during and after a transaction occurs. A database will be at the centre of the system and the web pages will contain code to allow them to read and update the database. One way of doing this is to use *Active Server Pages* (ASPs).

Here is an example of ASP code.

```
' get item price

pPrice          = getPrice(pIdProduct, pIdCustomerType,
pIdCustomer)
' gets item details from db

mySQL="SELECT description, details, listPrice, imageUrl,
imageUrl2, imageUrl3, imageUrl4, sku, formQuantity,
hasPersonalization, freeShipping, isDonation, searchKeywords
FROM products WHERE idProduct=" &pidProduct& " AND active=-1
AND idStore=" &pIdStore

call getFromDatabase (mySql, rsTemp, "ViewItem")
```

The code in the example reads the database and looks up the item price and details.

The CD contains a folder called *Comersus*. This is a piece of open source software to run a transactional web site. Because it is open source anyone

'Comersus' software

can download it and use it freely. It is possible to run a store online using
this software. The screenshots in this section are from that software.

It should be possible for your school or college to install *Comersus* on its
intranet. If you have a suitable computer yourself it is possible to run the
software on a single machine. Access to this software will help you
understand the processes much better.

Maintenance of the virtual shopping basket

As a customer moves through an online store ordering goods, it is necessary
to hold the details of the items to be purchased. The idea is rather like a
supermarket trolley on a computer screen. Items are placed in the trolley
but until the customer has finished shopping, then he or she purchases what
is in the trolley.

The following processes are involved in maintaining the trolley:

▶ items are added;
▶ prices are totalled;
▶ stock is reserved so that it is not sold twice;
▶ items can be removed;
▶ delivery costs may be added.

These processes can be shown in a flowchart.

■ **Figure 2.17**

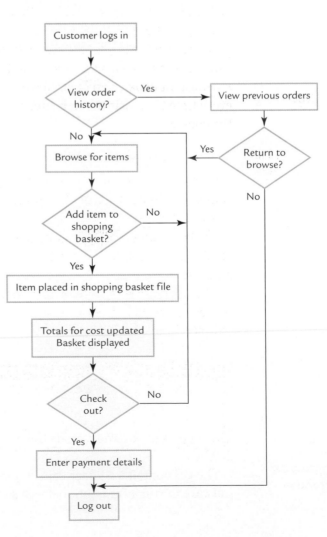

```
comersus_addItem.asp
comersus_cartRecalculate.asp
comersus_cartRemove.asp
comersus_checkOut.asp
comersus_goToShowCart.asp
comersus_shippingCostExec.asp
```

In the Comersus application (on CD-ROM these activities are carried out through the active server pages (ASPs) shown in Figure 2.18.

portfolio_tip

Start by listing all the things a shopping trolley needs to do. Then try to place them into a sequence.

Identification and authentication routines

When a customer enters a transactional web site, it is important to identify and authenticate the customer. Even if the customer does not have to log into the web site, it is important that the connection to the computer on the Internet is maintained and not mixed up with other connections.

Servers on the Web use two basic ways of identification and authentication.

HTTP: This type of authentication produces the familiar login/password browser sequence. This is where a user is asked for a password and an ID to access the server.

Cookies: These can be placed on the customer's computer but are typically set using an HTML form and Common Gateway Interface (CGI) script. Many users, due to privacy concerns, often view cookies with suspicion and they may reject them.

The big advantage of cookies is flexibility. Because the whole process is controlled by the web site, more control over the system can be gained. A persistent cookie can be used which can save the users having to log in every time they visit the web site. This works until the customer deletes the cookie.

What is a cookie?

It is a way for a server or a web site to place information on the client computer. Cookies are small text files that are stored on the user's hard disk by the web server.

Cookies contain information about the user, normally in the form of an identification number. When the user visits the web site again, the cookie is read. The web site can then access a database of cookie information to look up the user's identity. Other information might also be recorded such as the number of visits to the web site or the items looked at. We will look at this more in Chapter 2.5.

■ Figure 2.19

dbSession : Table

	idDbSession	randomKey	idCustomer	sessionData	sessionType	dbSessionDate
+	1	96258181	1235		web	20/4/2005
+	2	88718813	1456		web	20/4/2005
+	3	26830691	34560		web	20/4/2005
*	(AutoNumber)	0	0			

Real-time tracking of customers' actions

Customers who are logged in may be tracked anonymously by using a random number sent in a cookie; in the Figure 2.19 this is held in the field `randomKey`. Other tables in the database will track the customer's actions. The best way of tracking customers of course is to make the customer log in. Once a customer is monitored in, the session can be monitored in much more detail. Actions can trigger data being written to the database. This information can be used in a variety of ways. Loyal customers can be rewarded by special offers.

There are other ways to record access to a web site for analysis (see page 137, Figure 2.14).

■ Figure 2.20

Create table in Design view	currencyStatic	products	visits
Create table by using wizard	customers	recurringBilling	wapCarts
Create table by entering data	customerTypes	relatedProducts	wapSessions
admins	customer_specialPrices	rentals	wishList
affiliates	dbSession	reviews	
affiliatesTransfers	dbSessionCart	screenMessages	
auctionOffers	discounts	serials	
auctions	discountsPerQuantity	settings	
blockKeywords	emails	shipments	
bundles	layout	stateCodes	
cartRows	newsLetter	stock	
cartRowsOptions	options	stockMovements	
categories	optionsGroups	storeNews	
categories_products	optionsGroups_products	stores	
conditions	options_optionsGroups	suppliers	
countryCodes	orders	taxPerPlace	
creditCards	payments	taxPerProduct	

Figure 2.20 shows the tables making up a commercial site database.

Make a list of the tables you think might be involved in tracking customers' actions.

Payment processing

The more ways a web site can offer to accept payments, the more customers it is likely to attract. Most web sites offer some kind of credit card payment system. Taking a payment by credit card is a relatively easy task, but the security of credit card data is very important. The web site will need to use secure data transfer methods using HTTPS and if the details are stored in the database then the table or field holding that data needs to be encrypted as well. This way, if the database is accessed by unauthorised people, the card details cannot be read.

■ Figure 2.21

Encryption & Decryption

Input string: hello
Encryption string: AJALWIYSJAH14256ASQQTYAL59700

Encrypted text: |3|203|61|24|219
Decrypted text: N/A

Encryption took: 0 (±55 msec)

To reverse the process shown above, the user needs to have the encryption key and the software routine.

Organisations will also have links to the card issuers using the Internet. They will have a merchant number and an account with the credit card firm. The transactional web site will be able to connect to the card provider and check the details on the credit card. To cut down on the possibility of goods being ordered with a stolen card, the address details will normally be checked and first time orders must always be delivered to the address held by the card company.

Once a card payment has been accepted, then the seller is guaranteed the money by the credit card company. Payments cannot be stopped unless the card has been stolen.

Stock control

Stock control refers to all the processes involved in ordering, storing and selling goods. An important part of the back office process is real-time stock control.

A web site's stock control system runs on a computer system. The objective is to ensure that there is always enough stock to meet demand, but too much stock will tie up money that could be used for other purposes in the business.

When there is a need to order replacements, the web site could have links to the supplier via the Internet so that replacement goods can be ordered automatically. Careful analysis of sales can help with the prediction of sales volume so that a minimum level of stock is maintained.

■ Figure 2.22

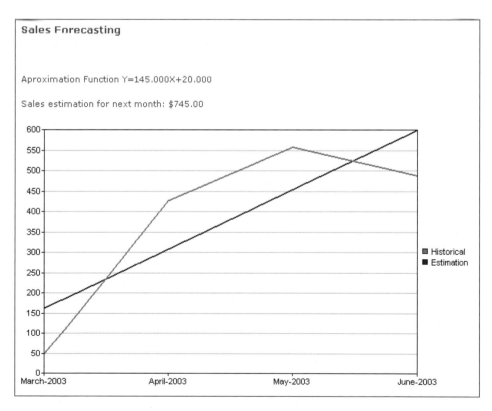

Sales Forecasting

Aproximation Function Y=145.000X+20.000

Sales estimation for next month: $745.00

Historical
Estimation

March-2003   April-2003   May-2003   June-2003

portfolio_tip

You should think about the information needs of the organisation, and how information flows between different parts of the system.

Despatch and delivery

This part of the process is largely a manual process. Address labels need to be printed along with dispatch notes and invoices. The goods need to be packaged and collected by courier. At this point, the organisation will hand the tracking over to them. The customer can be informed via email or by logging in to the courier's tracking system so that the customer can track the progress of the consignment (see Chaper 1.1 page 20).

■ **Figure 2.23**

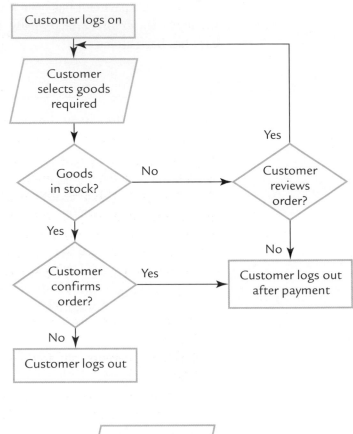

■ **Figure 2.24**

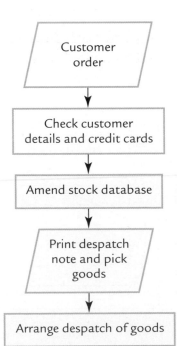

portfolio_tip

Figure 2.25 is an example of an information flow diagram. You should include similar diagrams to this in your account of the web sites that you investigate.

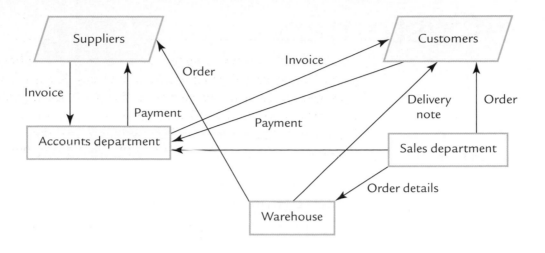

Portfolio evidence

The evidence for this section of your portfolio is mainly in the form of diagrams. You should make sure that your diagrams are clearly labelled and set out. You will need to make sure you can convert your diagrams into one of the file formats that is acceptable to the exam awarding body. You can find most of the standard symbols for these diagrams in Microsoft Word, and you can then convert your file to PDF.

To obtain good marks in this section, your diagrams must be clear and easy to follow. They should give a complete and accurate picture of the system, covering:

► the chain of events leading up to an online purchase (for example Figure 2.23);
► the chain of events that an online purchase triggers (for example Figure 2.24);
► the information that flows into and out of the organisation and between areas/departments as a result (for example Figure 2.25).

The information need not all be on one diagram, it might be easier to follow if it is broken down into sections.

e-Customers

Aims

■ To examine how businesses attempt to understand and build up relationships with their customers.

Introduction

Conducting business successfully requires knowledge of the customers: their wants, their needs and what motivates them to buy. This sort of market intelligence can be gained by face-to-face contact or by various statistical processes. For the statistical processes to be reliable, the company selling the goods or services must collect plenty of accurate information. There are lots of well-tried methods available from the world of traditional transactions. For example, using the incentive of entering a prize draw customers and potential customers can be persuaded to fill in questionnaires that reveal their buying habits. This information can be used for future marketing and product development activities.

Such data collection can be extended to the world of ebusiness, but the involvement of IT allows much more data collection and processing to be done. It also allows the automation of much of the intelligence gathering. Theoretically, ebusiness should allow vendors to refine their selling techniques to a much greater degree than traditional methods.

Basic transaction necessities

All businesses need to sell goods or services in order to survive. This means that they need to interact with customers. If a transaction is conducted remotely as with mail order or ebusiness, certain basic information must be collected in order to collect and fulfil the order, to deliver it to where it is required and to collect payment. At the very least, this must involve:

▶ obtaining the customer details, such as name and address, so that the purchase can be delivered;
▶ making arrangements to collect payment.

But before this can happen, the customer must:

▶ know about the goods or services;
▶ be persuaded to purchase.

The focus of this chapter is to look at the ways that ebusinesses can build up a picture of their customers: actual and potential.

When a transaction is conducted online, the business is able to add to a database of customers. The names, addresses, email addresses and purchases made can be used later to promote products in which the customer has already demonstrated an interest. So, as well as taking basic details, businesses try various methods to build up a picture of their customers. Some of these methods are made obvious to customers, but there are other methods that customers do not always know about.

Analysis of purchase histories and sales information

A person watching a TV advertisement is unlikely to take much interest in it unless it is about a product that is already of interest, or the advertisement uses such a striking technique that it draws attention to itself. The same is true of newspaper advertisements and posters. Mail shots will often go straight in the bin unless they are about something that the reader is already interested in.

Targeted advertising is much more likely to catch someone's attention than random advertisements. This requires information about existing and potential customers. This information has monetary value. This is why businesses are prepared to spend heavily in order to acquire it.

CASE STUDY

Dave gets lots of junk mail every day. This month, his car insurance is due and lots of the mail shots he recently received were about how much money he could save if he changed to a different company.

From time to time, he gets discounts coupons through the post from his supermarket. Sometimes they offer extra loyalty card points for making certain purchases. He noticed that this month they were all for cat food and cat litter. This was quite handy because his family likes cats a lot and has two of its own. The pictures of the kittens on the advertisements appeal to his daughters, who make their Dad think, 'I must remember to take these with me next time I go shopping'. Any coupons that Dave uses in the shop will be collected and counted. This way the shop can tell if sending out the coupons worked. The coupons might have a bar code on them, in which case the shop can work out that Dave used his coupons. In the trade these are called 'bounce back coupons'.

This week, they received a charity appeal from their local cat rescue centre.

Like many men, Dave dreams of getting an expensive sports car one day. Funnily enough, he gets lots of promotions in the post from car companies offering test drives and containing glossy brochures.

Dave has an 18-year-old son, Richard. Richard loves cars too. He recently received two advertisements in the post promoting cheap car insurance for the over 50s. They all had a good laugh about that.

ACTIVITY

Using the case study, make a list of ways that the different advertisers could have found out that the family

- likes cats;
- needs car insurance right now.

What might have gone wrong with Richard's insurance adverts?

A database of past purchases can be very useful in order to target people with promotions in which they are likely to take an interest.

Conversely, these databases can be used to find out what certain people do *not* buy. Suppose a shopper is on a database that records purchases of organic vegetables. It might be worth seeing if that person might be interested in purchasing a compost bin. Perhaps ecologically minded customers might be thinking of growing their own vegetables. The business can further try to attract the customer's attention by offering a discount coupon. If this coupon has a serial number on it, the company can monitor if it has been used and further build up intelligence on the customer.

■ Figure 2.26

Loyalty schemes

We are all familiar with the loyalty cards used by big retail organisations like supermarkets and petrol companies in order to persuade customers to return. Customers get points for the money that they spend and they can exchange them for special offers or money off. Much more important to the company is the shopping intelligence that they can provide. Software can interrogate databases and associate customers with purchases. Most loyalty schemes require the customer to fill in an application form before getting the card. The application forms provide yet more intelligence on the customer such as occupation, date of birth and, crucially, the postcode. Your postcode says a lot about you: your likely income, your insurance risks and even your lifestyle and interests. If your postcode shows that you live in a flat, you probably won't be interested in advertisements for lawnmowers.

With big organisations, this sort of relationship is not possible. Equally it is impossible when conducting ebusiness. Customers are never seen so many methods, mostly involving IT, have been developed in order to try and keep a good picture of customers' profiles.

Offering a personalised service

We have already seen how loyalty cards can be used to generate discount coupons that reflect a customer's buying habits and possible new interests. These not only stimulate interest in products that the customer might not have thought to buy, but they can feed back intelligence about whether buying habits have changed.

When you visit an ebusiness web site, you will not necessarily see the same web site that everybody else sees. Most ebusiness web sites carry advertisements, both from the owner of the web site and often from other businesses that have paid for space. The advertisements that you see may well vary according to the intelligence that has been gathered about you. As we have seen, this can be most easily done by using cookies to identify you. This is a simple process but runs certain risks for the vendor, for example:

▶ you may have set your browser to reject cookies;
▶ you may have deleted your cookies (you can do this through the browser, manually from the operating system or by using one of the many privacy programs that are available);
▶ you may be browsing from a different computer (common enough if you do some Internet shopping from work or an Internet café).

It is more effective to run an ebusiness web site that requires customers to log in. That way, software can always associate the customer with a history file and offer a personalised service.

A very good example of this is the book and music vendor *Amazon*. When a previous customer logs in, the shopping process is made much easier:

▶ Previous books bought are known, so new books of a similar type or by the same author can be recommended.
▶ Your credit card details are retained so there is no need to type them in again.
▶ Your name and address is known plus any other addresses that you may have used for previous deliveries. You can then chose which address to use without having to bother typing it in again.
▶ You can view a history of previous transactions which can help you track your own behaviour or perhaps print out details for the taxman.

All sorts of elegant touches are possible by means of the sensitive use of data collected by Internet transactions. Some of us with less common names get used to having our names misspelt throughout life. It always irritates slightly as it suggests that the person concerned can't be bothered to take care. If you enter your details yourself online, it can be a refreshing change to find that everything is correct on invoices and letters! You might book a hotel room online and find that when you arrive, not only are the details correct at the check in but you are greeted by name (correctly!) in a message on the television in your room. Little touches like this can make a good impression which is good for business.

■ Figure 2.30

Some businesses send emails to you when you have bought their products. The online electronics vendor *ebuyer* does this. Every week you get an email that details some product or special offer that is likely to interest you. When you buy software online, you often get reminders when upgrades are available.

Persuading customers to spend more

Businesses have developed many ideas to persuade their existing customers to spend more. Lots of these ideas translate well to the world of ebusiness because they can be automated. If you are buying a product and have added it to your shopping basket, then the web site might suggest other items you might like to add. For example, if you are buying something that needs batteries then the web site could offer to add them to your order.

Discounts

Most mail order and ebusiness companies charge for the delivery of their goods. One way to encourage customers to buy more is to reduce or waive the charge altogether if they purchase goods over a certain value. For example, a wine company charges £5 for each delivery to a particular address whether the customer has ordered one or ten cases of wine. Sometimes, the delivery charge for small orders is unrealistically high in order to encourage a bigger spend.

Suggestions

The virtual shopping environment can be made helpful to encourage shoppers to think about buying similar things that they may not have previously considered. *Amazon* has a note by each book that says 'customers who bought x also bought a, b and c'. You may not have realised that an author you like has written more than one book on a topic that interests you, so the web site can notify you.

Ratings

Web sites often invite customers to submit reviews of the items that they have bought. Lots of people cannot resist a chance to air their opinions so a set of positive ratings about a book, a computer or a hotel can add a lot to the interest of a web site.

Promotions

If you have bought a particular item or service, you may be sent emails to encourage you to buy again, particularly if the company concerned is trying to boost sales in a slack period. Some hotel chains promote amazingly cheap offers such as a limited number of rooms at £5 per night to previous customers. If a hotel group has empty rooms it is better to let them out cheaply than not at all and maybe the customer will feel special in being invited to partake of a limited offer.

Providing more information

Some products lend themselves so well to IT analysis, that it can be helpful to present the findings to the customers. A good example of this is in the world of financial products.

CASE STUDY

Fund management

A financial management company promotes investment by its customers in a number of funds. A fund is made up of shares in a group of companies. Typical funds might be an American fund, a European fund or a fund made up from undervalued companies that are expected to improve. The management company employs fund managers who buy and sell shares within these funds in order to maximise profits for the investors. A typical fund management company may have dozens of different funds available and the customers can log onto their web site and check the performance of all the funds over long and short terms. Clicking on a fund generates a graph over a choice of time periods.

Interested investors can use this facility to do some trend spotting for themselves and may be attracted to invest more in order to try to maximise their profits.

Predicting market trends

Sales success depends on having the right product available at the right time and at the right price. Getting the time right is crucial. Some timings are obvious, for example, supermarkets need to be ready for increased salad sales in the summer. Textbooks need to be ready for the new academic year. Other trends are less obvious and IT can help.

If a company has a big enough database, software can be used to plot trends and extrapolate possible future demand. If the data is detailed enough, trends can be spotted quickly by plotting charts which would be too time consuming to do manually.

Reducing wastage

If a company has good intelligence about its customers, it will be better able to predict its likely sales in the future. It is good economic sense for companies to stock only enough of a product to meet its likely needs. Excess stock is idle money. In some cases the stock has a limited life and excess stock represents a total loss. This does not just apply to perishables such as fresh food, it also applies to other time sensitive goods. For example, a textbook written to support a particular syllabus or specification is not going to sell once that syllabus has been updated or replaced. Any online business that maintains stocks of that book needs to ensure that it does not overstock. The past buying behaviour of the schools and colleges or indeed individual customers can provide information about when the busy sales periods are. Outside of that time, it is safe to run down stock levels.

eConsumer awareness

Aims

■ To consider how personal information can be misused and some of the measures that can be taken to protect it.

Introduction

Information is easily copied and transmitted by computer systems. Criminals have found many ways to exploit this for profit. Ebusiness has to do what it can to protect its interests and customers against the theft and misuse of information. New issues have arisen in the Information Age that were less important in the past. Theft is much harder to detect. When most things are stolen, you know they are gone. With information theft, you still have the information so you may not notice that it has been stolen.

This chapter is concerned with issues concerning personal data rather than trade secrets.

What information is held about you by organisations?

In order to do business with a customer, a business must have access to a certain amount of information. Additional information is helpful in order to protect itself, improve its product range and develop marketing strategies. We have looked at some of this in Chapter 2.5. Only some of this information is provided by the customer. The rest is either generated by the business transactions or obtained from third parties. We do not necessarily know what is stored about us unless we go to the trouble of finding out. Even then, you can never be completely sure.

Personal information is that which applies to a living person and can be identified with that person. As you will see in this chapter, there are very good reasons why care needs to be taken of personal information.

At the very least, a business transaction made online requires the name and address of the customer. Without this, the goods cannot be delivered and an invoice cannot be raised.

Online businesses will store various other items of personal information. What they store will vary a lot depending upon the nature of the business, for example, an online business is an ebusiness which clearly needs to know its customers' standing orders, direct debits, account balances and transaction details. It will have a good idea about your income, or at least the income that gets paid into your account. The bank cannot give you the best possible service unless it knows these things, but you would not want others to know them!

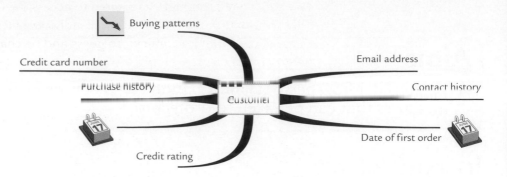

Your car insurance company has to know the make and model of your car, the year of registration, the engine size and other details in order to calculate your premiums correctly.

> **ACTIVITY**
>
> Find out what personal information is held on you by your school or college. You may be surprised about just how much there is.

On the whole, most of the information that businesses store about us is necessary at least in a second-hand way. If their knowledge of our buying habits is good, they may be able to give a better service and offer us other goods or services that we want. If we looked at the information, there would probably be few surprises except at the extent of it all. After all, no business wants to be responsible for upsetting its customers. The main concerns that econsumers should have are more to do with the security and accuracy of the information.

How the information is protected

For legal reasons, as well as just doing good business, companies that hold personal data need to take care of it. There are many well-tried methods to keep computer data secure, but new ones need to be produced in order to outwit the increasing numbers of IT-knowledgeable criminals.

Not only do businesses need to take care that their trading information is safe from criminals, they also need to make sure that it is safe from corruption and loss.

CORRUPTION: The alteration of data as a result of malfunction or a malicious act.

Physical security measures

A lot of security measures are common sense, but there are always individuals and organisations that neglect some of the most obvious precautions. Computers that have access to personal and private data should be in rooms that are locked whenever unattended. Only individuals who need to work on the data should be given access. Some organisations install biometric security locks that a fingerprint or similar has to be presented before the lock will open.

Storage media such as disks and tapes should be kept in lockable fireproof safes. There are more details about security measures in Chapter 2.7.

Procedural security measures

► A valid login ID should be required to access the computer systems where sensitive data is stored and also the individual files.
► Passwords should be difficult to guess and be changed regularly. It is not a good idea to use your birthday, pet's name or favourite football team as a password. One strategy is to combine an easy to remember password with an unrelated number.
► Levels of access can be set so that only members of certain departments or groups can access private files.
► Logged-in computers should not be left unattended; at least a password protected screen saver should be used.

ACTIVITY

What measures are taken in your school or college to make log-in secure? Do you know anyone else's password? Can you guess any?

Back-ups

There should always be up-to-date back-up copies of important files. The organisation should choose a suitable back-up strategy that works for them. This includes how often a back-up is carried out, the media used and how much of the data is backed up. A total back-up can take a long time, but an incremental back-up may be all that is needed most of the time (this is where only new or altered files are backed up and added to the stored copy).

CASE STUDY

Sunridge Information Systems backs up the data on its servers every night. The back-up strategy uses one tape each day, Monday to Thursday. Each day, the last week's day tape is overwritten. Another set of tapes is used for Fridays: there are four tapes used in rotation for this, so back-ups cover four weeks. The office is closed Saturday and Sunday so no changes are made to the system on those days.

ACTIVITY

Sunridge Information Systems is considering moving from brick to click and trading online. What are the implications for their back-up system?

Back-ups should be kept in a secure place. If the data is particularly vital, this can mean storing it off site, so if there is a fire, there is still a copy.

Firewalls

If a computer or network is connected to another network, and especially if it is connected to the Internet, there is the danger that someone will try to gain access to the files. People who do this are usually called hackers and often succeed by trying to guess passwords, sometimes by using software to make millions of guesses. Firewalls can prevent this threat. They are a

IP (INTERNET PROTOCOL) ADDRESS: The Internet and many internal networks use a set of rules or protocol to allow the connected devices to communicate. Every device has a unique number or address and it is one of the jobs of the protocol to define the exact format of these addresses. IP addresses consist of four numbers, each in the range 0–255, so a typical IP address might be 125.78.86.67.

combination of hardware and software that can be configured to block access to a network or individual computer to all except known IP addresses.

More and more people now have broadband Internet access. This is often left on for long periods. This makes it a possible target for hackers who may steal private information or use your PC as a launch pad for spam. Home users nowadays need to have firewalls just as much as businesses do.

Firewalls can also be configured to block outward access thereby controlling the web sites that employees can visit.

Encryption

Some personal data, such as credit card numbers, is often encrypted. The data is scrambled according to an algorithm and it can only be translated back to the original by a computer that has the correct unscrambling software. The software usually needs access to a security code called a key so that it can make the necessary transformations, (see Chapter 2.7 page 171).

How accurate is the information?

Customers have an interest in the accuracy of the information that is kept about them. This is particularly important if it has to do with accounting procedures. They don't want to get the wrong bills or be pursued for debts that they have already paid.

Obviously, a well-run company will have procedures in place to make sure that when invoices are paid, the facts are recorded correctly. The weak link in this process is always the human factor. The process of billing can be better automated with online systems than with more traditional methods. If a customer makes certain selections from a sales web site, as long as the underlying database contains the correct prices of the items, the software will calculate the correct total and bill the customer's credit card correctly as well. The total will be displayed to the customer before the final agreement so it is very unlikely that mistakes will be made.

The most likely source of error is if the original data in the database is entered incorrectly. One of the authors of this book looked up room prices at a good hotel in New York and was quoted $3.28 per night. Either someone had keyed in the wrong data or this was the bargain of the year! Incorrect data entry can be much reduced by entering it all twice, preferably by two different operators. Software can compare the two versions and flag up any inconsistencies.

> Verification is the checking of data that has been entered. It is often carried out by humans although they can use computer checks to compare two versions of the data.

Keeping information up to date

Customers can help in keeping their details up to date more easily with web-based businesses. They can log in and check their details themselves and make changes when necessary. This is much more likely to produce an accurate database than when operators copy details off forms. Occasionally, the company may contact the customers to get them to check details, but there is always the danger that scammers will pretend to do this in order to get customers to reveal information.

When completing a sale online, some companies display the user's details and ask them to confirm that the details are still correct.

What is the information being used for?

People are increasingly concerned about what their personal data is used for. This is because it is so easily passed around and some companies do not always behave in the most professional way.

We have much less personal privacy than we used to. It is easy to gather information about us. Usually we accept this as a price to pay for greater convenience, but there are good reasons to be concerned. Most of the privacy issues are simple annoyances. We often get cold calls from companies we haven't heard of touting for business. These calls always seem to come during dinner or during our favourite TV programmes and we sometimes wonder how they got our phone number!

CASE STUDY

The electoral register

Ben was caught accidentally exceeding the speed limit by just a couple of miles per hour by a speed camera. He received a fine and points on his licence. He was so annoyed about this that he wrote an angry letter to a national newspaper. The paper published it with his name and town. A few days later he received letters through the ordinary mail taking issue with his point of view. He wondered how on earth these readers got hold of his address. The fact is, there are online versions of the electoral register which anyone can view. It is now possible when filling in the registration form for the electoral role to indicate that you do not wish to be listed other than in the copy held at the local council offices. However, this option is not very clear on the forms.

There is even a database that can be viewed which shows who has voted in recent elections. This enabled scammers to fill in stolen voting papers in the fair assumption that the people concerned would never notice as they don't normally bother to vote.

Privacy issues are not likely to go away. Indeed they will probably increase as more people have access to more personal information. There is legislation that stipulates the limits to which personal data can be used when an organisation holds personal data. This legislation is there to try to protect people's privacy, but as more and more data becomes available in the public domain, the effectiveness of this legislation is much reduced.

Who has access to the information?

As discussed, a certain amount of data is available to anyone and it is likely that the amount will increase rather than decrease. Despite the laws intended to protect privacy, data increasingly 'gets out' either through interpreting the rules in a casual and elastic way, carelessness or malpractice.

Data that is sold to others

Many organisations that collect personal data pass it on to others. This is prohibited by most countries' legislation, but it can be done if the individual concerned has given permission or, more likely, failed to tick the box withholding permission. Lists of potential customers for various products can easily be compiled and they are worth a lot of money in helping companies to target their advertising. The selling of such lists is itself a good business and a useful source of income to the organisation that originally collected the data.

Collecting email addresses

Some types of information can be collected automatically, such as valid email addresses. These are useful for spammers. Software can trawl web sites in order to look for email addresses on web pages and store them in a database. Other software can generate random email addresses for well-known domains such as hotmail.com. If an address is invalid, a delivery failure message may be sent back, thereby confirming which addresses are real ones.

Credit card details

The amount of credit card fraud is enormous. This is a particular problem because of the way that sales can be confirmed over the phone or the Internet without the card actually being present. Knowledge of a card number plus its expiry date is often all that is needed to confirm a sale. Criminals use all sorts of methods to obtain card details, not least from burglary and muggings. But, they do not even need to go to this trouble. Carelessness can bring even richer pickings.

Old PCs

CASE STUDY

PCs are everywhere and nearly all organisations use them. Getting rid of old ones poses many problems, not least the removal of all data from the hard disk before disposal.

A farmer who knew only a little about computers recently bought a second-hand one at an auction. He found it difficult to set up so he asked his brother-in-law who was a computer expert. He found a hotel database on the hard disk complete with two years' worth of transactions containing customer names and addresses plus credit card details.

Just deleting data from a hard disk is not enough. The directory entries are marked as deleted, but the data still remains. Even formatting a disk may leave traces that can be recovered.

Researchers at the University of Glamorgan analysed some 100 randomly-sourced PC hard disks, and discovered that more than half contained data from organisations such as multinational companies, universities and a primary school.

Data on the disks included:
- staff records, passwords, internal emails and financial details;
- school reports, a list of pupils, and letters to parents;
- a document template for university degree certificates.

Attempts had been made to destroy data on nearly half the disks in the study, but significant material remained intact.

Computing, 17 Feb 2005

Other than using government and military deletion standards, the only sure way to make sure that old data cannot be used is to remove the hard drive and smash it to pieces.

Identify theft

One fast growing crime is identity theft. In this, criminals use the details of real people in order to open credit card and bank accounts and then use up the credit in fraudulent transactions. The real person then gets sent the bills. Another scam is to find out someone's Internet banking details and then empty the account.

There are lots of ways to find out real personal details. As mentioned in Chapter 1.3, some criminals employ people to go through rubbish bins to steal utility bills and old bank statements. Trojan horses (see Chapter 2.5) can record keystrokes, such as for passwords, and email them to the originator's address.

 Visit www.telegraph.co.uk/news/main.jhtml?xml=/news/2005/05/01/nfrau01.xml and www.telegraph.co.uk/news/main.jhtml?xml=/news/2005/05/01/npost01.xml to read more about identity theft.

Legislation

There have been many attempts by many governments to pass laws that regulate IT transactions. This shows that there is an acute awareness that the Information Age has special problems that are different from those in the past. On the whole, these Acts of legislation are only partly successful as there are often ways around them or transgressions are difficult to detect.

Legislation has largely focused on the exchange of information by IT because of all the reasons to do with security and privacy that have already been explored.

Data protection

Most countries have some laws that cover the protection of personal data on computer systems. The data protection law in the UK are fairly typical. For a full coverage of the Data Protection Act and the Computer Misuse Act, look at pages 64–65 in Chapter 1.3.

There are weaknesses in the data protection legislation.

Some of the personal information in the public domain cannot be called back as there is no obvious 'owner'. We have seen that it is easy to obtain names and addresses. It is also easy to track down a lot about many people simply by doing a Google search or by visiting:

www.118118.com

Civil rights

There are government organisations that do not have to comply with the full rigour of the data protection legislation. We have already seen that the DVLA is in possession of the insurance details of people's cars as well as the basic vehicle details. The security services may have access to personal information that can be completely unverifiable. A suspicion or an accusation about someone could be on file without the person's knowledge. There have been suggestions, which will no doubt resurface from time to time, that many government agencies will be able to share information about people.

In the UK, there has been much debate in recent years about the introduction of a compulsory ID card. Many take the view that this is a further unwarranted intrusion into our privacy, allowing authorities faster access to a host of personal details. Some argue that this is no more than exists in other countries and that it would help the police and security forces prevent terrorist attacks.

Credit ratings agencies keep lists of people who have defaulted on debts or have bad credit records. These lists can make it impossible to get credit. Mistakes sometimes happen and people get included when they should have a perfect credit record. It can be very difficult to find out about these and get mistakes put right.

Whatever point of view you take about these issues, there are big implications for our civil rights and the amount of freedom and privacy that we have as individuals.

Distance selling

Ebusiness has allowed us to purchase goods and services as easily from the other side of the world as it is from our own high street (see Chapter 1). This has allowed us to have more choice and can also bring prices down. There are, of course, potential problems with long distance selling, especially when transactions are conducted across more than one country. Because different countries have different trading laws, there is always going to be the question of which country's laws apply to a particular sale. There can sometimes be ambiguity about whose taxes need to be paid. There is lots of work for legislators and lawyers here for years to come, but settlements need to be made to allow transactions to be made without too much difficulty.

There are laws in the UK covering distance selling in order to provide consumer protection. They are extensions of existing consumer legislation such as *The Consumer Protection (Distance Selling)(Amendment) Regulations 2005*. Regulations include:

▶ the right to receive clear information about goods and services before deciding to buy;
▶ confirmation of this information in writing;
▶ a cooling off period of seven working days in which the consumer can withdraw from the contract;
▶ protection from credit card fraud.

www.dti.gov.uk/ccp/topics1/facts/distancesell.htm

In Europe, the existence of a political and trading community makes things a little easier because there is already a forum where decisions of this sort can be made. It will take longer to work out the implications on a global basis and there will probably never be total agreement.

> **portfolio_tip**
>
> This section contains some information about the laws passed to protect customers' data. You need to list the laws that help protect data and should have a conclusion which says how effective you think it is.

Security

Aims

■ To examine the possible threats to security.

■ To examine ways that an organisation can minimise the risk.

Introduction

Security threats are often due to weaknesses in an operating system which people can exploit to affect your system in some way. Hackers might try to use these weaknesses to run a program on your system, or access your confidential data, such as passwords and user IDs. Some operating systems have well-known weak points that can be exploited over the Internet. Email programs such as Microsoft Outlook have been exploited many times to distribute viruses. When these weaknesses are identified, software manufacturers normally release updates, patches or hot fixes that will help to protect your computer.

Wireless networks are now common and are used by home users as well as larger organisations. These networks have many advantages for their users but they provide easy access to a system if security measures are not put into place.

Internet access via a wireless network can allow other unauthorised people to use an unprotected connection. Any computer close enough to pick up the signal can use the connection. People living close to each other can easily 'freeload' a neighbour's Internet connection. This may seem as if it is a minor problem, because if a connection is always on and a fixed fee is paid then what does it matter if someone nearby has access to your connection? But what if they use it to carry out illegal downloading, such as child pornography? The police will track it down to your IP address.

Also if you are using an insecure wireless network your own PC is exposed, particularly if file sharing is enabled.

portfolio_tip

This section describes some of the protective measures a company can use. For your portfolio, you will need information from other sections as well as to cover laws protecting data.

■ **Figure 2.33**

Apr/08/2005 14:02:07	Unauthorized wireless PC try to connected 00-0B-6B-6A-14-61
Apr/08/2005 14:02:07	Unauthorized wireless PC try to connected 00-07-CA-04-29-AA
Apr/08/2005 14:02:08	Unauthorized wireless PC try to connected 00-0B-6B-6A-14-61
Apr/08/2005 14:02:10	Unauthorized wireless PC try to connected 00-0B-6B-6A-14-61
Apr/08/2005 14:02:10	Unauthorized wireless PC try to connected 00-07-CA-04-29-AA
Apr/08/2005 14:02:11	Unauthorized wireless PC try to connected 00-0B-6B-6A-14-61

Risk assessment

To improve the security of systems, it is a good idea for organisations to carry out a risk assessment. Doing this will help to identify potential risks faced by the organisation's systems. It is also important to consider what might happen if valuable data is lost or the system suffered a major failure.

Carrying out a risk assessment is quite simple and most precautions are a matter of common sense.

The first step is to identify any possible threats to the data and computers. These can include:

► human error, such as deleting the wrong file;
► physical threats such as a fire or lightning striking the building;
► unauthorised access via wireless links;
► who has access to the Internet, emails, etc;
► whether employees work off-site or travel with laptops.

Once the risks are identified, they are classified as high, medium and low. Spending on protection can then be prioritised. A recovery plan should be drawn up with steps to be taken should systems fail or in the event of data loss. Risks and security safeguards should be reviewed regularly to allow for changes in operations or equipment. It is important to remember that threats can come from inside the organisation as well. It is much harder to protect systems from a rogue employees, especially if they have a high level of access to the system. When employees leave a company special care needs to be taken to ensure that their IDs are removed from the system and checks made to make sure that they have not left any alternative ways into the system (known as 'back doors').

> **portfolio_tip**
> These links will give you an idea of the types of threats facing organisations.

www.dti.gov.uk/bestpractice/technology/security.htm
www.caci.com/business/ia/threats.html

Physical security

Organisations need to think very carefully about physical security. Passwords might prevent an unauthorised person deleting files but they will not prevent a person with a sledgehammer smashing up the file server!

Examples of physical security include:

► equipping premises with an alarm system;
► keeping computers out of public view;
► locating the server in a room with controlled access to essential personnel only;
► storing back-up tapes away from the server.

A server room should have a particularly high level of security. A large network is useless if the file servers are disabled. To provide adequate protection, a secure server room should have a strong door with high security locks and no windows. Fans and air conditioning should be used for ventilation.

Laptops used by staff present more difficulties; they are very portable and easy to steal, or leave behind on trains! Members of staff who make use of laptops should ensure that passwords are used to control access. Extra care

> **portfolio_tip**
> You need to describe some of the steps an organisation can take to protect customer data.

should be taken if the laptop has Bluetooth or infrared communications as other laptop users within range of these might be able to access data.

ACTIVITY

Prepare a leaflet that contains advice on physical security of data systems.

This link may be useful: www.caci.com/business/ia/threats.html.

User ID and access rights

When logging on to a network, the user ID is used by the system to identify the user. Each user has access rights and permissions that are set by the network administrator. These are vital in controlling the way the system is used and how secure the data is. All networks come with several standard user profiles that can be used to set up users quickly and easily with some degree of control, however most network administrators will make small changes to customise the system to best suit the needs of the organisation.

■ Figure 2.34

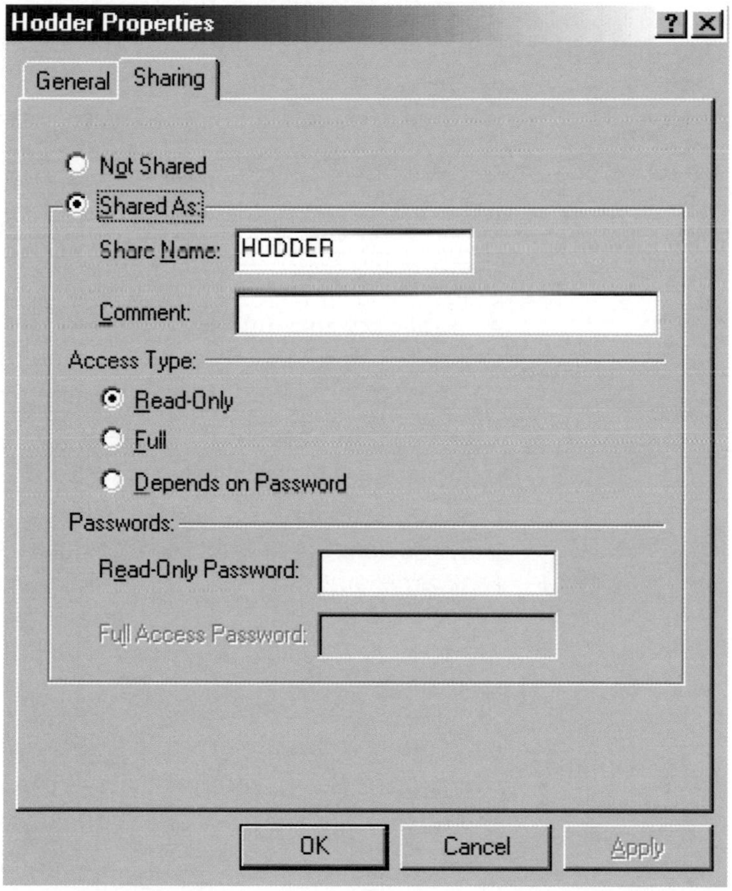

Figure 2.34 shows some of the access properties available in Microsoft Windows. In this example, the folder can be accessed by anyone across the network, but access is read-only. Everyone has the same level of access. More detailed access rights can be set on dedicated network systems.

It is possible to give staff different access levels according to their role or job within the company. For example, sales staff should be able to access the prices and amount of stock for items, but would not be able to access the files containing staff pay information.

Other methods of log on are now available including fingerprint recognition, where a user registers a fingerprint on a small scanning device normally built in to the computer. If the computer recognises the print then the user is logged on. This has several advantages, the user cannot forget a password, and fingerprints are unique and cannot be guessed like passwords.

Encryption

Some information must be kept secret, such as:

▶ sensitive company information;
▶ private correspondence;
▶ personal details;
▶ credit card information;
▶ bank account information.

Encryption uses the science of cryptography. This has been around long before the Information Age started. Governments have used it for military purposes and secret intelligence for a long time. Encrypted codes were used extensively during the Second World War.

These days, computers use cryptography extensively and the encryption of data plays a very important part in ensuring secure communication on the Internet.

Computer encryption systems in regular use are divided into two categories:

▶ symmetric key encryption;
▶ public key encryption.

Symmetric key encryption

Each computer has a secret code or key that it can use to encrypt information. This is then sent over a network to another computer. The key needs to be on both computers so that the message can be read because the code provides the key to decoding the message as well as coding it.

www.pgp.com

Public key encryption

Secure Sockets Layer (SSL) is a regularly used form of public key encryption. It is an Internet security protocol used by Internet browsers and web servers. Before entering a credit card number or other details a user should look for a letter 's' after 'http' in the address.

■ Figure 2.35

At the same time, a small padlock should appear in the status bar at the bottom of the browser window.

■ Figure 2.36

Secure electronic transactions (SET)

If a customer has a browser which is SET enabled, for example Netscape Navigator or Microsoft Internet Explorer, and the site being accessed has a server that is SET enabled, then this system can be used for the transaction.

■ Figure 2.37

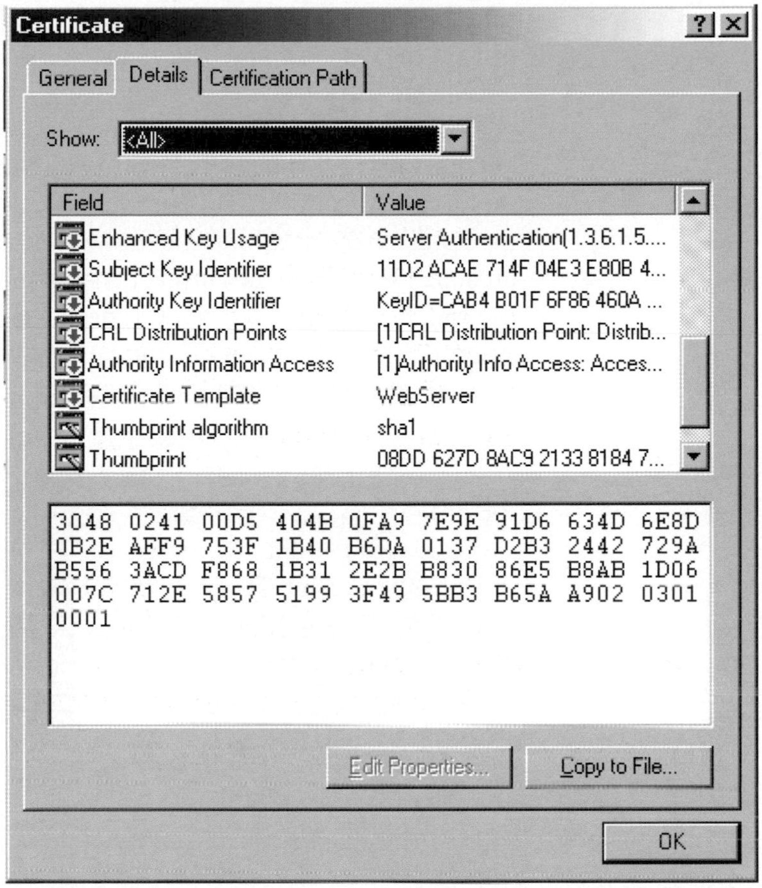

The customer opens a credit card account and receives a digital certificate. This is an electronic file which is used as a credit for online purchases or other secure transactions. It has a public key and an expiration date. Sellers also receive certificates from the credit card company. These include the seller's public key together with the bank's public key. When the customer places an order online, the browser confirms that the seller is valid using the seller's certificate. The payment information and details of the order are encrypted with the bank's public key so that the payment can only be used in this specific instance.

The seller identifies the customer by verifying the digital signature on the customer's certificate. The order message is then sent to the bank. This includes the bank's public key, the customer's payment information and the seller's certificate. The bank verifies all the information and the transaction is completed.

Firewalls

A firewall is used to control access to networks. A firewall has two mechanisms: one that blocks traffic, and one to allow traffic. In other words it enforces an access control policy.

There are many people with the Internet who will try to access and hack into the computer systems belonging to others. An organisation needs to protect the data it holds. The whole point of a firewall is to keep these people out of your network while still allowing work to be done.

Most firewalls are set up to protect against malicious log-ins from the outside world. This helps to stop hackers logging into machines on a protected network. Internet firewalls block traffic from the outside getting in, but allow users behind the firewall to communicate freely with the outside. Firewalls do not protect against attacks that are passed through the firewall. For a firewall to work, it needs to form part of an overall security system. Firewalls cannot offer any protection from internal threats by employees who copy data to disks.

■ Figure 2.38

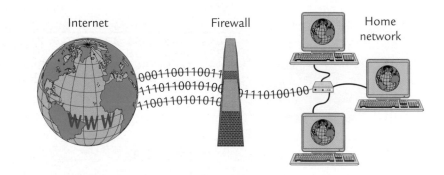

Virus protection

A virus is a program which is able to self-replicate. It then spreads by various methods such as by hiding copies of itself in executable code or documents. Viruses have become more and more ingenious over the years. To begin with they spread via floppy disks, now they use web pages, emails, downloads or even transmit themselves over a network from machine to machine.

Because new viruses are being written all the time and new security loopholes exploited, it is important to not just have a virus checker, but also to keep it up to date at least daily, or even more often. Organisations can buy such a service from companies that allow servers to update at intervals throughout a day and to distribute the update automatically across a network. Updating the checking software alone will not give any protection, the scanner must be run regularly or use a system of on-access scanning, where every file is scanned as it is opened and closed. This will of course slow things down, but the benefits are well worth the small sacrifice of speed.

The database

Aims

- ■ To examine the nature of a database that supports online transactions.
- ■ To build a suitable database to hold a predefined data set.

Introduction

Behind most business IT systems there is a database. In order to understand how a transactional web site works, it is necessary to have a good idea about what a database is.

A database is a store of data on a computer system. The data is usually structured in some way in order to make processing it more effective. The data is added to the database and processed by software. The software lets us extract the information we want from the database. Databases are powerful tools for many purposes, not just in business. They are easy to keep up to date and it is also easy to combine information from many parts of a database to provide us with many different views of the data.

A school or college will have a database that contains details about pupils and students, courses, rooms, staff and finance. If the office is well run, the information will always be up to date. The staff can use this database for any number of purposes. A few examples show how versatile databases can be:

- ▶ The location of a pupil or student can be looked up at any time.
- ▶ The phone number of a parent can be found.
- ▶ A list of all the pupils or students in a particular group can be printed.
- ▶ A list of pupils taking Edexcel examinations can be emailed to the examining body.

One of the good things about databases is that if a new requirement arises, for example the government decides it wants to know how many pupils passed GCSE ICT in one year or how many staff teach subjects for which they are not qualified, there is always a way to extract the information.

The basic need for data is just as important for a transactional web site as it is for a traditional business. The database is mostly not visible to either the customer or the administrators of the business because it is handled by software that provides a user-friendly front end. This way, the underlying data is protected from accidental damage.

Most databases are relational. This means that the data stored in them is divided up into linked tables: a separate table holds data about each component or *entity* in the database. The data, in its tables, is manipulated by software called a *database management system* or DBMS. Sitting on top of the DBMS are the applications that the users work with, such as modules to order goods, to access personal details or produce management reports.

Each table comprises a number of *fields*. These are the items of data that are stored about each item in the table. All the data about one item in the table makes one *record*.

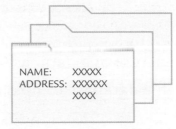

NAME: XXXXX
ADDRESS: XXXXXX
          XXXX

Most pupils, students and many professionals use Microsoft Access to make database systems. Microsoft Access itself is the database management system. You create forms, queries, reports and modules to do the things that you need the database to do, but they work through MS Access and require MS Access to be present in order to function. Microsoft Access, the DBMS, does all the clever things such as indexing and sorting and lets the developer concentrate on making the system do the job that is required.

A transactional web site will work by connecting its front end (the web site that the customer sees) to the underlying database. The back office processes (fulfilling orders and generating invoices) will also connect to the database.

The specific jobs that have to be done with the database are carried out by software *applications*. An application is computer software that is designed to do a particular job for the user. For example, in a transactional web site, there may be an application that updates the stock, an application that accepts orders and an application that maintains details of customer credit cards. One of the great advantages in using relational databases is that everyone (the staff as well as the customers) is using the same set of up-to-date data. The diagram below shows the relationship between the database and the software on a transactional website.

■ Figure 2.40

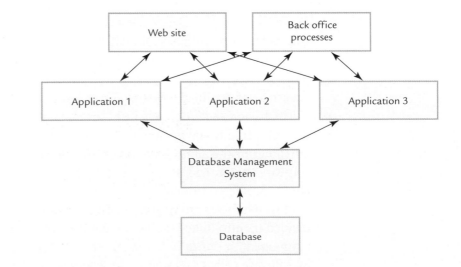

By dividing the data into tables, it is also possible to protect it more effectively by giving different groups different permissions. For example, the customers will not have access to the invoicing application. They will have restricted write access to the order tables (only being able to add data to orders that they have placed).

When designing a table to go into a relational database, it is necessary to make a number of decisions. The data in a table must be all about one entity. If you include data about names and prices of goods in the same table as the details about orders, it will become impossible to keep the whole database up to date. This is because the same data (names and prices) will occur in a number of different places. Unwanted duplication of data is called *redundancy* and we need to avoid that if the system is to be reliable. There is a process called *normalisation* that you can undertake to make sure that you remove all redundancies. Most databases contain lots of tables so that everything is kept separate. It is always possible to combine data when you extract it.

Each table will normally have a primary *key field*. This is one or more fields that can uniquely identify a record. Often, a key field is a reference number of some sort. A primary key field can be linked to another table so that data that should go together can always be kept together. For example, a table of stock does not need the name and address of the supplier stored with every item of stock. It is much better to keep the supplier information in another table where each supplier is stored just once. You then create a field *Supplier Number* in the stock table and link it with the correct supplier in the supplier table. A field that is not a primary key in one table but links to the primary key of another is called a foreign key.

■ Figure 2.41

Table: Stock		
Field name	**Field type**	
Stock number	Number	Primary key
Stock name	Text	
Number in stock	Number	
Supplier number	Number	Foreign key

link

Table: Supplier		
Field name	**Field type**	
Supplier number	Number	Primary key
Supplier name	Text	
Telephone number	Text	
email address	Text	

Other examples of good primary keys are driving licence numbers, book ISBNs, car registrations and National Insurance numbers. Names do not work as primary keys as they will not be unique.

A typical transactional web site will have at least three tables to deal with orders. There will probably be even more in order to deal with other matters such as re-ordering from suppliers.

Products and prices

It makes sense to keep a master list of all the products that the company sells. For many transactional web sites this will be a huge list (made possible by the lower cost of running an out of town warehouse). The list will probably often change as new products are taken on and old ones dropped.

The product and prices table will be used for:

▶ **Customer enquiries:** The web site will give the customers read-only access so that they can view the products, but of course not change them.
▶ **Invoicing:** The prices of chosen items will be looked up by the system in order to calculate the customers' bills.
▶ **Stock checks:** The names of items will make it easier for physical stock checks to be carried out.

Each item in stock will be given a stock number as a key field.

> **ACTIVITY**
>
> Think of some other times when the products and prices table will be accessed.

Stock levels

The quantity of each item that is in stock should be stored so that the company always has enough of each product to satisfy demand. Customers do not want to wait ages to receive an order because the company is out of stock. On the other hand, the company does not want to hold so much stock that too much of its money is tied up in stock instead of earning interest.

On transactional web sites, it is easy to tie in stock levels to sales. Every time an item is despatched, the software that handles the order process can reduce the stock record by an appropriate number. Similarly, when items are delivered from the suppliers, the stock levels can be increased. Every so often the stock has to be physically checked against records in case of loss or theft.

Stock levels can be stored in the same table as products and prices because there is a one-to-one relationship between a stock item and the quantity of that item in stock. This means that every stock item has a stock level that refers to no other item of stock.

Customers

A separate table is necessary to hold customer details. This is because customer details may be required many times and for many purposes. Every time an order is placed or a bill produced, the customer details will be needed. It makes sense to have these details stored just once in a customer table so that they can always be accessed in their most up-to-date form.

In order to make sure that each customer is stored uniquely and can be unambiguously referenced, each customer will be given a number. Each time a new customer is registered, a new record is created for that customer and a unique number given to that customer. This means that no customer has the same number although they may have the same names.

Orders

Each time an order is placed, a new record will be stored in an orders table. It makes sense to keep orders separate from the rest of the data because otherwise data redundancy will occur. It makes no sense to store the names and prices of products again and again every time a new order is made up.

> Remember, data redundancy is the unnecessary repetition of data in a database. This is a bad thing because it is very difficult to be sure that you are working with the most up-to-date version of a data item.

Each order relates to items in stock as well as a customer, so we do not want that data duplicated for every order. Linking to it in the stock and customer tables is more efficient.

Each order will have a unique order number as a key field.

Designing and creating a database

To finish this Unit, you have to design and create a database that is suitable for holding a particular set of data and also to answer certain enquiries. There is a data-set on the CD which contains data about customers, products and prices, and orders. It concerns an online business that sells computer network components.

Select appropriate field types and formats

When we set up a data table, it is necessary to make certain decisions so that the table will hold the data we want and allow us to manipulate the data in the ways that we want.

Field types

ASCII (AMERICAN STANDARD CODE FOR INFORMATION INTERCHANGE): This is a well-known code where numbers from 0–255 are interpreted as characters. For example, 65 = A, 66 = B and so on.

> Why have field types?
> To a computer, data is just data. It is stored and handled as 0s and 1s. We can however, assign a *type* to data in a field so that when the computer works with it, the data is handled as we want it to produce meaningful results. For example, we can say that a particular combination of 0s and 1s must always be looked up in an ASCII table and be translated into characters. So 01000001 is treated as the letter 'A'. Alternatively, we can say that a group of 0s and 1s should be interpreted as a whole number or integer. In that case, 01000001 is interpreted as the number 65.

Different computer systems have different field types. If you are setting up a database in Microsoft Access, some of the more common choices are:

▶ **Text:** This accepts anything that can be typed at a keyboard, numbers, letters and symbols. If your data has letters in it anywhere, you must choose this data type. For example, a postcode must be text because it contains letters. A telephone number must be text because it may have a leading zero or spaces.

　　When you choose a text field type, you should also choose the size of the field. This is the maximum number of letters that you want in the field. If you do not choose, Microsoft Access defaults to 50, which is usually too much and wastes storage space.

▶ **Number:** This can be in several formats depending on how big a number you want and whether you need decimal places. It accepts only numbers and is needed if you want to do calculations on the data.

▶ **Currency:** This is a special case of number data where you always want two decimal places and probably a currency symbol as well.

▶ **Date/Time:** This stores combinations of dates or times. You can format it in different ways so that you can display a date as 23 April 2005 or 23/04/05, or in other ways.

▶ **Yes/No:** Sometimes called Boolean, this accepts one of just two values, Yes or No, or True or False.

▶ **Memo:** This can contain long passages of text, for example when you need a long description of a product.

The customer details on the CD have fields. Some example data looks like this:

Title	Surname	Forename	Initials	Address1	Address2	Address3
Mr	Raybould	James	J	Flat 1	34 Jersey Close	Oldham

Postcode	Tel	Email	Credit_Limit
0L9 8YU	0635463212	james@hotnet.co.uk	900

A suitable structure for a customer table, containing data like this is as follows (shown in Figure 2.42).

ACTIVITY

Use the help facility of your database software to see what alternative field types are available and what different types of number format can be chosen.

Here are examples of the data that is held in the other two tables of our ordering system.

product_price

Part_Number	Description	Category	Price	No_in_stock	Re_order_level	Re_order_quantity
AE424657	Netsolutions OfficeConnect wireless 54 Mbps travel router	Networking connections	£ 39.99	26	22	30

order

Order_Number	Part_Number	Quantity	Customer_Number	Date
376797	AE424657	1	576	29/04/2005

Field Name	Data Type	Description
Customer_Number	Number	Unique number - key field
Title	Text	Combo box for validation
Surname	Text	Max 30 characters
Forename	Text	Max 30 characters
Initials	Text	Max 10 characters
Address1	Text	Max 30 characters
Address2	Text	Max 30 characters
Address3	Text	Max 30 characters
Postcode	Text	Max 12 characters - must be text as text and numbers
Tel	Text	Max 30 characters - must be text for leading zeroes
Email	Text	Max 60 characters
Credit_Limit	Number	No more than 10000

tblCustomer : Table

Field Properties

General | Lookup

Field Size	Long Integer
Format	
Decimal Places	Auto
Input Mask	
Caption	
Default Value	
Validation Rule	
Validation Text	
Required	No
Indexed	Yes (No Duplicates)

A field name can be up to 64 characters long, including spaces. Press F1 for help on field names.

portfolio_tip

You should include screenshots of the design of at least two tables.

ACTIVITY

Choose suitable field types for the product price and the order data tables. Set up all three tables using your database software. Make sure that you name them tblCustomer, tblProduct_Price and tblOrder.

Create simple validation rules

We have seen a definition and examples of validation in Chapter 2.1. Many errors can be stopped at the input stage if the database is designed carefully. There are many ways of validating data as it is input. If you are setting up a database in Microsoft Access, it is often easiest to set up validation rules during the table design.

Type of validation	Reason	How to set up in Microsoft Access
Length check	This prevents text being entered that would exceed the space allocated for it.	Setting the field size for a text field limits the size that can be input.
Range check	Number must be within stated range.	Set maximum in table design and insert suitable error message.

| Presence check | Field must be filled in. | Set 'Required' field to 'Yes' in table design. |

portfolio_tip

Your database portfolio should include screenshots to show the validation checks you used. You should include some error messages that occur when bad data is entered.

There are many ways to validate input. The more you use, the less likely it is that errors will occur.

Creating one-to-many relationship between tables

We have seen how the tables in a relational database are linked. This allows the data from one table to be associated with that in another thereby reducing redundancy. A customer is a single individual so there is only a need to record his or her details once. The customer places many orders, so each order only needs to be linked to the customer details. The details do not need to be copied into each order. This way, the customer details do not run the risk of being changed in different places.

Links can be shown in an entity-relation diagram.

■ Figure 2.46

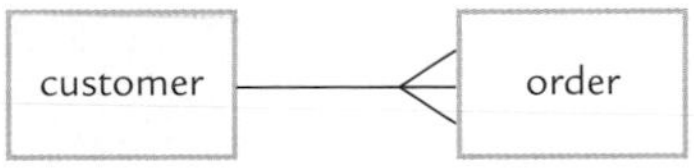

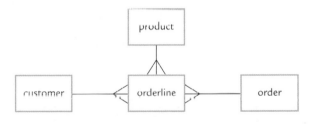

portfolio_tip

When you design your database structure, you will need to make it fit the data that you are provided with.

The 'crow's foot' at the order side of the diagram shows that there are many orders for one customer: a one-to-many relationship.

To produce a fully working system to support orders, you will need four tables. As well as the ones already mentioned, you will need an extra one called tblOrder_Line in which each record is one line of an order. This way you can have orders with many products on them.

The entity-relation diagram will now look like this:

■ Figure 2.47

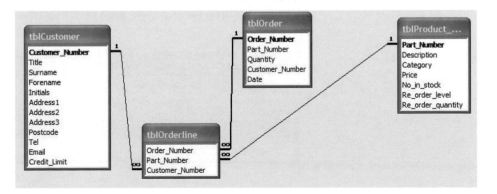

The details of the tables involved can be seen in Figure 2.48. The infinity sign shows the 'many' end of a one-to-many relationship.

■ Figure 2.48

In most cases, relational databases are made up from one-to-many relationships. A one-to-one relationship can exist between a customer and a customer telephone number (assuming that the customer only quotes one number), for example. If that is the case, the number may as well go in the same table as the other customer details.

Many-to-many relationships can exist. An example is products and orders. Orders can be made of many products and a product can occur on many orders. This is a very difficult situation to process, so this is why it is better to split the tables as shown in the diagram in order to avoid a many-to-many relationship. You can set up relationships between fields in Microsoft Access, by selecting Tools > Relationships ... from the menu bar.

■ Figure 2.49

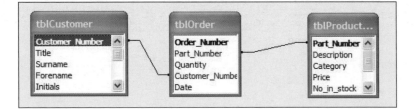

portfolio_tip

You should include a screenshot in your portfolio of the relationships that you make in your database.

You then link the fields by clicking and dragging. You connect the primary key of one table to the foreign key of another. If you had a simple system with just one product per order, it would look like this:

■ Figure 2.50

Importing a given data-set

The data tables that you have set up need some data in them. On the CD, there is data for the three tables described earlier. They are supplied in Microsoft Excel and CSV formats. If you have set up the tables properly, you should be able to import the data very easily. All you have to do in Microsoft

■ Figure 2.51

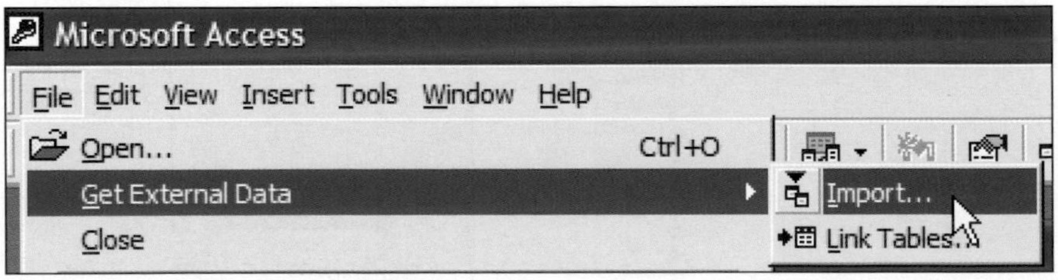

Access is to select File > Get External Data > Import from the menu bar. You then look on the CD for the file that you want.

■ Figure 2.52

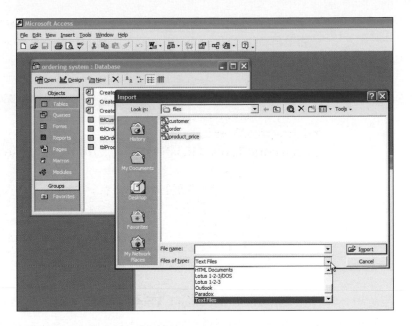

You then follow the instructions given by the wizard to import the data.

---

portfolio_tip

Make sure that you show some data in your tables as evidence that you have imported it. For example, you could include a screenshot like this one.

tblCustomer : Table

Customer_Nur	Title	Surname	Forename	Initials	Address1	Address2	Address3	Postcode	Tel
101	Mr	Raybould	James	J	Flat 1	34 Jersey Clos	Oldham	OL9 8YU	0635463212
132	Mr	Allen	Tom	T	8 Glebe Drive		Warwick	CV69 7FG	0407619993
176	Mr	Tomlinson	Jack	J	9 Ironbridge Ro	Redditch	Worcestershire	B97 2DE	0447270450
254	Mr	Barnaby	Ian	I	75 Cathedral Cl	Wolverhampton	West Midlands	WV4 6FQ	0291649554
266	Dr	Washbourne	George	G	75 Caravan Roa	Camberley	Surrey	GU2 6FR	064066866
296	Mr	Pidman	Stu	S	8 Pelham Stree	Colchester	Essex	CO8 7KL	0933043899
324	Mr	Hill	Henry	H	47 Pinewoods A	Harborne	Birmingham	B77 8RF	0936907567
333	Mrs	Barlow	Leah	L	46 Solent Road	Gornal Wood	West Midlands	B98 7FD	0340095746
336	Miss	Keir	Trudy	T	10 Brimstone C	Bewdley	Worcestershire	DY 79 8UB	0580540274
345	Rev	Girling	Rob	R	27 Murcroft Roa	Selly Oak	Birmingham	B99 9YU	0151420676
354	Mr	Vooght	Heinrich	H	56 Dark Lane	Guildford	Surrey	GU7 3SW	0122172156
357	Mr	Woodrow	John	J	67 New Road	Dudley	West Midlands	DY6 8MN	0501598238
455	Mr	Ollerton	Chris	C	61 Meadow Roa	Worcester	Worcestershire	WR99 8YY	099357764
456	Mr	Eland	Steve	S	69a Terne Closi		Lincoln	LN00 7RR	0079046006
476	Mr	Roberts	Jesse	J	45 School Drive	Tonbridge	Kent	TN8 7SE	0268395361
477	Ms	Cook	Jeannie	J	25 Farm Road	Coundon	Coventry	CV7 8JN	0579558878
487	Dr	Moloney	Dilys	D	75 Southcrest F	Cheltenham	Gloucestershire	GL06 4ES	0756280893
566	Ms	Orange	Stella	S	4 Mayflower Ro	Barnt Green	Worcestershire	B75 6TT	03924817
576	Ms	Hake	Julia	J	25 Barnt Green	Halesowen	West Midlands	B88 8UU	0756950724
577	Mr	Patel	Zubin	Z	42 Monarch Cre	Weymouth	Dorset	DR6 7GN	0331031165
578	Ms	Capewell	Jenny	J	36 Gerald Road	Douglas	Isle of Man	IM8 9TY	0675426966
587	Mrs	Drysdale	Helen	H	75 Watkins Wa	Swinton	Manchester	M66 6NU	0224383323
678	Mr	Welch	Gary	G	664 Greatfiled F	Reading	Berkshire	RG6 7HU	0412021597
789	Prof	Griggs	Stuart	S	20 Southall Ave	Ealing	London	W5 6FF	0313789388
966	Ms	Radley	Bertha	B	Flat 2 Magnolia	Poole	Dorset	BH8 8DE	0645974922
986	Mrs	Harrell	Stephanie	S	36 Rockford Dri	Old Hill	West Midlands	B98 7DF	059070234

Using sorts to group and order data

The data in a database is normally stored in the order that it arrives. Sorting is not usually done as it takes time and is not necessary. It is more usual to use indexes which are separate files that indicate the desired order. The main data stays where it is but the index can be looked up to show the data in any order that is wanted. In Microsoft Access, you usually use queries to show data in order. In that case, an index is set up in order to display the data in the order required. The actual data is not moved at all which is safer. Queries are also useful for selecting and extracting data.

You can sort data in Microsoft Access, but it is not usual.

For example, suppose that you wanted to sort the stock_price table so that you can see the number in stock displayed in increasing order. You select the field and then select Records > Sort > Sort Ascending.

■ **Figure 2.54**

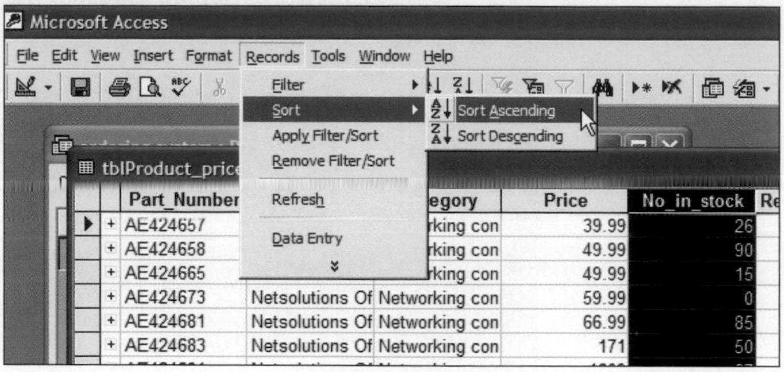

You can sort on any field. This could be useful if you want to group together all the categories of products.

ACTIVITY

Try a number of different sorts on the data to produce some meaningful groupings. For example, you could try to sort the customers according to credit limit.

Using searches to extract valid and meaningful information

Queries can combine data from different tables. You can set up a new query in design mode, then add the tables you are interested in. For example, suppose you want to show all the orders before 2 May, with the customer name, telephone number and the product ordered, so that you could phone up if there is a delay in despatch.

You add all the tables and drag the fields you need into the ‘query by example’ grid. You can choose to display it in surname order at this stage, if you want.

Under the Date field, you type in <02/05/2005. This selects the records before that date.

■ **Figure 2.55**

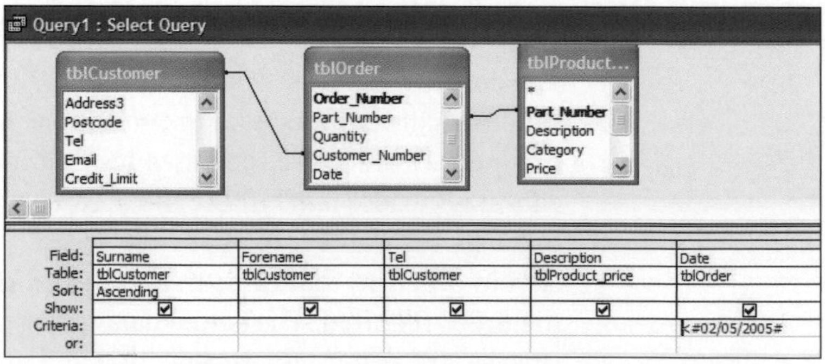

As you can see, fields have been included from different tables and the end result shows customers listed in alphabetical order by surname.

■ Figure 2.56

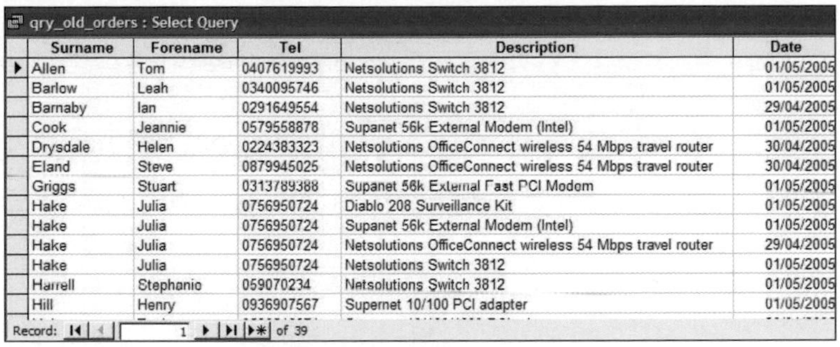

Surname	Forename	Tel	Description	Date
Allen	Tom	0407619993	Netsolutions Switch 3812	01/05/2005
Barlow	Leah	0340095746	Netsolutions Switch 3812	01/05/2005
Barnaby	Ian	0291649554	Netsolutions Switch 3812	29/04/2005
Cook	Jeannie	0579558878	Supanet 56k External Modem (Intel)	01/05/2005
Drysdale	Helen	0224383323	Netsolutions OfficeConnect wireless 54 Mbps travel router	30/04/2005
Eland	Steve	0879945025	Netsolutions OfficeConnect wireless 54 Mbps travel router	30/04/2005
Griggs	Stuart	0313789388	Supanet 56k External Fast PCI Modem	01/05/2005
Hake	Julia	0756950724	Diablo 208 Surveillance Kit	01/05/2005
Hake	Julia	0756950724	Supanet 56k External Modem (Intel)	01/05/2005
Hake	Julia	0756950724	Netsolutions OfficeConnect wireless 54 Mbps travel router	29/04/2005
Hake	Julia	0756950724	Netsolutions Switch 3812	01/05/2005
Harrell	Stephanie	059070234	Netsolutions Switch 3812	01/05/2005
Hill	Henry	0936907567	Supernet 10/100 PCI adapter	01/05/2005

Record: 1 of 39

ACTIVITY

Make a list of all the customers and their addresses who ordered the product with the Part Number AE424657.

Try some other queries to extract useful information.

Producing reports to present information clearly

You can use Microsoft Access to produce printed reports from your data. These can be much easier to understand than the raw output from a query. You can base a report on a saved query and use it to group the data and display it in all sorts of ways.

Access provides Microsoft useful wizards to help create things like reports. You could use this to make a printed report of old orders to show to management.

■ Figure 2.57

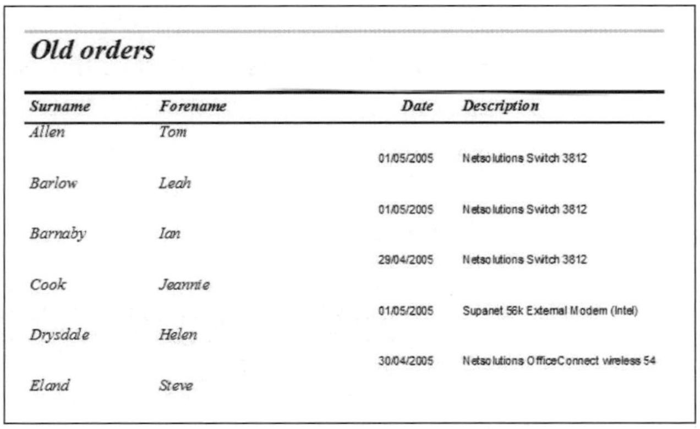

Old orders

Surname	Forename	Date	Description
Allen	Tom		
		01/05/2005	Netsolutions Switch 3812
Barlow	Leah		
		01/05/2005	Netsolutions Switch 3812
Barnaby	Ian		
		29/04/2005	Netsolutions Switch 3812
Cook	Jeannie		
		01/05/2005	Supanet 56k External Modem (Intel)
Drysdale	Helen		
		30/04/2005	Netsolutions OfficeConnect wireless 54
Eland	Steve		

Grouping is very useful in making a report easy to read. You can, when you set up your report, group together all the orders made by each individual customer. In order to do this, all you have to do is to tell the wizard that you want to group by surname.

Figure 2.58

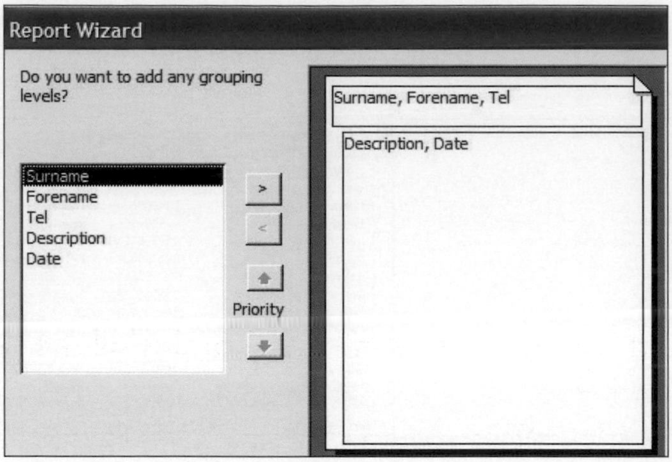

Figure 2.59

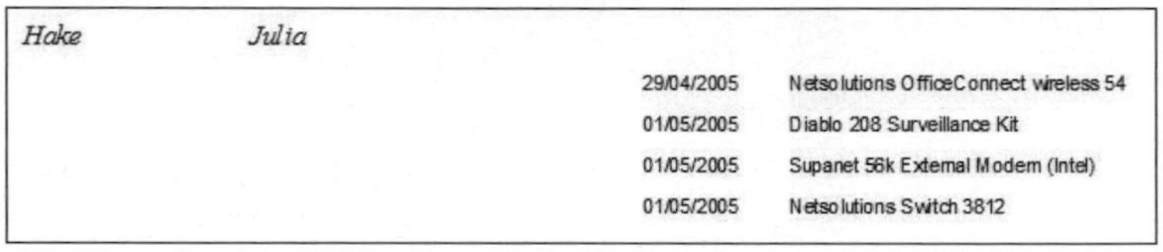

> **portfolio_tip**
> Make sure that you include some well-formatted reports in your portfolio. Be sure to use an appropriate heading for your report which explains clearly what the report contains.

You can make adjustments to a report in design view. This allows you to tailor it to fit its intended audience. You might want to change the font to the house style if your report is going into a company document.

Know-how

You should be able to interpret the output from a database and identify patterns from it. One example that you can try from the examples given in this chapter is to identify items in stock that need reordering. You can use the expression <[Re_order_level] as the criterion in a query grid. This checks each item's reorder level and only shows the product if it is low on stock.

Figure 2.60

Field:	Part_Number	Description	No_in_stock	Re_order_level	Re_order_quantity
Table:	tblProduct_price	tblProduct_price	tblProduct_price	tblProduct_price	tblProduct_price
Sort:					
Show:	☑	☑	☑	☑	☑
Criteria:			<[Re_order_level]		
or:					

You can add to this query to get the reorder quantity and put this into a report to show what needs to be ordered.

> **ACTIVITY**
> Try to make a report that shows what needs reordering and how much to order.

ICT skills

Aims

- To ensure that your portfolio contains all the evidence that you need for Unit 2.
- To build a suitable database structure to hold a given data-set.

Introduction

As you worked through the previous eight chapters, you should have performed most of the activities to prepare you for this part of your portfolio. The purpose of this chapter is to make sure that everything is covered and you score the best marks that you can for this part of your assessment.

There are five parts to this section of your portfolio. The first three are to do with your investigation of the transactional web site and the other two are to do with your database.

What the specification says

Your eportfolio for this unit should include:

For the transactional web site

(a) A description of the main features of the web site's design and an evaluation of its effectiveness, including some suggestions for improvements.

(b) Diagrams illustrating the chain of events leading up to and triggered by the online purchase of a product and the associated flow of information.

(c) A description of potential threats to customer data collected by organisations via their web sites and an evaluation of measures being taken, including legislation, to protect it.

For the database

(d) A database which has been designed, built and tested to store a given set of data.
Evidence that you have successfully imported the data.
Evidence that you have used the database to produce meaningful information, identify significant trends and make recommendations based upon them.

(e) An evaluation of the performance of the database and your own performance on this unit.

Hint: It is important that you work independently in order to achieve the higher mark bands. You must choose your own web sites and all your evidence must be completely your own work.

The web site: objective (a)

In Chapters 2.1 to 2.7, you have taken a look at some transactional web sites and seen many examples of the important issues surrounding the successful and secure operation of them. It is important that you select your own choice of web site for investigation and inclusion in your portfolio. You should make sure that you include good descriptions of:

► the layout of the web site and how the customer navigates around it;
► the nature of the goods or services that are on sale;
► the types of transaction that can be carried out;
► the techniques and strategies used by the web site in order to keep the customers interested and coming back often;
► how the web site captures data from the customers;
► how easy it is to use, taking into consideration a range of possible customers;
► the security measures that are clear from the customer's point of view;
► the overall effectiveness of the web site in achieving what it sets out to do, including an assessment of individual features of the web site.

You should also include

► enough screenshots to make the report clear;
► an evaluation of each of the features of the web site;
► an evaluation of the total experience of the web site for the customer with comments on any particular strengths and weaknesses that you have noticed;
► some suggestions about how the web site could be improved or added to.

Tips for success

To do well in this section of the portfolio, you should have chosen the web site yourself and demonstrated that you really understand what the makers of the web site are trying to achieve and exactly how they are trying to achieve it.

The web site: objective (b)

For this part, you have to use diagrams to illustrate the processes that take place before, during and after a web site transaction. To help you do this, it is a good idea if you make use of some standard symbols commonly used by analysts to produce flowcharts. Using the correct symbols will help you to keep clear about what you are describing.

To develop a better understanding of the processes that take place, you can use the Comersus software on the CD to set up a transactional web site. If you do so, you will have real practical experience of the processes involved and therefore understand them better.

Produce diagrammatic representations of systems, events and information flows

There are various ways in which you can show how data moves around and how things happen in any business process. We have already seen in Chapter 2.4 how diagrams can be used to show the sequence of events when ordering goods on a web site.

You have to be able to show in diagrams how information moves from one part of a business to another and how information moves between the business and the customer.

Information flow diagrams

One way to illustrate a process, such as ordering goods from a mail order or online company, is to use an information flow diagram. These can be made from simple boxes and arrows to show what information goes where. The trick is to keep the whole diagram fairly simple to avoid having lines crossing each other. You may have to move boxes around quite a lot when making diagrams, so it is a lot easier if you have access to drawing software.

■ Figure 2.61

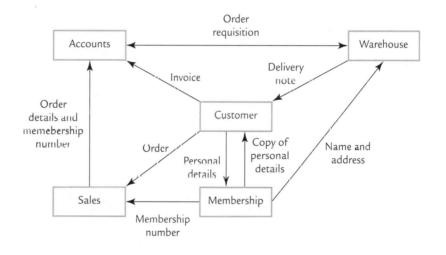

Data flow diagrams (DFDs)

A more detailed flow diagram can be made with the special symbols that systems analysts use. These can be put together into what is known as a data flow diagram or DFD for short. DFDs show how external entities (in this case such things as customers and warehouses) are linked to the processes and stores of data that make the web site work. There are different systems that analysts use to represent things in DFDs, but one common methodology uses the following shapes:

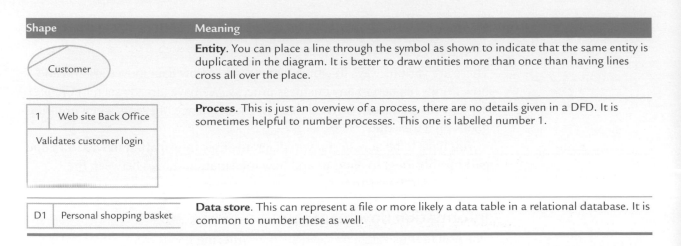

Shape	Meaning
Customer	**Entity**. You can place a line through the symbol as shown to indicate that the same entity is duplicated in the diagram. It is better to draw entities more than once than having lines cross all over the place.
1 Web site Back Office Validates customer login	**Process**. This is just an overview of a process, there are no details given in a DFD. It is sometimes helpful to number processes. This one is labelled number 1.
D1 Personal shopping basket	**Data store**. This can represent a file or more likely a data table in a relational database. It is common to number these as well.

Putting some of these shapes together, it is possible to show how things happen.

■ **Figure 2.65**

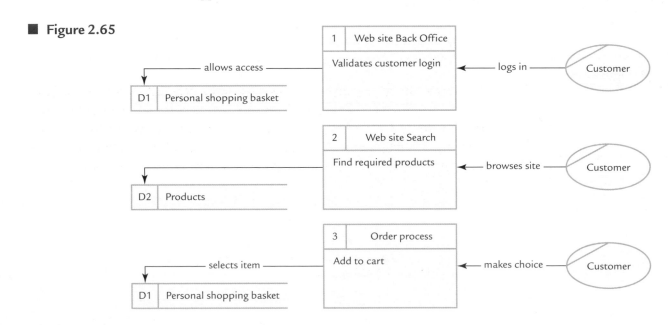

You can use a series of DFDs to show the various jobs that have to be done in the transactional web site that you have chosen.

System flowcharts

You may want to include system flowcharts to show rather more detail of the processes. For example, the customer log-in can be shown in greater detail than in the DFD. The symbols used for system flowcharts can also vary slightly. There are different analysis and design methodologies that favour slightly different symbols. Some common ones are shown here, again with typical labels added.

portfolio_tip

There is no requirement that you have to use special DFD symbols; a straightforward information flow chart will be sufficient. However, you may find it helps to focus on the separate elements of a system and it allows you to duplicate entities more easily to avoid lines crossing.

Shape	Meaning
Customer table	**Direct access data store**. In other words this normally means disk storage. It will contain the name of a table or file.
Enter user id	**Keyboard input**. This will contain a verb, as there is an action to perform.
Check valid user id	**Process**. This will also contain a verb.
Customer details	**Screen output**. This will contain a brief description of what is to be output.
Printed confirmation letter	**Paper document**. This will also contain just a brief description of the document concerned.

The shapes can be put together to show in more detail how files are used in order to make a process happen. A system flowchart is more concerned with detailing how we get from input to output. For example, we can use one to show how a customer logs in and brings up personal details. Remember that the labels in all these diagrams should be very brief (just a few words).

■ Figure 2.71

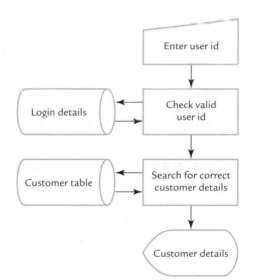

How to make a flowchart
You can make a flowchart quite easily if you use graphic software for the job. You may have your own favourite software for this. The diagrams in this chapter were made using Microsoft Visio, but you can get most of the shapes you need from the drawing toolbar in Microsoft Word.

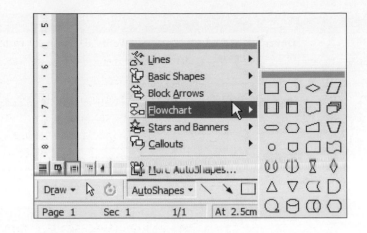

portfolio_tip

When you have made a flowchart, group all the symbols and connecting lines together. That way, the chart won't break up if you edit your document.

If you right click on a symbol that you have created, you get a pop-up menu which lets you add text.

You must make sure that you produce diagrams that show both the stages leading up to an online purchase and the stages that follow. You should include the actions that:

▶ maintain the shopping basket or cart;
▶ identify and authenticate the customer;
▶ track the customer activity;
▶ process the payment;
▶ control the stock;
▶ handle the despatch and delivery of the items.

The web site: objective (c)

In this section, you should make sure that you have written a report on the safety of customer data. It should be subdivided into sections that cover:

▶ the threats to customer data;
▶ the protective measures that can be taken;
▶ the laws intended to reduce these threats;
▶ the meaning of each of these laws;
▶ the effectiveness or otherwise of each law;
▶ a weighing up of these issues in which you arrive at an overall assessment of the issues.

The database: objective (d)

In this section, you must use database software to fulfil some quite specific tasks. This is a separate issue from the work on the web site. You will use a database management system that should be familiar to you: probably Microsoft Access. You will be supplied with a set of data and you will have to carry out some specific operations on that data. These operations are set out in the specification and most of them have already been covered in Chapter 2.8 using the data-set provided on the CD that goes with this book. If you have carried out the exercises, plus a few more outlined in this chapter, you should be able to do the same with any other set of data that is supplied.

Create simple relational database structures

This is all about setting up tables that are suitable for the data-set that you are given. You must remember that each tables should normally only contain data about one entity. Make sure that each include screenshots that demonstrate the design of your database. The screenshots should make it obvious that you have made sensible choices about field names (make them meaningful), data types (be careful to use Text if there is any text or spaces at all in the data) and field size (in the case of text fields).

You should make sure that there is a primary key in each table that you have set up. It can often be a mistake to let the software make an 'autonumber' field for you. You may need to have a text field as a primary key or you may be importing data that already has a suitable primary key.

Relationships

If you go to the Tools menu in Microsoft Access, you will be able to link the tables (see Chapter 2.8). You should show screenshots to prove that you did this correctly. Drag the tables around the screen so that all the relationships are clear with no crossing over.

Set field characteristics

Chapter 2.8 covered this at length and it is important that you should take the greatest care in getting this right. It is very easy to make errors, the most likely being that you might choose a different field type for a primary key from the foreign key in another table with which it is supposed to be linked. Remember that there are various number types and different formats as well. Experiment with what is available: you do not have to accept the defaults and indeed it is often a bad idea to do that.

Create simple validation rules

Chapter 2.8 covered a variety of validation possibilities. Remember that you *must* include some evidence of validation and ideally use a variety of validation methods. Again, use some screenshots to show how these were set up and include some demonstrations of error messages to prove that the validation is working.

You should provide a set of tests that shows that you have comprehensively tested the validation rules. You can set this out as a table.

Test number	Test action	Expected result	Actual result	Page reference of evidence
1	Enter Sm9th in surname field	Error message 'Numbers not allowed'.	Error message is displayed, data cannot be entered.	124

Testing

It is vital that you have carried out enough testing in order to get the highest marks possible. Use a table to record your tests and provide plenty of screenshots to back it up.

Make sure that you have tested the database structure completely. You should make sure that:

▶ the fields required are all there (look at the data set supplied);
▶ the field types are correct;
▶ the validation rules correctly stop invalid data from being input;
▶ the relationships work (make sure that a link between tables is between fields of the same data type).

All the tests should be recorded with documentary evidence.

Import data

portfolio_tip

Carefully study the data-set as it is presented and think about the structure needed to import it.

Chapter 2.8 included details about how to import the data files that are provided with this book. You should be able to use the same method to import any other data but it won't work unless the tables have been set up exactly to match the required data.

You should be able to import data either from a spreadsheet or from CSV files.

To demonstrate that you have successfully imported your data, you will need to provide screenshots showing the data in your tables.

Sort on single and multiple fields

Chapter 2.8 gives an example of how to use a query to combine data and display just a subset of it. The query was also set up to show how to sort the data into customer surname order. You will need to sort data for your portfolio, and to demonstrate this you should produce screenshots showing the query design and the output from the query.

As well as doing simple sorts, you should also set up some sorts where more than one criterion box is used. This way, using the example on page 184, you could set the sort field on the date field as well. This way, the customers would be displayed in order and also, for each customer, the orders would be displayed in date order.

Search on single and multiple fields within a table to extract information

It is often necessary to perform quite complex searches on databases to retrieve the records that match requirements. In Chapter 2.8, we used queries to extract order information from a query that linked more than one table.

Queries also make it easy to apply multiple criteria. All you have to do is to enter the criteria in the QBE (Query By Example) fields and run the query. All the conditions will be applied. Obviously, the more conditions you set, the fewer records will appear in the results.

This example looks at the customers and orders tables to find the names and telephone numbers of all customers who ordered more than five items over two weeks ago. It displays the customers in alphabetical order and shows the reference number of the items ordered.

■ **Figure 2.73**

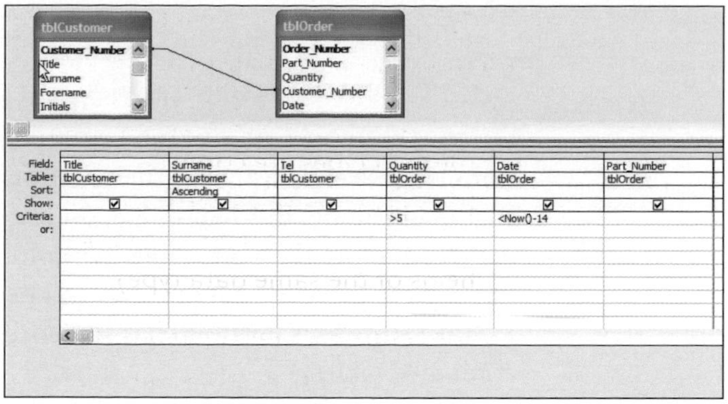

You can see the results of this query in Figure 2.74.

■ **Figure 2.74**

	Title	Surname	Tel	Quantity	Date	Part_Number
	Prof	Griggs	0313789388	7	01/05/2005	AF524801
	Ms	Hake	0756950724	6	01/05/2005	AE424747
	Mrs	Harrell	059070234	7	01/05/2005	AE424747
	Mr	Hill	0936907567	8	02/05/2005	AF524829
✎	Mr	Pidman	0933013899	6	01/05/2005	AF524781
*						

Your portfolio should contain screenshots like these to demonstrate the accuracy of your queries.

■ **Figure 2.75**

Query1 : Select Query

	Part_Number	Description	No_in_stock	Re_order_leve	Re_order_qua	Price
	AE424683	Netsolutions Of	50	40	70	171
	AE424691	Netsolutions Of	67	57	100	1609
	AE424747	Netsolutions Sv	78	70	100	629
	AE424755	Netsolutions Sv	49	46	70	1019
	AE424756	Netsolutions Su	70	68	100	1339
	AE424761	Netsolutions Su	53	52	70	2348
	AF524812	Diablo 206M Mi	58	55	80	219
	AF524824	Diablo 207 Netv	34	28	50	514
	AF524830	Diablo 208 Surv	64	58	90	1600
	AF524837	Diablo 208 Outc	5	2	10	509
	AF524841	Diablo 209 Aud	89	80	100	109
	AF524845	Diablo 209A Ou	72	65	100	189
▶						

portfolio_tip

Any work you want to include in your portfolio must in one of the formats specified by Edexcel. Make sure when you are collecting evidence that it can be converted later if needed.

When you set up a query, it is translated into a statement in a language called SQL (Structured Query Language). The query in Figure 2.75 translates to this statement:

```
SELECT tblProduct_price.Part_Number,
tblProduct_price.Description, tblProduct_price.No_in_stock,
tblProduct_price.Re_order_level,
tblProduct_price.Re_order_quantity, tblProduct_price.Price
FROM tblProduct_price
WHERE (((tblProduct_price.No_in_stock)>[Re_order_level]) AND
((tblProduct_price.Price)>100));
```

You do not have to know any SQL for this unit, but it is worth a quick look and it is very easy to understand.

You can write programs to set up automated queries in SQL to make a better system although you don't have to do this for this specification.

Search on related tables to extract information

We have seen how queries can be used to link tables. We can make use of the links that we established in the relationships or we can set up new links in that query alone. In Chapter 2.8, on page 184, we used a query to extract data from more than one table. We combined tblCustomer, tblOrder and tblProduct_price in order to show related details from each of these tables.

Make sure your portfolio has screenshots showing some information from combined tables.

Use logical and relational operators

When you set up queries, you will make use of logical and relational operators even if you don't actually see them. You should know what they are and what they are doing. The SQL example for the last query shows some of these.

```
WHERE (((tblProduct_price.No_in_stock)>[Re_order_level]) AND
((tblProduct_price.Price)>100));
```

A logical operator is part of an expression that compares two values. For example, the SQL statement contains the line
The first line checks to see if the number in stock is greater than the reorder level. It uses the logical operator 'greater than' or '>'.

It then looks to see if the price of the records found is greater than 100 (in the second line).

To apply **both** of these conditions, we also use the relational operator AND. Examples of logical operators are:

Operator	Meaning
>	greater than
<	less than
=	equals
=>	equals or greater than
<=	less than or equals

The common relational operators are AND (where we require two conditions both to be true), OR (either condition can be true) and NOT (where we are looking for a condition not being true).

> **ACTIVITY**
>
> Try altering a simple query in SQL View to change the conditions.

Different software systems have others as well and may use different symbols.

portfolio_tip

You must include some evidence that you have identified trends from your reports. You also have to make recommendations on the basis of these trends. In Chapter 2.8, we saw how we could output a list of stock items that were running low by using a query that showed products where the number in stock was below the reorder level. Try to include a range of examples of trends and recommendations.

Produce reports to present information

Microsoft Access and other database management systems can produce printed reports. Chapter 2.8 covered how reports can be useful and how to set them up with a wizard. Your portfolio should have examples of reports based on queries to present required information in a neat way. Don't forget that the best way to set up a report is often to start out by using the wizard and then going into design view to fine tune it the way you want.

Try to include a range of examples of trends and recommendations.

Save information retrieved from the database appropriately

When you make a search on a database using a query, it is not usual to save the subset of the data. This is because the next time you run the query, the underlying data might have been updated and you will want your output to reflect that. However, you may want to make the output of a query or a report, or even a whole table, available to a Microsoft Word document or an Microsoft Excel spreadsheet. You can do this quite easily by selecting the database object, such as the query, that indicates the desired data and selecting File > Export from the menu. You have to indicate the format that you want. You may want CSV, RTF (Rich Text Format) or Microsoft Excel format.

■ **Figure 2.76**

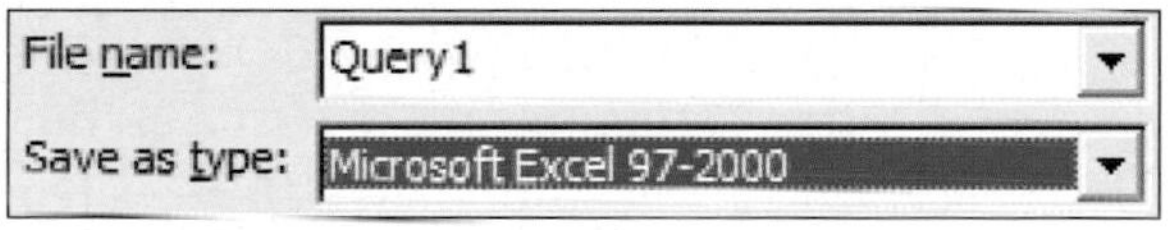

The data extracted by a query can be viewed in a spreadsheet.

■ **Figure 2.77**

	A	B	C	D	E	F
1	Title	Surname	Tel	Quantity	Date	Part_Number
2	Prof	Griggs	031378938	7	01/05/2005	AF524801
3	Ms	Hake	075695072	6	01/05/2005	AE424747
4	Mrs	Harrell	059070234	7	01/05/2005	AE424747
5	Mr	Hill	093690756	8	02/05/2005	AF524829
6	Mr	Pidman	093304389	6	01/05/2005	AF524781
7						

The data can be saved in CSV format and viewed in a text editor.

■ **Figure 2.78**

```
File  Edit  Format  View  Help
"Prof","Griggs","0313789388",7.00,1/5/2005 00:00:00,"AF524801"
"Ms","Hake","0756950724",6.00,1/5/2005 00:00:00,"AE424747"
"Mrs","Harrell","059070234",7.00,1/5/2005 00:00:00,"AE424747"
"Mr","Hill","0936907567",8.00,2/5/2005 00:00:00,"AF524829"
"Mr","Pidman","0933043899",6.00,1/5/2005 00:00:00,"AF524781"
```

Create, edit and format word-processing documents

Often, you need to include database output in a word-processed document. You can add data by exporting it as explained above, or you can use mail merge. Some documents require multiple copies, each one containing information from a different record. You have probably performed many mail merges in the past. Microsoft Word is able to take as a data source any Microsoft Access table or query, so you could send a letter with personal details added to all customers who have not yet received their orders.

All you have to do is to aim the mail merge at the required Microsoft

Access database file during the Get Data stage. You will then be able to choose whichever table or query you want to act as a source of records.

■ Figure 2.79

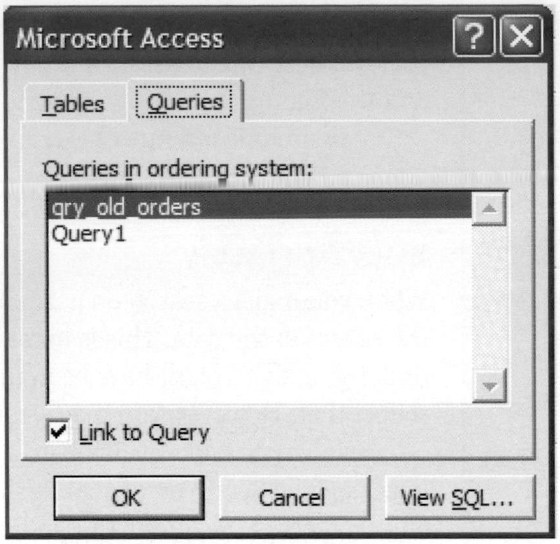

portfolio_tip

Always check the output before making decisions based on it.

Check accuracy

You should never rely totally on any output from a computer system unless you have used some common sense to make sure it is what you want. It is not that computers make mistakes, but people do. Maybe you haven't selected the correct fields or maybe there were mistakes at the data input stage.

Combine and present information

The examples in this chapter and also in Chapter 2.8 have made reference to combining information. We have used queries to combine data from different tables. We have used reports to present this information in an easily understood format. Make sure that you have enough evidence of this in your portfolio.

Add information from one type of software to information produced using different software

There are many ways to combine information from different software packages. In a Microsoft Windows-based system, you can simply copy and paste. We have also seen some other examples of how we can make a file from various sources of information.

We have used:

► export from Microsoft Access tables and queries;
► mail merge.

You can also make use of various embedding and linking facilities that are available in most office software. The Insert menu option allows you to insert a suitable file or an object into a word-processed document. With Insert > Object, you can link to an existing file so that you can edit it from within the word-processed document. All you have to do is to double click on the object.

For example, you may have started a report like this one:

■ Figure 2.80

Old orders

Surname	Forename	Date	Description
Allen	*Tom*		
		01/05/2005	Netsolutions Switch 3812
Barlow	*Leah*		
		01/05/2005	Netsolutions Switch 3812
Barnaby	*Ian*		
		29/04/2005	Netsolutions Switch 3812
Cook	*Jeannie*		
		01/05/2005	Supanet 56k External Modem (Intel)
Drysdale	*Helen*		
		30/04/2005	Netsolutions OfficeConnect wireless 54
Eland	*Steve*		

You select 'insert object' from the word processor menu:

■ Figure 2.81

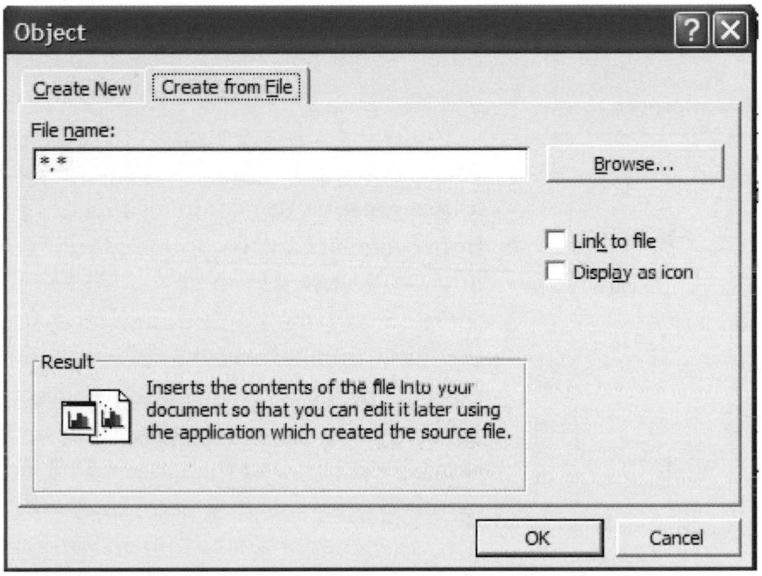

Object [?] [X]

Create New | Create from File

File name:

.   Browse...

☐ Link to file
☐ Display as icon

Result

Inserts the contents of the file into your document so that you can edit it later using the application which created the source file.

OK | Cancel

Then you have the original data in your document ready to work on.

■ Figure 2.82

Output from database showing customers whose orders were placed over two weeks ago. Note that there are only five in this category.

Title	Surname	Tel	Quantity	Date	Part_Number
Prof	Griggs	031378938	7	01/05/2005	AF524801
Ms	Hake	075695072	6	01/05/2005	AE424747
Mrs	Harrell	059070234	7	01/05/2005	AE424747
Mr	Hill	093690756	8	02/05/2005	AF524829
Mr	Pidman	093304389	6	01/05/2005	AF524781

The database: objective (e)

The final part of your portfolio for this unit must be an evaluation. This has to cover a number of points.

▶ **The performance of the database:** Here, you ask yourself whether the outputs from the database showed you useful information that was correct and helpful in identifying trends and facts and also provided a good basis for recommendations.

The software will work, you will not need to evaluate the performance of Microsoft Access! But, maybe some of the queries were not able to show exactly what you wanted because the data fields originally supplied did not give the facts you needed.

portfolio_tip

You could start with a self assessment of your database skills at the start of the project, then at the end you can write about new skills and how your existing skills have improved.

▶ **Evaluation of your own performance**: You have to make a report on how well you performed in doing these tasks. Be honest about it, even if you think that you did everything perfectly, you may be able to comment on how easy it was or how long it took you. There must be comments on this in your portfolio.

▶ **Witness statements and other feedback**: Include any comments from others about how useful the database was and possibly how easy it was to use. Again, add these to your portfolio.

You could ask one of your friends to use your database and write a short review of it. Also ask them if they have any suggestions for improvements. You could also record an interview as evidence.

▶ **Improvements and recommendations**: You will probably have produced a fairly effective system. If you worked well on it, you may not think that there are too many improvements that could be made. However, possibly the data supplied was in a format that made it difficult to process. One example of this is where addresses are supplied in a single address field. Splitting them up as we did in Chapter 2.8 makes it possible to do more extensive processing such as sending letters to everyone who lives in a certain town.

It is very important to remember that it is the system you are evaluating. Do not be afraid to say that some things did not work as they should. If something did not work, then say why it did not work.

UNIT 3
The knowledge worker

Problem solving

Aims

- To introduce computer modelling.
- To show how a spreadsheet can be used for modelling.

Introduction

We are all knowledge workers. We all take in information from the outside world and process it so that we can make decisions. We watch television, talk to our friends, read newspapers, letters and bank statements, etc., and absorb information in thousands of other ways. From this information, we decide things such as whether to go out (it might rain), whether to go clubbing (can I afford it?), whether to watch the TV (is there a good film on?).

We have seen how computers store and process data. The processing can turn the data into information. We, as humans, accumulate lots of information and make judgements and generalisations about it all. This big picture that we make is knowledge. It is never static. We grow in knowledge all the time as we adapt to our surroundings.

People have always acquired knowledge. The more able are conscious of this and are able to take advantage of their knowledge for their own and others' benefits. What is different in the Information Age is that there is much more information readily available to everyone. It is more than can be absorbed by an individual. We can make use of Information Technology to help us sift and process all this information. With luck and good judgement, we should be able to make more informed decisions than in the past.

What this unit is about

This unit looks at how we can make use of IT tools in order to help us grow in knowledge and make better decisions. IT is not going to change us as human beings, it is unlikely that we are going to behave better or be happier because of technological developments. However, we can learn how to make better decisions in specific cases if we know how to collect and process facts from the vast amount of information that is available.

The unit examines some examples of how we can use IT to help us. These ways focus on identifiable tasks which try to make us more conscious of what to do when making decisions. They should help us to collect the right information and know what to do to get the best out of it, and, most importantly, communicate it and our recommendations to others.

If you are making decisions for yourself alone, you may not have to convince anyone else that you have acted sensibly. Most of the time, however, we need to carry others with us and that means either having enough charisma to convince people to trust you or to set out reasons for a course of action that are themselves convincing.

A computer system will not help you to make the big decisions in life. There is no software that guarantees choosing a lifelong partner. Humans will continue to make decisions based on gut feeling or countless other motivations, and they will continue to make mistakes. Computer systems are limited in what they can do and it pays to know the limitations very clearly.

Assessment

This unit does not require you to produce anything for your portfolio. Instead, you will take a practical examination in which you have to use a spreadsheet to work out a sensible course of action from data that will be provided. You will get some practice at doing this as you work through this unit.

Modelling

If a car manufacturer wants to try out a new design of air bag to see if it prevents injuries better than older versions, it could crash real cars with real drivers and then assess the injuries. It is unlikely that many people would volunteer to take part in these tests! In the past, crash test dummies were used that were made to behave in much the same way as human bodies. These were very expensive and they were never exactly right. Wrecking cars is expensive too.

Today, as with many real-life situations, is often possible to simulate crashes mathematically. If we know:

▶ the mass of the car
▶ the thickness of the metal in the bodywork
▶ the strength of the metal
▶ the speed of the car
▶ the direction of impact
▶ the mass of the driver and passengers
▶ the strength of various tissues such as bones
▶ the trajectory of the body when decelerated

 Figure 3.1

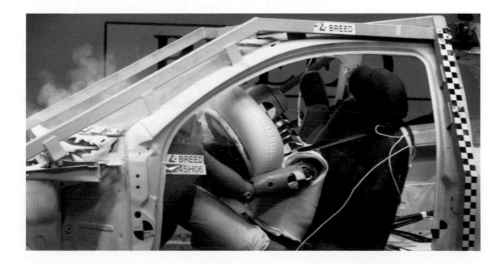

and many, many other factors, it is possible to calculate the likely effects of a crash in different circumstances. Turning a situation into a set of equations is called modelling. Modelling is cheaper and safer than carrying out tests in real life.

There are many ways to crash a car and people are all different so many calculations are needed. When we model any situation, we cannot be sure that all the correct things have been taken into account.

Using a computer to help

Processing data is what computers are good at. They do all the calculations we tell them to do at amazing speeds. Modelling with computers has been one of the great success stories in the development of the Information Age. Nowadays, computers are used to model almost everything, including:

- a country's economy
- aircraft
- the weather
- river flooding
- bacterial growth
- mortgage repayments.

■ Figure 3.2

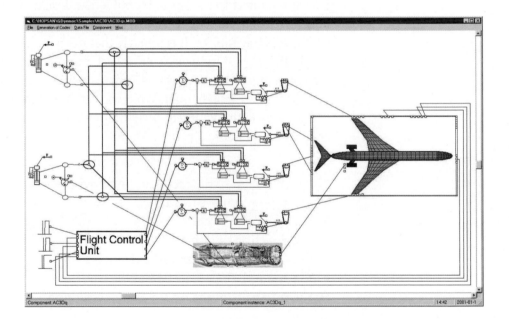

The degree of success to which these models simulate real life varies according to:

- how much data we have and how accurate it is;
- how well we have translated real events into mathematical formulae.

ACTIVITY

Think of a list of at least five real-life situations that can be modelled on a computer. Rank them in order of their reliability and comment on reasons for this.

Spreadsheets

Modelling can involve colossal amounts of data and huge numbers of calculations. A good example of this is the modelling of the atmosphere in order to produce weather forecasts. Our understanding of the atmosphere continues to improve and more data is available than ever before from satellite monitoring and ground stations. Even so, weather forecasts are seldom accurate beyond a week or so. We would all like to be able to model global warming so that we could make better decisions, but there is not enough data available.

Many modelling situations, like the atmosphere, require huge computing power and specially written software. Anybody can carry out their own modelling in a smaller way on a PC. A supermarket might want to model throughput at the checkouts in order to decide how many staff to employ in its branches. It is easy enough to write a small program to model this, but it is even easier to use a spreadsheet.

Spreadsheets were developed for PCs so that users could perform complex calculations and make the most of the processing power available. Many businesses bought PCs in the early 1980s so they could run one of the first spreadsheet programs: Lotus 1-2-3.

portfolio_tip

By the end of this unit, make sure that you can set up a spreadsheet to model many different scenarios. This skill is crucial.

A simple model can be set up to answer the standard question 'What-if...?'. You have probably tried this before. Suppose we have a budget of £2000 to furnish a room. We can set up a spreadsheet to find out what we can afford (Figure 3.3).

	A	B	C	D	E	F	G	H
1	Model to furnish a room						VAT	17.5%
2								
3	Item	Unit cost	Number	Total ex VAT	VAT	Total		
4	Chair	£ 50.00	1	£ 50.00	£ 8.75	£ 58.75		
5	Sofa	£ 500.00	1	£ 500.00	£ 87.50	£ 587.50		
6	Easy Chair	£ 350.00	1	£ 350.00	£ 61.25	£ 411.25		
7	Table	£ 400.00	1	£ 400.00	£ 70.00	£ 470.00		
8	Cupboard	£ 250.00	1	£ 250.00	£ 43.75	£ 293.75		
9								
10	Total					£1,821.25		
11	Budget					£2,000.00		
12	Balance					£ 178.75		

■ **Figure 3.3**

This simple model was set up using formulae and one function.

A formula is made from instructions to perform some operation on data in the spreadsheet cells. For example,

```
=D4+E4
```

tells the spreadsheet to add together the contents of cells D4 and E4.

A function is a ready-made set of instructions that you can call by name. For example

```
=SUM(F4:F9)
```

tells the spreadsheet to use the SUM function to add up all the numbers in the cells between F4 and F9.

The room modelling spreadsheet looks like Figure 3.4 if you show its formulae:

	A	B	C	D	E	F	G	H
1	Model to furnish a room						VAT	0.17
2								
3	Item	Unit cost	Number	Total ex VAT	VAT	Total		
4	Chair	50	1	=B4*C4	=D4*VAT	=D4+E4		
5	Sofa	500	1	=D5*C5	=D5*VAT	=D5+E5		
6	Easy Chair	350	1	=D6*C6	=D6*VAT	=D6+E6		
7	Table	400	1	=B7*C7	=D7*VAT	=D7+E7		
8	Cupboard	250	1	=B8*C8	=D8*VAT	=D8+E8		
9								
10	Total					=SUM(F4:F9)		
11	Budget					2000		
12	Balance					=F11-F10		

■ Figure 3.4

You will notice that the formula in cells E4 to E8 refer to a cell that we have named VAT. It often helps to name cells so that we don't have to remember where they are.

We can use this model to try out different purchases. For example, if we decide that we want two easy chairs we can change the 'number' cell for the chairs (Figure 3.5). We can immediately see that we have gone over budget: in this case, we have formatted the 'balance' cell to show up in red if it is negative. The important cells have been marked.

	A	B	C	D	E	F	G	H
1	Model to furnish a room						VAT	17.5%
2								
3	Item	Unit cost	Number	Total ex VAT	VAT	Total		
4	Chair	£ 50.00	1	£ 50.00	£ 8.75	£ 58.75		
5	Sofa	£500.00	1	£ 500.00	£ 87.50	£ 587.50		
6	Easy Chair	£350.00	2	£ 700.00	£ 122.50	£ 822.50		
7	Table	£400.00	1	£ 400.00	£ 70.00	£ 470.00		
8	Cupboard	£250.00	1	£ 250.00	£ 43.75	£ 293.75		
9								
10	Total					£2,232.50		
11	Budget					£2,000.00		
12	Balance					£232.50		

■ Figure 3.5

Changes can be made very easily until an acceptable result is obtained.

Defining a problem

It sounds obvious, but if there is a problem to be solved, there is not much chance of a successful solution unless the problem is fully understood in the first place. Many attempts to solve problems have been doomed from the start because nobody ever fully understood exactly what the problem was. Some problems are more obvious than others.

Example 1 – A trip to New York

I want to visit my friend in New York. I promised her I'd go soon but we didn't really make any firm plans. I'm beginning to feel guilty. What's the problem? It is actually making it happen. Some people might be fortunate enough to be able to say, 'OK, I'll buy a ticket and go, then find a hotel and stay for a week.' For most people, their lives aren't quite that simple. There are problems that have to be identified and dealt with before the whole project can come to a successful conclusion. Let's have a look at the problems:

▶ I shall need a week off work.
▶ I need to be able to afford the air fare.
▶ I need to find a flight at the right time.

This doesn't look too bad, but each of these problems has sub-problems of its own. I can break them down in a chart (Figure 3.6).

■ Figure 3.6

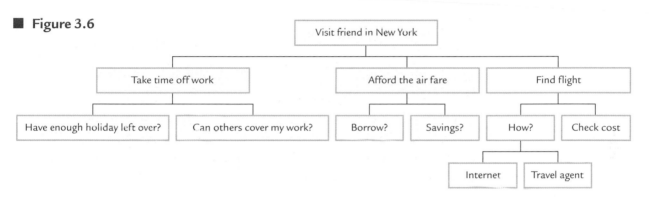

It's looking a bit more complicated now, but I still haven't considered that:

▶ I need to find a hotel to stay in.
▶ I need to make sure that my friend is free at the same time.

Things could get a lot worse! There are hundreds of possible flights to New York and they vary in price according to the time of year, the day of the week and the time of day. There is also the choice of economy or business class. You might get a better bargain if you are prepared to travel to a different airport at the start of your journey. Do you fly to JFK, LaGuardia or Newark?

In reality, some of these decisions are quickly made, but it just shows how much has to be taken into account when solving any problem. You can rarely *just do* something, there are always constraints that determine what you can and cannot do. That is one of the key things about understanding a problem: the idea that some constraints are fixed and some are variables. In our example, we shall look at just a few:

▶ Fixed constraints
   Starting location (home)
   End (friend's apartment – NY)
▶ Variable constraints
   Date to go
   Airline
   Flight
   Time

Departure airport
Arrival airport
Class of travel

Once we have itemised as many of the constraints as we can, it is possible to go through them one at a time, do some research and make some decisions.

Not enough information

In this example, we will probably forget to factor in a lot of other constraints. It is easy to think of some that we have missed. We haven't checked that we have a passport or whether we need a visa.

ACTIVITY

Make a list of five other things that we should think about when planning our trip.

Too much information!

If you look up a hotel to stay in while you are away, you will find that if you spend long enough at the task, there are absolutely hundreds of possibilities. You can make choices about:

► location
► price
► type of room
► size of room
► smoking or non-smoking
► leisure facilities
► restaurant

A Google search will turn up thousands of combinations of these factors. You have to be able to narrow your search down unless you want to spend the next year planning your trip.

Internet search engines can help. You can enter a search string that includes logical operators. If you enter

```
hotel New York
```

you will get far more 'hits' than you can cope with. If, however, you enter

```
hotel Manhattan three star
```

you will have fewer 'hits' to sift through because the software filters the results based on your decision criteria.

Inserting the word AND between each of the words in the search string means that **all** your conditions are to be met. Search engines have various advanced features to help you find what you want as quickly as possible.

ACTIVITY

Look at the advanced options in Google to find how to narrow down a search. How can you be sure that you only find web sites with .com as a suffix?

Notice that to do all this successfully, we need to know

► more or less what we want to do;
► how to get the information;
► how to sift for the information most likely to help us.

There are other ways to use the Web to find out what we want. You can use various web sites to check flights, hotels and hire cars, for example:

   www.expedia.co.uk

ACTIVITY

What are the advantages and disadvantages in using a travel planning web site such as Expedia?

Example 2 – Buying a train ticket

If you live in the UK and ever need to travel by train, you will know that arranging a journey for example, from Worcester to London, is almost as complicated as booking a multi-centre holiday in the Far East!

► You can go via Birmingham or Oxford or Stroud. You can use up to three different train operating companies.
► The journey time can vary considerably.
► You may want to include an Underground travel card.
► The cost varies according to the time of day you wish to travel.
► The cost might vary if you pre-book your seat and then according to how far in advance you book it.

Season tickets are just as complicated.

ACTIVITY

● Find out how much a three month season ticket costs between Cambridge and London. Use any of the booking services that are available on the Web.
● What additional information did you need to provide apart from the time period, the start and the destination stations?
● How long did it take you?
● What do you know now that you didn't know before (apart from the season ticket cost)?

Both of our examples are relatively easy. It is possible to find out what you need to know and safely ignore some obvious blind alleys. We know we cannot consider everything and in the end we have to do as much research as we feel we have time for and then make decisions on that information.

Example 3 – The NHS IT system

Don't worry! We will not consider all the needs and constraints in this one! The NHS (National Health Service) provides a publicly funded medical service for UK citizens. Everybody is covered, whether they pay contributions or not. (How many people is that?)

The Government is spending taxpayers' money on a new IT system for the NHS. It is intended to address a long-standing problem. Doctors, nurses, dentists, surgeons and all the other health professionals keep their own records about patients and their treatments. If you are visiting a town far away from your home and you are taken ill, it is not easy for doctors to access your records. They may have to ask you if you are allergic to penicillin and you may be unconscious.

How can we make it possible for all health professionals to have access to all the information they require in order to provide a quick and efficient treatment for a patient?

Don't spend too long on this but just think how many different requirements there are in order to solve this problem. Think about things like:

▶ access points;
▶ the information that needs to be stored: about you and about treatments;
▶ communications;
▶ security;
▶ training;
▶ willingness to use it (the health workers may like their own systems, they may not want to bother with a new system);
▶ operating platform;
▶ compatible hardware;
▶ compatible file types;
▶ database structures.

Already *billions* of pounds have been spent on this project. Many IT and health professionals wonder if it can in fact be done, or if anyone really wants it. It is more important than ever to make sure that the problem is fully understood when it is a big one, otherwise colossal sums of money are wasted. Remember throughout this unit that a problem must be fully understood before you can get the best out of an IT solution.

The decision-making process

Aims

- To provide an overview of the decision-making process.
- To introduce topics covered in later sections of the unit.

Introduction

This section outlines some of the processes involved in making a decision, the sections that follow explain in more detail using examples based on a model which is on the CD.

The process can be summarised in these steps.

- ▶ Step 1: Define the problem.
- ▶ Step 2: Identify alternative solutions to the problem.
- ▶ Step 3: Evaluate the alternatives.
  Will the alternative being considered resolve the issues?
  Will the alternative being considered create any new issues?
- ▶ Step 4: Make the decision.
- ▶ Step 5: Implement the decision.
- ▶ Step 6: Evaluate the decision.

Example

The doctors in a surgery are thinking about installing a computer network to help in the management of their medical practice. The practice manager has been given the task of investigating the costs of setting up such a system. Following a week of research, a report is drawn up explaining how a network of computers could be connected to the Internet. It explains in detail the advantages and disadvantages of using an Internet-based database for the diagnosis and treatment of illnesses.

Understanding the situation

Before making any decision, it is important to answer the following question: What exactly do you have to decide?

This might seem like an obvious question, but it is possible to waste a lot of time and effort if the situation is not clearly understood from the start.

ACTIVITY

Do you think the report in the example answers the right questions?

The key to the report is establishing exactly what is required. Whilst there is not very much to go on it appears that the practice management wants information about the cost of buying and setting up a network.

Search for information related to the problem

Today, more than ever, the knowledge worker has a vast amount of information available. The aim of any search should be to increase knowledge about the situation. Increasing this knowledge will help with the decision making process and enable better recommendations to be made.

It is very tempting in the Information Age to go straight to the Internet where there are vast amounts of information. However a good knowledge worker will use a wide range of sources including paper-based examples such as books, maps, newspapers, magazines and academic papers.

It is possible that someone else has already researched a similar situation and reading this research might save a lot of time.

Information is required about the costs of a network, so it would be a good idea to look for information from equipment suppliers to find the cost of what is needed. It might be necessary to invite some of the company sales representatives in so that they can quote for new equipment. However, it should be possible to obtain some information from web sites.

Establish and evaluate sources of information

Once a search has been carried out, many sources of information will be available, some useful and some not so useful. Some may even be misleading. It is, therefore, important that the information sources are evaluated to decide if they are worth using. To be of use, sources of information need to be up-to-date, unbiased and relevant. Care must be taken to establish the source of the information. This is especially important when relying on Internet resources because anyone can put information onto a web site; they do not need to have it checked first.

Commercial sites that sell goods or services must comply with certain laws which relate to advertising and they should not make false claims. However, they will be biased towards their own products. One mobile phone company is hardly likely to tell you that calls are cheaper with a competitor. This is why a range of sources needs to be used and comparisons made between them.

Identify gaps in your knowledge

Once you have done some research, a review of the situation should be carried out to remind yourself what you are doing. It is easy to become lost when faced with lots of information, and to think that you have covered everything completely. There may be some important information missing, so you should reassess your initial thoughts and try to match the information collected to the situation. You should also look for any important gaps in your knowledge.

It is important to take note of any missing pieces of information so that you can decide how important the information is. Would having the missing information make a difference to the decision you need to make? If it makes no difference, the information is irrelevant so there is no need to waste time looking for it. If it does make a difference, try to assess how much of difference it might make.

It is possible that the practice manager is not a computer expert and so might not know much about networks and setting them up. It would be a good idea therefore to research about networks and what is needed to set one up. It need not be too technical but enough to give an idea about what is involved.

Sales representatives will help to explain what is needed but it is a good idea to have some background knowledge first. After all, a sales representative's job is to sell things.

Other factors and constraints to consider

Read carefully through any information that has been collected and study the model you have set up or have been given. Is there anything else that might need to be looked at? You may not have a complete model and therefore any decision will be based on an incomplete assessment of the situation. It may be that this is the best you can achieve in the time given. In which case you need to point this out in any presentation or report you might produce.

If possible, the model should be adapted to take into consideration any external or internal factors that might affect the outcome. Further information may be needed, in which case you will need to gather this information and assess its usefulness. Then adapt your model to take this into consideration.

In a doctor's surgery, security of the data is a vital factor (more so than the physical security of the equipment). This is a factor that needs to be considered when installing new equipment. Added security may have a cost implication for the system.

Select the information you will use

At this stage, the information available should cover all necessary aspects of the problem. You will possibly have too much information at this stage so it is important to carefully select the information you need.

Consider any duplicated information by comparing one set to another. Choose the set that gives the clearest view. In this unit you will be using a spreadsheet to model a situation. You will need to select the information that best fits into the model you have. You always need to study the model and see how the information fits into it. You might need to change the format of the information to fit the model, or adapt the spreadsheet to accept the data you have.

In the final report to the practice, the manager will need to select information about the cost of installing and purchasing any equipment for the network. He may have prices from different companies, so the manager will need to select which ones are going to be used in order to make the final decision. The manager might also have some information that is simply not relevant to the task.

In this example, the final report was not about costs but looked at how a network of computers could be connected to the Internet. It explained in detail the advantages and disadvantages of using an Internet-based database for the diagnosis and treatment of illnesses.

This report contained information that might be interesting but is not what was asked for, it should have been filtered out by this stage.

Analyse the information

You should study the information you have and try to make a summary of it. There are various ways that you can do this. You could make notes or draw a chart to break down the information into manageable chunks.

The important thing about any method you use is to list the key factors. Some of the data in your model will have more of an effect on the outcome than other data. It is a good idea to experiment with the model, changing one thing at a time, to see what effect any particular change has. Once you have seen how the model behaves you can start to look at your information and analyse it according to the effect it has on the model.

Identify alternatives

One of the purposes of a model is to help identify alternatives. Sometimes there might be many different options and the easier it is to try them out the better. The good thing about a computer model is that the options can be changed over and over again and you can always go back to the start by loading up the original.

It is important to evaluate each alternative option. You should look at the positive and negative points for each. It is unlikely that you will find one option that will solve the problem but you should find one solution that is better than the others. Differences might be small and you should not be afraid to base the final decision on your personal findings. What matters most is that you can justify your decision to others.

When you look at the positive and negative points, you need to make clear what you know to be a fact and what you only believe is true.

Make the decision

In trivial situations, it may be that you will have all the facts that you need in order to make a decision. In more complex cases, you will have to make assumptions to save time. Assumptions may or may not be reliable so as soon as you start making assumptions, you introduce the possibility of making mistakes. There is no avoiding this if you want to make a decision in a reasonable time frame.

Use the information you have been given or have found to reach a decision in a considered way. Do not jump to choose the first solution. The whole idea of using a computer model is the ability to try out alternatives: so try out several. You might write down the advantages and disadvantages of each as you go. Think carefully about double checking each solution. Make sure that the model is working correctly.

Justify the decision

When you have reached a decision you will need to justify why have you chosen this outcome. It is important to have the facts about your solution

portfolio_tip

Do not make changes to the original model: use a copy. That way you can start again if you make a mess.

If you reach a point that provides something of interest which might be useful, then save a copy at that point.

summarised in a form that is easy to demonstrate to others. If you are using numbers then graphs and charts are often a good way to do this.

You should cover what reasons there are for your decision and any assumptions you have made about the situation. When it comes to making a decision, there are no hard and fast rules. What you think is the right decision may differ from that of the person next to you. Very few decisions are made with total certainty; every decision involves a certain amount of risk.

The information presented to the doctor's practice should have been about the cost of the new system and the cost of setting it up. It should have included the name of the recommended supplier and a quote from it. A summary of one or two other suppliers' quotes should have been included for comparison to show that the practice is getting good value for money.

Explain decisions to others

Once you have reached a conclusion you will need to explain it to others. It is important that when doing this that you do not just list the benefits. You should also include any drawbacks you can see and any assumptions that you have made. You should also discuss any information you think is missing from the model and how you might go about obtaining this extra information. You will need to think about the best method of presenting your conclusions. This is explained further in Chapter 3.10.

Understanding a situation

Aims

- To consider ways of understanding a situation.
- To introduce a case study.

Introduction

It is vital to be able to identify the decision to be made and the goals to be achieved. This unit is about using spreadsheets to model a situation and to make decisions based on that model.

Much of this chapter uses an example model on the CD. It is about a computer networking company called *Livewires*. You will use the scenario given to follow through the process of making a decision and explaining it to others.

CASE STUDY

Livewires

Livewires is a computer cable company that specialises in installing the network cables for computer systems.

The company director is looking at how the company charges customers for installations. The market is very competitive and it is important to get the balance right between the charges they make for installing cables and the cost to themselves of the materials.

At present they use a simple system to work out the cost of the installation, based on the number of sockets a customer wants. The system they use has a fixed charge for each outlet regardless of the distance from the server cabinet to the computer. Using this system saves time for *Livewires* since they only need to know the number and type of socket required to complete a quote.

They want to move to a new system that charges the customer according to the materials used and the time the job takes to complete. The company director thinks that this method will result in a more consistent profit margin for the company. He has looked at the sales and site reports for a number of sites where they have worked and found that the profits are much lower on some sites than others.

What you need to decide

Here are some examples of different types of decision that a knowledge worker might be asked to help with:

A **recurring decision**: This is one that needs to be made repeatedly, sometimes at fixed intervals (for example, weekly, monthly or yearly). An example would be a finance minister or the Chancellor making decisions about taxation in the yearly budget.

A **non-recurring decision**: This is a one-off decision which you will not be asked to repeat. You will need to use a new model, new data and new information each time you make this type of decision. The *Livewires* example is like this.

To make any decision, you need to understand the situation you are facing. Unless you understand what you are being asked to decide, any attempt to make a decision is likely to be incorrect because it is based on errors about the reality of the situation.

The first step is to find out what needs to be decided. You then need to build up an accurate and full description of the situation.

To help your understanding, you should now write down any questions you might have about the situation. By doing this, you can go over the information again and look to see if the answers are given to you or if you need to look for answers elsewhere.

Livewires – Questions	
Question	**Possible answer**
How much does it cost for materials?	In the description but not the model.
How is the labour cost worked out?	In description but not clear.
Is there any information about a site?	Space in model, data to import is available.
...	...
...	...

Are there different viewpoints?

As well as collecting facts, it is important to consider those who will be affected by your decision. Ideas from these will supply you with more information and help you to examine the model from different viewpoints.

There are several viewpoints to be considered in the case study. Here are a few extracts from the study:

The sales staff: John and Paul, who are sales staff, think that the amount of time taken to visit the site should also be taken into consideration.

The engineers: The engineers say that there is no such thing as a typical site; each site presents new problems and unique challenges.

The director: The company director thinks that this method will result in a more consistent profit margin for the company.

Open the file 'Livewires start'. This is the basic model that you are provided with. In your examination, you will be provided with a different model.

Does the model cover all the viewpoints above?

<u>H</u>ow does this decision compare with similar ones you have made before?

Your own experience of solving problems needs to be put to good use to guide you. Although you have only recently been introduced to this scenario you will have used spreadsheets before. You will have some experience of using 'What if... ?' models to investigate a situation.

The screenshots show how a similar model was used to arrive at the cost of labour in the scenario. The first decision needed for the new system was the cost of labour, since this was not taken into consideration in the old way of charging. Part of the model was used with a small set of data. The labour was set at £25 per hour and the screenshot (Figure 3.7) shows this resulted in a lower profit being made than the old system.

■ Figure 3.7

live wires labour.xls

	A	B	C	D
1	Item	Old method	New method	
2	Total Costs	£581.16	£581.16	
3				
4	Charges to customer	£815.00	£807.70	
5				
6	Profit made	£233.84	£226.54	
7				
8				

This was not seen as a good starting point since the cost of surveys would be higher in the new system and the profit needs to reflect this. The cost per hour was set at £27 resulting in the increase shown in Figure 3.8. The sales staff felt that this was not enough so eventually the labour cost was set at £30 per hour for the new system.

■ Figure 3.8

	A	B	C
1	Item	Old method	New method
2	Total Costs	£607.16	£607.16
3			
4	Charges to customer	£815.00	£846.70
5			
6	Profit made	£207.84	£239.54
7			

portfolio_tip

This unit is assessed by examination. You will be given a copy of the model and some information before the examination. You should spend time experimenting with the model and practising some 'What if... ?' type questions.

<u>A</u>re there variations from time to time or place to place?

Any model must be as complete as possible and take into account as many variables as possible. In this scenario, it is important to realise that not all sites are going to be the same. Look at the following extract:

> *The timing is based on a typical installation; sometimes the engineers complain that they take much longer than allowed, especially if there are a lot of walls to drill through.*

It is clear from the extract that there are some variations from one site to another. Another variable in the model is the length of cable runs. This varies from room to room, even on the same site.

On some sites, the customers want the work done out of office hours to cut down on disruption to their own activities, therefore another consideration is how much the engineers are paid. If they work late at night or long hours, they might need to be paid more per hour. This is not taken into consideration in the model you have been given.

How important do you think the rates paid to the engineers are?

Do you think the model could be adapted to take this into consideration? If so, how?

<u>How long do you have to decide?</u>

Most decisions are time-constrained. In other words you need to reach a conclusion by a deadline. As the amount of time decreases, less time is available to examine and to compare possible options. The decision-making process needs to be modified to allow for this. It may mean ignoring some alternatives altogether and basing the decision on a reduced set of information.

Many people try to collect far more information than is required to make a decision. When too much information is obtained, problems can arise. Computers enable us to collect an almost limitless supply of information, so we have to be selective in what we use.

portfolio_tip

In the assessment for this unit you will have 2 hours to present the facts, reach a decision and convey that decision to others.

► The decision might be delayed because of the time taken to obtain and examine the information.

► Something called 'information overload' can occur and because so much information is available it becomes impossible to process it all in time.

▶ Too much information cannot be held in a person's memory so some is lost and it is possible to forget vital things.

What resources are at your disposal?

To help you make a decision you will have a number of resources available to you. It is a good idea to make a list of the resources and make a note of how you might use them.

In the *Livewires* example you have the following available:

▶ a part completed spreadsheet model;
▶ a description of the scenario;
▶ some files containing data about two sites.

You will need to spend some time looking carefully at the materials. You will need to:

▶ add formulae to the model because it is not finished;
▶ import data files into the model;
▶ read the scenario carefully.

As you work on this example you will be adding to and using the model to develop your skills.

Sources of information

Aims

- To examine the need for knowledge about a situation.
- To look at how to identify gaps in your knowledge.
- To consider the reliability of information.

Introduction

When you are making a decision, the first thing you need to work out is what you already know and what you need to find out. If you can identify any gaps in your knowledge then you need to establish ways to fill these gaps if necessary. You will need to make judgements about the accuracy and usefulness of any other sources of information.

It is important to realise that there is a difference between the terms data, information and knowledge. Information is when data is processed in some way to give it meaning.

Data can be given meaning by putting it into context.

```
1, 35, 2, 73, 70
2, 66, 2, 88, 132
3, 25, 2, 70, 50
4, 33, 1, 72, 33
5, 82, 1, 96, 82
```

For example, the data given is just a list of numbers, however if you put into the context of the *Livewires* scenario and then into the model it becomes information about the cable runs at a site.

■ Figure 3.9

	A	B	C	D	E
					live wires2.xls
1	Run number	Distance (m)	Sockets	Time mins	cable used
2	1	35	2	73	70
3	2	66	2	88	132
4	3	25	2	70	50
5	4	33	1	72	33
6	5	82	1	96	82
7	6	84	2	97	168
8	7	85	1	98	85

Processing information and interpreting it, by using a set of rules that apply to a situation produces knowledge.

In the cabling example shown in Figure 3.9, the worksheet provides information. When you know how the time taken to lay a run of cable is worked out using the formula in column D, you have acquired knowledge about the situation. Figure 3.10 is the image of the spreadsheet with formulae turned on and shows how the time for a run is worked out.

■ Figure 3.10

D2	▼	=	=IF(B2<30,70,70+ROUNDUP((B2-30)/2,0))	
	A	B	C	D	E
1	Run number	Distance (m)	Sockets	Time mins	cable used
2	1	35	2	=IF(B2<30,70,70+ROUNDUP((B2-30)/2,0))	=C2*B2
3	2	66	2	=IF(B3<30,70,70+ROUNDUP((B3-30)/2,0))	=C3*B3
4	3	25	2	=IF(B4<30,70,70+ROUNDUP((B4-30)/2,0))	=C4*B4
5	4	33	1	=IF(B5<30,70,70+ROUNDUP((B5-30)/2,0))	=C5*B5
6	5	87	1	=IF(B6<30,70,70+ROUNDUP((B6-30)/2,0))	=C6*B6
7	6	84	2	=IF(B7<30,70,70+ROUNDUP((B7-30)/2,0))	=C7*B7
8	7	85	1	=IF(B8<30,70,70+ROUNDUP((B8-30)/2,0))	=C8*B8

You will need two sets of knowledge in this unit: knowledge about the scenario and knowledge about how spreadsheets work.

What do I need to know?

There are several reasons you might need to gather knowledge about a particular situation:

▶ to help with a decision;
▶ to make recommendations;
▶ to give yourself better knowledge.

For this unit you will need to obtain information to help make a decision using a model you have been given.

The *Livewires* scenario starts with an incomplete model. Before you can use the model it is important to look at what is already there. You have to understand that the company installs computer cabling. If you have no idea what network cabling is then it would be a good idea to do a small amount of research to increase your knowledge about computer cabling systems. Doing this might give you a better idea of how the model can be used.

You will also need knowledge about how a spreadsheet works. Here is a list of some of the features of a spreadsheet you might need.

▶ How to load and save workbooks.
▶ The difference between workbooks and worksheets.
▶ How to format cells to match data types.
▶ How to enter formulae.
▶ How to check formulae.
▶ How to replicate (fill) formulae.
▶ How to use functions.
▶ How to use absolute and relative cell references.
▶ How to sort data.
▶ How to produce graph and charts.
▶ How to print parts of a spreadsheet.
▶ How to insert and delete rows and columns.
▶ How to format data.
▶ How to validate data.
▶ How to use filters.

This site covers a lot about cabling. Have a look at the site to improve your understanding of the subject.
www.datacottage.com/

<u>What relevant knowledge do I already have?</u>

As well as knowledge about the scenario, you will need knowledge of how spreadsheets work, and in particular how the *Livewires* spreadsheet model works. You will need to be able to use formulae and add them to a spreadsheet, as well as investigate the existing formulae and check if they are working.

You will also need knowledge about presentation software and how to use a suitable package to produce a report on the decision you have made.

Look at the scenario and the model carefully and spend time looking at how it works. Try to work out the rules governing the model. Remember that it is the rules that help you turn information into knowledge.

In the models you are given, there will be some quite complex formulae to work with. You will not need to create ones that are as complex as these but you should be able to understand them.

<u>What are the gaps in my knowledge and can they be filled?</u>

Once you have a clear picture of the knowledge you hold about the situation you can start to work out what is missing. Later parts of this chapter will help you fill gaps in your knowledge about spreadsheets and give you a better understanding of the rules that make the model work. It is important to strike a balance between too much knowledge and too little. Clearly some knowledge is vital to the model, other knowledge might be of no use at all and therefore do not waste time looking for it.

In the scenario it is vital to know the details of the sites and the lengths of cables used. However the name of the company director is not given. Knowing this will not improve the performance of the model so it is irrelevant. Changes to the quote system may or may not affect sales, but if the system produces quotes that are much higher than before then your competitors might take business away from you.

ACTIVITY

Use a table like the one below to record any gaps you think you have in your knowledge at this stage.

Missing Information	How vital is it?	How easy can find out?
Site details	Cannot work without details	Very easy
Time taken to install cable	Needed for model to work	Very easy
Name of director	Not at all	Not available

You need to deal with missing information using a strategy.

First write down what pieces of information are missing. Then decide how important that item is to your model. Ask the questions:

▶ Will the model work without it?

▶ Does it make a difference to the decision you need to make?

▶ How big a difference will it make?

Next, try to work out if it is difficult to find the information. Remember you have a fixed amount of time so if the information is not important do not waste time looking for it.

You will be provided with a scenario and a partly completed model about 2 or 3 weeks before the examination day. During this time, you will be able to experiment with the model and become familiar with it. You should try to add data to the model and see what happens.

What information do I already have access to?

Study the situation carefully and extract all the information you can find. Make a list of where the information is to be found. In the case study it could be in the scenario, in the spreadsheet model or in the other files.

There are several ways to carry out this task, the exact way will depend on your own style of learning.

Make tables, for example:

Item of information	Where found	Used for
Cable is in 300 m boxes	Scenario brief	Working out cost
Labour is £30 per hour	Scenario brief	Working out new costs
John is a member of sales staff	Scenario brief	Not needed
…		

Draw a chart or diagram, for example,

■ **Figure 3.11**

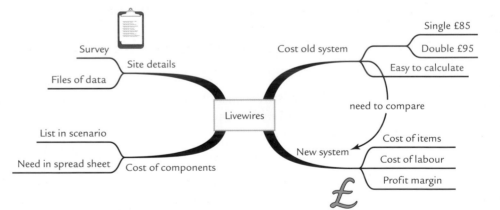

Create a numbered list, for example:

1. Old system (need to compare with: new system)

    1.1 Fixed cost

        1.1.1 Single £85

        1.1.2 Double £95

    1.2 Easy to calculate

2. New system
   2.1 Cost of items
   2.2 Cost of labour
   2.3 Profit margin
3. Cost of components
   3.1 List in scenario
   3.2 Need in spreadsheet
4. Site details
   4.1 Survey
   4.2 Files of data

Where will additional information come from?

In order to make any decision, the knowledge worker must have access to information about the situation. This information can be in a variety of formats.

Before searching for information you should establish the following:

▶ clear objectives;
▶ the extent of existing information.

Information can be obtained from the original source. In this case, the scenario and the incomplete model. This information comes from a direct source.

Other information will come from processing the data sets provided. The profit made by *Livewires* and the difference between the two methods of charging will be found out when the model is complete and the data from the two sites is processed.

Additional information will be provided in the examination which you will need in order to complete the tasks set.

Evaluation of sources for reliability

Any sources of information need to be assessed for reliability. Ask yourself if the information is:

▶ accurate
▶ relevant
▶ complete
▶ detailed enough

Also remember the computer term GIGO (which stands for Garbage In Garbage Out). If the data you are using for the model has errors in it then the results of your efforts will be no use at all. At best they will be misleading, but they could be totally worthless.

You are provided with two data files about sites. This data may contain errors. It is a good idea to check any data first using other information about the system. For example in the scenario you are told that sockets are installed as singles or doubles. So check the numbers in the column headed sockets, it should only contain a 1 or a 2, any other number is incorrect. You can look at the data and perform a visual check or you could set up a validation rule for the data. See page 180 for details of how to do this.

Other factors to consider

Aims

■ To examine more factors that affect decision-making.

Introduction

Very few people make decisions in a textbook-like way. Many major decisions in company boardrooms all over the world are made quite quickly based on experience rather than any complex formal process. Very often people know what they are doing, but are unable to explain the reasons to others.

Gut feeling

Sometimes people make decisions without wading through a lot of facts and figures. They often react to a situation using instinct or because of years of experience.

Example 1

A driver travelling along a road sees a ball roll out in front of him. He brakes hard. A split second later a child runs out after the ball. The car has already stopped.

The driver reacted instinctively based on a notion that when a ball rolls into the road a child is often following. He had no proof that this was going to happen just a feeling based on experience. The events that followed proved him right.

Example 2

A senior nurse in a hospital is nursing a recently admitted sick child. No one really knows what is wrong: the doctors are performing many detailed tests to try and find out. The nurse has a suspicion and persuades a doctor to start using some antibiotics. She just cannot explain why, but her gut reaction is to follow that line of treatment. A few days later the results of the tests arrive and show the child has a very serious condition, which once it takes hold can be fatal in matter of hours. The early treatment without any evidence prevented the infection taking hold.

The nurse cannot say why she did this. It was a gut reaction based on the many years of experience with sick children.

The lesson is that gut reaction can be a useful way to make decisions, but it can often go wrong. Sometimes it is a good idea to take account of the gut feelings of others if there is not enough solid information available at the time.

Emotion

Good decision-making is not purely a matter of facts and figures. The good knowledge worker is aware of how emotions might help and hinder the decision-making process. Some people say that emotion can clutter up the process of gathering information in a logical way to make a decision.

In life we make frequent decisions. Sometimes we are logical about them and rely only on the facts and figures. Decision-making is a process where the final result is a choice made from more than one option. Different people have different preferences, which will affect the approach they take to making a decision.

Logical decision-making is a process using only a clear and predetermined reaction to facts to make decisions. This method attempts to rule out emotions. Emotions involve all sorts of influences that are hard to identify and specify. Using only the data from a statistical model or from mathematical tools such as a spreadsheet should result in a totally logical process of decision-making. Computers do not have emotions and can only produce results based on data that is entered into them and the rules that we program into them.

Emotional decision-making is where your feelings about a situation are used to help produce the decision. Emotional decisions might use some logic, but the main reason for the final choice is based on feelings. These feelings are not to be dismissed. They may have developed as the result of experience.

There are two extreme types of decision-makers.

'Thinkers' who make decisions using logic only. Thinkers see no other way of making a decision. To them, things are a matter of yes or no. They do not like situations that are not clearly defined. They prefer to use a set of clear rules. They will set up models based on data and rules and use them carefully, in a planned way, to investigate the situation.

'Feelers' make decisions based on their own thoughts and emotions They trust their feelings and take account of how others might feel. They do not like rules and models and prefer to judge a situation on its merits.

Emotions can sometimes get in the way of objective decision-making. The following can all play a part in the process:

▶ A person's own likes and dislikes.
▶ Personality clashes.
▶ Emotive issues based on ethical issues.

These are the two opposite ends of the decision-making spectrum. There is a whole range of methods between them with the balance between logic and emotion shifting continuously. The balance changes not only between people, but the same person will use a different mixture of logic and emotion in different situations. No two decisions will have the same balance.

Example

A person buying a car might gather lots of facts and figures about the running costs, the finance, the reliability and the performance. He might spend many hours looking over these. Then driving past a garage, one particular car stands out: the right colour, the right price. Within ten minutes the deal's done: the car's sold.

What others will think?

When making a decision, not everyone is going to agree with you. If you always worry about what others will think about your decision, then you will never actually make a decision. Everyone is entitled to have an opinion and to have an individual approach to approaching a task. However, it is not possible to accommodate all opinions and some people will be disappointed if an outcome does not agree with their views.

Most people like to work with others when making a decision and it is often helpful to take other people's thoughts into consideration when making a decision.

Information and feedback from others can be valuable, but remember that an opinion is just an opinion and it may be wrong or misguided or unhelpful. It is important to hear what others say. You should consider if it is relevant and then make up your own mind.

Unfortunately people often make bad decisions because they are concerned about what other people might think. If the decision is not going to be popular with colleagues at work then the path of least resistance is often chosen even though it might not be the best solution.

Example

A large company has just made the Internet available on all 100 workstations in the offices. This means that all staff now have access to the Internet during working hours. One of the managers notices that some staff appear to be spending a lot of time surfing when they should be working. The company has an acceptable use policy which allows the use of the Web for personal use provided that the use is 'reasonable'.

He speaks to the network manager about restricting the availability to the Web to improve the situation. The network manager produces some statistics that show many hours are being wasted. The obvious decision here is to set up the restrictions. However the manager knows that this will be unpopular and cause friction between him and some of the staff so he decides to do nothing.

ACTIVITY

Make a copy of the table below and complete it to show the positive and negative points of setting up restrictions from the company's point of view.

Positive points	Negative points
More work is done.	Work force feel they are constantly being watched.

Look again at the *Livewires* example.

How do you think the sales staff might feel about the new system?
● Is what they think going to have an effect on how the model performs?
● How might you modify the model to take account of what they think?

Ambition and career consequences

The knowledge worker must be able to take responsibility for decisions made in real life. That also means accepting the consequences.

The management structure used in many companies today has certain implications on the morale of the staff. Junior workers have more responsible and more interesting jobs. This greater level of responsibility carries with it more accountability for the individuals concerned. They find themselves reporting directly to a company director and this can pose problems.

Accepting and taking risks is not easy but it is increasingly likely to happen at some point in your career. Whatever the decision is, you should use all the information you have and carefully examine all the outcomes before making a decision. If you do take any risks, they should be calculated ones and you should be able to use any knowledge and information you have to justify it to others.

Often when faced with making a decision, people will look at how their own career prospects will be affected by the outcome. It could be that a decision is made so as to improve promotion prospects and increase salary. This is when ambition to succeed plays a major role in the decision-making process.

Example

Janet is a sales manager. She is responsible for a team of sales staff covering a large part of the country. She is looking at the sales statistics and notices some patterns in them. Further analysis shows that there are two better ways to deploy the sales staff but both will mean changes in the way they operate. However, since she is paid bonuses based on the amount that the sales team generates, she chooses the option that will increase her bonuses the most in the next year. Even though this is not the best long-term solution she is looking for promotion in the next year and these figures will look good.

Lack of knowledge: are the gaps significant?

In the Information Age, technology is changing rapidly. It is common to find that you lack the knowledge to do a particular task. The way to deal with a lack of knowledge is to try to understand each step of the task that you are doing. If you follow the advice in this unit to break down the task into sub-problems it is easy to identify the gaps in your knowledge. Often what seems to be a major gap turns out to be something quite small when you think about it.

For example, if you do not understand how the time taken for a cable run is worked out in the *Livewires* example, it is still possible to use the model. It is only significant if you want to change the way that the time to do a job is calculated. On the other hand, if you do not know how to import the data for the two sites into the model then you are unable to carry on and need to plug that gap in your knowledge.

It is important to understand the situation fully before you test or modify the model. If you can identify any major gaps in your knowledge of the situation then you will need to follow them up. Lack of knowledge is often used as an excuse for poor decision-making. When the decision is questioned many people find it easy to say, 'Oh! I did know that' or 'I'm not sure I was part of that initiative'. Often this is simply laziness on the part of the decision maker and is the result of poor research.

Making a decision

Aims

- To look at the final stages of decision-making.
- To consider how a spreadsheet model can aid decision-making.
- To make a decision based on a simple model.

Introduction

You should have now reached the point where you have gained as much information as possible about the situation. The next stage is to analyse the information and test out different solutions to the problem to find out which is best. It may be that you have only two alternatives to choose from, as in the *Livewires* scenario. This is where you either change to the new method or leave things alone. However, you might have a situation where there are several possibilities to choose from. In this case you will need to try as many of the possibilities as you can in the time available before you reach a decision.

Spreadsheets are very powerful tools that can help in this type of decision-making. They will allow many different sets of data to be used in order to model a situation and help you to arrive at a good decision. You need to realise that the spreadsheet is just one part of the process. You will need to use all the other information available to you as well.

To look at some of the aspects of this final process a simple scenario is going to be used to make a decision and it will illustrate some of the possible problems that you might encounter with a spreadsheet model.

The scenario

Chris has decided to convert his family car to run on LPG (liquified petroleum gas). He knows that the gas is much cheaper than petrol and it is better for the environment. The price of a conversion however is about £1400. He would like to consider different ways of financing the conversion and to get an idea about how long it will take to recover the cost of the conversion. He has three options:

▶ **Option 1:** Take the money out of the interest gained from a savings account and use the amount saved in fuel costs each month to pay the money back. Interest will then be lost on the money taken out of the account.

▶ **Option 2:** Use a credit card and pay back a fixed amount each month. The credit card company will charge interest until the money is paid back.

▶ **Option 3:** Borrow the money from a bank as a loan and pay it back over two years. The amount paid back and the interest is fixed at the start of the loan.

To help with the decision, he recorded his mileage each time he filled up with petrol for a period of two months. He also made a note of the cost of both petrol and gas at the service stations where he filled up. He has set up a simple spreadsheet model with this information in it.

Correct logic

The first stage in the process is to look at the model and consider its logic and how well the spreadsheet does the job. There are two worksheets in the model: *savings* and *method*. We will examine each of these in turn to see how they contribute to the decision.

There are several versions of the spreadsheet on the CD at various stages of completion, make sure you use the right one at each stage in this unit.

Figure 3.12 is taken from the spreadsheet `convert1.xls`.

■ **Figure 3.12**

	B	C	D	E	F	G	H
1	**Mile reading**	**litres**	**p/litre**	**£**	**petrol p/l**	**saved**	**miles**
2	34378	26.3	33.5	£8.81	79.9	£12.20	
3	34610	40	33.5	£13.40	79.9	£18.56	232
4	34785	27.5	33.5	£9.21	79.9	£1,276.00	175
5	34822	8.5	33.5	£2.85	84.9	£4.37	37
6	34872	7.5	33.5	£2.51	79.9	£3.48	50
7	34993	21.4	33.5	£7.17	79.9	£9.93	121
8	35177	28	33.5	£9.38	79.9	£12.99	184
9	35294	22	33.5	£7.37	76.9	£9.55	117

The image shows part of the model. It is a simple model with columns holding weekly data about mileage and the number of litres of fuel used. Some cells hold data and some hold calculations.

ACTIVITY

Make a list showing which of the columns you think hold calculations and which you think are the results of calculations based on this data.

When you have completed the list, load the spreadsheet `convert1.xls` and check your answers.

---

portfolio_tip

In the examination, check the spreadsheets to make sure there are no errors in the model or the data that you have been given.

When you look at the spreadsheet carefully, you should see that in row 4 a massive saving was made on one fill up with fuel. Do you think that is likely that a saving of over £1000 was made on 27.5 litres of fuel? Now look at row 2. The amount of fuel was almost the same and the saving was £12.20. This should give a clue to the problem.

Having seen a possible problem, the next step is to try to fix it. Since the calculations in the other rows seem about right it could be the formula in cell G4 that is wrong.

Column G should now look like this if you show the formulae in the cells.

■ **Figure 3.13**

G
saved
=((F2*C2)-(D2*C2))/100
=((F3*C3)-(D3*C3))/100
=((F4*C4)-(D4*C4))
=((F5*C5)-(D5*C5))/100
=((F6*C6)-(D6*C6))/100
=((F7*C7)-(D7*C7))/100
=((F8*C8)-(D8*C8))/100
=((F9*C9)-(D9*C9))/100

The problem is now obvious. All the other cells are divided by 100. Cell G4 is not. How this has happened is not important at this stage but fixing the problem is, so edit the formula.

When you look at the formulae in this column, it appears that the design of this sheet may be part of the problem. There are lots of opportunities for errors in this formula because it is calculating the cost of both gas and petrol and then working out the difference all in one go. The cost of gas is already worked out in column E, so why do it again? A better approach would be to break the calculation down, by adding a column for the cost of petrol. Then the difference can be calculated with a simple subtraction (see Figures 3.14 and 3.15).

G	H	I
£ Petrol	**saved**	**miles**
£21.01	£12.20	
£31.96	£18.56	232
£21.97	£12.76	175
£7.22	£4.37	37
£5.99	£3.48	50
£17.10	£9.93	121
£22.37	£12.99	184
£16.92	£9.55	117

■ **Figure 3.14**

G	H	I
£ Petrol	**saved**	**miles**
=F2*C2/100	=G2-E2	
=F3*C3/100	=G3-E3	=B3-B2
=F4*C4/100	=G4-E4	=B4-B3
=F5*C5/100	=G5-E5	=B5-B4
=F6*C6/100	=G6-E6	=B6-B5
=F7*C7/100	=G7-E7	=B7-B6
=F8*C8/100	=G8-E8	=B8-B7
=F9*C9/100	=G9-E9	=B9-B8

■ **Figure 3.15**

These images are taken from the improved version of the sheet and show how the formulae are made much simpler. The improved version is on the CD called `convert2.xls`.

Using the spreadsheet

This first part of the worksheet allows Chris to calculate the amount saved over a number of weeks.

To use the worksheet effectively, however, some totals are needed. It would make sense to make a total of the savings made over the eight visits to the petrol stations and then use this amount to work out an approximate monthly saving. The easiest way to do this is to use the SUM function in cell H10. This gives the total saved over two months so add we can add another formula in an appropriate cell to divide this by 2 to give the monthly saving.

ACTIVITY

Using the file `convert2.xls` make the changes needed to do the calculations for the monthly saving described in the text.

When complete the sheet should look like Figure 3.16.

Formula Bar	H
£ Petrol	saved
£21.01	£12.20
£31.96	£18.56
£21.91	£12.76
£7.22	£4.37
£5.99	£3.48
£17.10	£9.93
£22.37	£12.99
£16.92	£9.55
	£83.84
Monthly Saving	£41.92

■ **Figure 3.16**

The worksheet now allows the monthly saving to be estimated using the model.

Chris has used the Internet to find out some figures for a bank loan and found the following information to add to the model. The monthly payment is fixed for the duration of the loan.

Loan amount:	£1400
Months:	24
APR:	14.9%
Monthly repayment: including interest:	£67.22

Note APR is the Annual Percentage Rate which is a standard way of giving an interest rate for comparison.

The credit card statement states that the current interest rate is 1.7% per month on the amount outstanding at the end of the month.

By taking the money out of savings, some interest will be lost on the money but Chris has decided not to build this into the model since the amount is quite small.

To help with the decision on the finance, another model is needed. The worksheet that handles this is called Method and is partly ready to use in the file `convert3.xls`.

ACTIVITY

Open the file `convert3.xls` and look at the main features of the model.

Spend some time looking at the formulae used in the model and also examine its layout.

The model shows the monthly amounts paid by each method. In the credit card section the monthly interest is added. The bank loan is a fixed cost and the money from savings method assumes that the money is paid back based on the amount saved per month in the trial period.

ACTIVITY
Add the following to the model:
- A formula to calculate the total paid back to the bank.
- A formula to calculate the break even time for the bank loan.

Features of the decision

The main decision to make is how to finance the purchase. Chris wants to do this in a way that reflects the projected savings. The model as it is set up shows that with the current data-set, the credit card is the most expensive way to pay. Taking the money out of savings costs less than other methods, because the lost interest is not taken into account. The break even time varies between 33 and 41 months with the data as given.

The credit card and loan methods both cost more than the projected savings, so Chris will have to find extra money each month.

Another important consideration here is the life expectancy of the car. The break even point is up to $3\frac{1}{2}$ years away, so to save money on the project he will need to keep the car longer than that, otherwise he will lose money. It is possible that Chris can sell the car for more money because of the conversion but this is not a certainty.

Other options

Apart from the method of payment, there are other options that can be investigated with the model. It is possible to pay back lower amounts on the credit card. As the debt reduces, the credit card company requires a minimum payment of 3% each month. This will increase the time taken to pay off the debit and increase the amount of interest paid.

ACTIVITY
Adjust the amount paid back on the card to £40 per month and see the effect on the time taken to pay off the debt. You will need to add more rows to the spreadsheet to do this.

Another possibility is to pay more back on the credit card and shorten the time taken to pay back the money. This will also reduce the interest paid.

ACTIVITY
Increase the amount paid on the credit card to £100 per month, and investigate the effect on the interest costs.

Bank loan options

Another set of choices is possible with the bank loan method. It is possible to change the length time taken to repay the loan. Here are some figures.

Months	Cost
18	£86.69
30	£47.86
36	£47.86

ACTIVITY

Use the figures in the table to see the difference made to the loan method of repayment.

Chris has also discovered that, when converted, his car would not have to pay the congestion charge in London because most gas converted vehicles do not need to pay the charge. The charge is currently £8 per day and Chris estimates on average he makes two trips per month into the zone covered by the London congestion charge.

ACTIVITY

Modify the model to take this into account. Obviously it will shorten the pay back time, but by how much?

The choices

Given the amount of savings made on running costs, Chris has decided to convert his car. Now he has to make the decision about the method to pay for the conversion.

Here are some of his notes on the methods.

▶ Credit card
  – Costs more if over a long time.
  – Can vary the payments if needed.
  – Does not use savings.
  – High interest rate.
▶ Loan
  – Fixed cost at start.
  – Interest rate is competitive.
  – Cannot vary the payments.
  – Time taken to pay back is fixed at the start.
▶ Use savings
  – Can vary payments.
  – Can stop payments if need to.
  – Less money in savings for emergencies.
  – Some interest lost.
  – Least expensive way.

Making the choice

To make a decision like this it is now important to weigh up the points in favour (the pros) and the points against (the cons).

ACTIVITY

Complete a table like the one below for each method putting the note into the appropriate column and adding others you might think of.

Method: Credit card	
Pro	Con
Can vary payments	High interest rate

ACTIVITY

Now you have all the information needed to make a decision. Look at the pros and cons of the situation and decide what you would do if you were Chris.

ACTIVITY

Imagine that you are an adviser to Chris. Produce a one-page document explaining which you think is the best way for him to proceed

Computer modelling

Aims

- ■ To understand the logic of a spreadsheet model.
- ■ To identify errors in a model.

Introduction

portfolio_tip

You should always take a good look at the results on a spreadsheet model and think about whether they look right. It is easy to miss errors and make wrong decisions on the basis of them.

Once we have a spreadsheet model to help us make decisions, we tend to put our trust in it. We might commit a department or company to a project on the basis of what we have found out from the model. We will probably have carried out some 'What-if… ?' analyses such as 'What if we purchase 200 PCs? Can we afford the new cabling that would be needed?'

What if the model is wrong? We could end up making very bad decisions that could land us in big trouble.

Developing a spreadsheet model has a lot in common with developing a piece of software by writing a program. We have to make sure that the model or the program takes in the right data, performs the right processing on it and delivers the right output. The bigger the program, or spreadsheet model, the more places there are where things can go wrong.

As we build a spreadsheet model, we take the output from one formula and feed it into another. Then probably pass on the result of that calculation into yet another process. If there is a mistake anywhere along the route, the output will be wrong and we are in danger of making wrong decisions.

CASE STUDY

Steve the plumber

Steve is a plumber who charges for his work like this:

Each job has a minimum charge of £35. This includes up to 1 hour of labour. If a job takes longer than 1 hour, the charge is £35 plus £30 per hour after that.

A spreadsheet can be set up to work this out using the IF function. The IF function works like this:

```
=IF(condition,result if true,
result if false)
```

Steve the plumber set up a spreadsheet to work out the charges for each job.

	A	B	C	D	E	F
1	Job number	Time taken	Charge		Basic charge	35
2	1	2	125		Hourly rate	30
3	2	4.5	200		VAT	0.175
4	3	6	245			
5	4	1	35			
6	5	1.5	110			
7	6	0.5	35			

■ Figure 3.17

CASE STUDY

The constant values are recorded in cells F1 to F3. To make it easier to construct formulae, we can name these cells Basic_charge, Hourly_rate and VAT, respectively.

There are no error messages or funny entries in the cells but when Steve charged his customers, some of them were not impressed! For example, a 2 hour job should not cost £125. Steve asked his son Tom to check out the model and he found that the formula in cell C2 was

```
=IF(B2<=1,Basic_charge,(Basic_charge+((B2+1)*Hourly_rate)))
```

Tom noticed that instead of taking away the first hour's charge (B2–1) which should be included in the charge, the formula added it (B2+1). To make it worse, this larger figure was then multiplied by the hourly rate, magnifying the error.

When the error was fixed and copied down, the calculations were correct.

	A	B	C	D	E	F
1	Job number	Time taken	Charge		Basic charge	35
2	1	2	65		Hourly rate	30
3	2	4.5	140		VAT	0.175
4	3	6	185			
5	4	1	36			
6	5	1.5	50			
7	6	0.5	35			

■ Figure 3.18

Data formats

A spreadsheet stores data as digital bit patterns. It displays the data in its cells according to either our instructions or its defaults. These formats may be completely wrong for our purposes. In the case study, the cells which hold sums of money may be better formatted as currency. Also, the cell that holds the VAT rate would be clearer if it is shown as a percentage instead of a decimal. These changes are easily made by using the menu or the toolbar. Compare Figure 3.19 with the Figure 3.18. The changes in formatting make the new one much easier to read.

■ Figure 3.19

	A	B	C	D	E	F
1	Job number	Time taken	Charge		Basic charge	£ 35.00
2	1	2	£ 65.00		Hourly rate	£ 30.00
3	2	4.5	£ 140.00		VAT	17.5%
4	3	6	£ 185.00			
5	4	1	£ 35.00			
6	5	1.5	£ 50.00			
7	6	0.5	£ 35.00			

Some formatting errors look even worse. You can produce the average of a column of figures by using the =AVERAGE function, but it will default to a ridiculously large number of decimal places.

■ Figure 3.20

	A	B
1	Job number	Time taken
2	1	2
3	2	4.5
4	3	6
5	4	1
6	5	1.5
7	6	0.5
8		
9	Average time	2.5833333

	A	B
1	Job number	Time taken
2	1	2.00
3	2	4.50
4	3	6.00
5	4	1.00
6	5	1.50
7	6	0.50
8		
9	Average time	2.58

■ Figure 3.21

It is always important to make sure that the number of decimal places is always carefully chosen so that the spreadsheet communicates as clearly as possible.

In the above example, formatting all cells to two decimal places would make the 'Job number' column display unnecessary digits. The following example does not look right at all and is confusing.

Syntax problems

You can communicate successfully with people in all sorts of ways. Even if you don't speak much of another language, such as Italian, you can often communicate with a native Italian speaker with a few half-remembered words and a bit of English. Humans are good at interpreting obscure meaning because there are all sorts of other signals to respond to such as gestures and tone of voice as well as the actual words.

You could write an order to a butcher for *half a kilo of stake* and he would assume that you can't spell and interpret it as 'steak'. You would probably get what you wanted.

Consider these two phrases: 'Put the kettle on' and 'Put the coat on'.

There is only one word changed but the actions needed are completely different. People often use the context in which words are used without thinking about the meaning. Computers cannot do this.

The rules of any language are called the *syntax*. If you make a technical mistake in expressing yourself, it is called a *syntax error*. Computers aren't very good at dealing with syntax errors.

Computers don't understand non-standard communications and they certainly don't respond to irony. With spreadsheets, just as with writing programs, it is essential that instructions are given in exactly the correct way.

Computers can't guess what you mean if you don't express yourself correctly. The most likely thing to happen if you give an instruction incorrectly is that error messages will pop up and you will have to fix things before you can go on.

Spreadsheets will try to help you with error messages if you do make a mistake, but they are sometimes difficult to understand.

Suppose we wanted to add two numbers and test to see if they added up to more than 5. We use the IF function to test for this and there are lots of ways to go wrong.

Suppose we enter it like in Figure 3.22.

■ Figure 3.22

ABS	▼	X ✓ =	=if(a1+b1)>5,too big,OK		
	A	B	C	D	E
1	4	5	=if(a1+b1)>5,too big,OK		

Excel tells us that something is wrong and gives us a few hints about where we might look to get some help.

If we then try to fix it, by getting the number of brackets right, there are still lots of little mistakes that we can make.

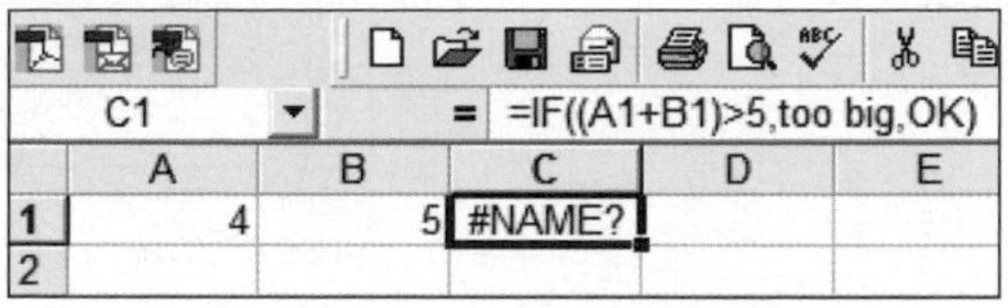

You can go to the function help screens to help you to construct a correct IF statement.

■ Figure 3.24

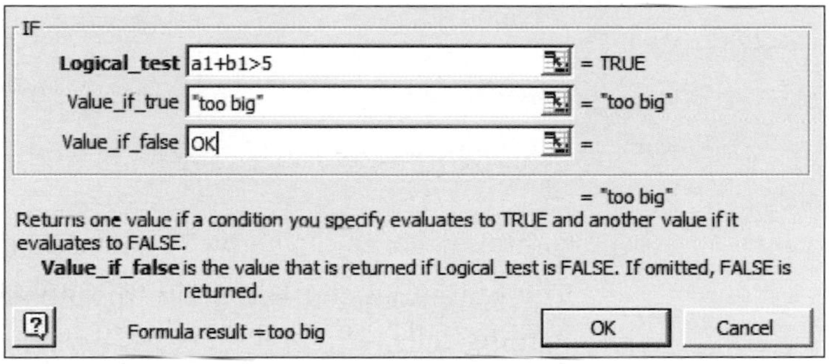

If you look carefully, you might notice that it has put quotation marks around the words 'too big'. If you carry on, it will do the same for 'OK'.

■ Figure 3.25

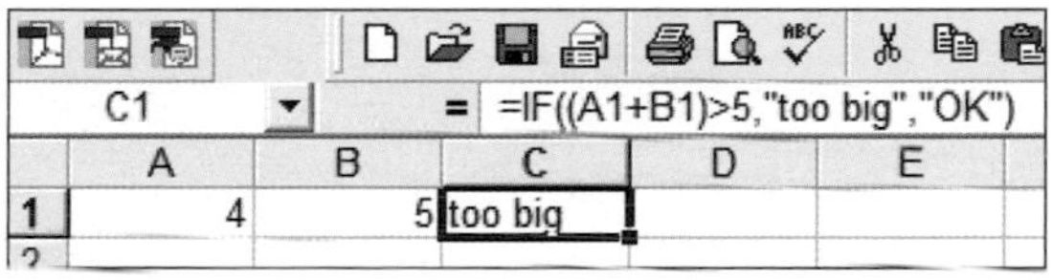

Tracking down syntax errors can take a lot of experience.

> **portfolio_tip**
>
> A spreadsheet model may have all the formulae and functions working without error but the model might still give the wrong results. It might be working out the answers to the wrong calculations! Check the model carefully before you rely on it.

Cell references

It is easy to make mistakes with cell references. If you have a formula or function that references the wrong cells, then obviously the results will be wrong. One common way that errors are made is when using the copy down action.

When you copy a formula down, it adjusts to reflect its new position. The spreadsheet works like this because that is usually what the user wants. However, this can lead to problems. In the case study, Steve may want to add a column to calculate how much VAT (Value Added Tax) should be added to the bills. He can do this in cell D2 and reference the cell where the VAT rate is in cell F3 with the formula

```
=C2*F3
```

This will multiply the total charge by the VAT rate. But, when this formula is copied down, it adjusts F3 to look at the next cell down.

■ Figure 3.26

D	E	F
VAT	Basic charge	35
=C2*F3	Hourly rate	30
=C3*F4	VAT	0.175
=C4*F5		
=C5*F6		
=C6*F7		
=C7*F8		

There is no data in F4 to F8 so the formula will fail.

■ Figure 3.27

D	E	F
VAT	Basic charge	£35.00
£ 11.38	Hourly rate	£30.00
£ -	VAT	17.5%
£ -		
£ -		
£ -		
£ -		

There are two good ways to fix this problem: absolute cell addressing and naming cells.

Absolute cell addressing

If dollar signs are added to a cell reference, then the reference will not change when copied. This is called absolute cell addressing and we enter

```
=C2*$F$3
```

■ Figure 3.28

D	E	F
VAT	Basic charge	35
=C2*F3	Hourly rate	30
=C3*F3	VAT	0.175
=C4*F3		
=C5*F3		
=C6*F3		
=C7*F3		

This is called absolute cell addressing.

Naming cells

If you give a cell a name, you can use that in a formula instead. That makes it easy to remember the cell and also it won't change if it is copied, for example:

```
=C2*VAT
```

Evaluating models

Often, people have to make use of models that others have set up. These models may or may not be well constructed, easy to use and contain all the variables needed to make a good decision. Looking at someone else's model can teach you a lot about what to do or what not to do when setting up your own.

The *Livewires* cost calculator can show you a lot about how to evaluate a model.

The process/scenario being modelled

You cannot properly evaluate a model unless you understand completely what the process is that is being modelled. In the *Livewires* example, we cannot begin to evaluate whether the spreadsheet is set up in the best possible way unless we realise such things as:

- *Livewires* installs computer cables;
- the company wants to save money by changing the way it calculates quotations;
- the old method is based simply on how many sockets the customer wants;
- the model is supposed to take many more variables into account than the old simple quotation system;
- this new method should better reflect the actual costs to *Livewires* than the old method;
- the model should be easy to use and not cause delays.

Examples of other models have been looked at in Chapter 3.6.

What it does

Once you understand the purpose of the model, you need to understand exactly how it performs its tasks.

In the *Livewires* model, you need to understand that:

- the costs to the customer are worked out twice, once using the old method and once using the new method;
- the whole model is subdivided into separate sections. For example, there is an output section (old totals, new totals, comparison), an input section (site details) and lookup tables (costs, material costs);
- the separate parts of the model are organised on separate pages (worksheets);
- the site details can be imported from a data file;
- the calculations are carried out on the output and site details pages.

How well it does it

There are several things to consider when you look at how well a model works. You can assume that the computer will correctly carry out the instructions it is given.

What you have to assess:

- Is the data that is input correct and how do you know that?
- Is there enough data to give a complete answer? In the *Livewires* model, you might consider whether all the variables have been taken into account to provide a totally accurate prediction of the costs. Look at cell D2 on the site details page. See how the time taken is calculated. It is based only on the distances involved. Suppose drilling through walls turns out to be a much bigger problem than originally thought. The model doesn't allow for that so *Livewires* might be out of pocket when they have to pay their technicians for more hours.
- Are there any mistakes in the formulae? You can assess this by working out the expected result by hand or with a calculator and comparing the result with the output of the model. If this is too complicated, you can at least assess whether the output looks 'reasonable'.
- Look carefully at data in columns. Often there will be a pattern. One cell might not follow this pattern and should be investigated.
- User friendliness. Is the output clear and easy to understand? Is it easy to input the data?

portfolio_tip

You should make sure that you thoroughly understand exactly how the model that will be supplied to you works before you start thinking about any shortcomings it has or what you need to add to it.

portfolio_tip

It is *much* easier to make a successful spreadsheet model if you separate the stages onto separate pages (worksheets). You should also immediately rename new sheets so that you can instantly see what they are about. Also, you will find it a lot easier if you rearrange the order of the sheets if they are not in a logical sequence. The time you spend in 'housekeeping' pays off later in understanding a complex model.

Remember: if in doubt, make a new sheet.

Can it be improved?

The main areas to look at here are suggested by an assessment of how well the model does its job.

Are there other factors that should be incorporated into the model? In the *Livewires* example, you could include how many walls need drilling through, how thick they are, what material they are made of. You can probably think of many other factors that could be taken into account. However, eventually you have to make a decision about how far to go. You can never think of everything and you cannot spend forever improving the model. The work has to get done and like everything in life, compromises have to be made and approximations accepted.

Some models need more attention to detail than others. If a model is going to be used for a life or death situation, such as modelling the design of aircraft wings, it is important to factor in as many variables as possible. Even then, there comes a point where you have to stop and get on with the modelling.

User friendliness can usually be improved. The *Livewires* model could automate the data input, or provide a clear form to display the output. Buttons could be provided to run automated processes such as data import.

Which variables can be input?

We have looked at how it is rare in a model of any size for all possible variables to be incorporated. We have seen how drilling through walls can produce all sorts of unforeseen problems. It could be that a particular installation might require some materials that are not at the moment part of the model. None of the working parts of a fully functional network are included. The company might want to include items like wiring cabinets, patch leads, switches and routers. The cable might be copper or fibre optic.

> **ACTIVITY**
>
> Make a list of other extra variables that might affect the cost to *Livewires* of carrying out an installation. Hint: the list *could* be almost endless.

What the output tells you

You have to understand exactly what the output from a model means. It is always a danger that the output from a model can be misunderstood. The output from the model of the atmosphere at the Meteorological Office includes predictions about atmospheric pressure, rainfall, wind speed, etc.. From these, an experienced meteorologist can make a weather forecast. There are things that a model does not do. It will have limits and it is important to realise what these limits are. The output from the atmosphere model does not include predictions of damage caused by high winds. Other processes have to be considered to extend the usefulness of a model.

The output from the *Livewires* model is the cost of a job, calculated in two different ways. This output can also tell you whether the old method of calculation is likely to produce more profit than the new way.

The output does not tell you which is the better way. You have to make your own mind up about that.

The decisions you could make using it

The *Livewires* model does not tell you which method you should accept. That is a human decision. Human decisions are also a form of modelling but they do not follow the exact rules that you put into a computer model.

It is possible to design a computer model to incorporate some aspects of human thought. Random functions can be useful. Eventually, experience and judgement have to be brought in. Computers will probably never be able to make important decisions about our lives that everybody will accept.

In the *Livewires* model, the director could look at the output and see which method is likely to produce a bigger profit. But that is not the only consideration. Once this figure is looked at, he might decide that the old method is so quick and simple that the customers will be happier. They won't have to wait so long for a survey to be carried out. Alternatively, the director might be so worried about tight profit margins that he decides that the more accurate model is essential for the company to stay in business.

ACTIVITY

What decisions are possible from the output from a weather forecasting model?

Using a model to consider alternatives

3.8

Aims

- To understand how a spreadsheet model can help to clarify decision-making.

Introduction

We have seen how computer models can be very helpful in providing us with facts on which we can base decisions. We have also seen how most computer models have shortcomings. This is because most situations are so complex that it is impossible to include everything when designing a model.

If you set up a simple model, you might be fairly sure that all the eventualities are covered. Even so, the output from that model can lead you into more complicated decision-making. Understanding how a model can affect the decision-making process can be looked at in the case of a very simple model.

CASE STUDY

Writing a textbook

An author is writing a textbook. His publisher has budgeted for 100 pages. When other similar books are looked at, it is found that about 500 words fit on each page. That means about 50 000 words for the whole book.

If the textbook is successful, the publisher intends to have it translated into Spanish to sell it in a fast growing market in South America.

The author uses a very simple spreadsheet model. It simply records the number of words in each chapter then calculates the total number of words and how many more are required to fill the book. The model is so simple that you might think that all eventualities are covered. It would certainly be difficult to make a calculation error with a model this simple.

When the author has finished Chapter 8, it looks like Figure 3.29.

	A	B
1		No. of words
2	Chapter 1	6456
3	Chapter 2	4046
4	Chapter 3	8675
5	Chapter 4	9675
6	Chapter 5	5434
7	Chapter 6	5786
8	Chapter 7	2342
9	Chapter 8	4657
10	Chapter 9	
11	Chapter 10	
12	Total words	47071
13	Target no.	50000
14	Difference	2929

■ Figure 3.29

The alternatives

The author has two chapters to go but there is only room for a further 2929 words. Most of his other chapters were much longer than this. The author and his publisher must make some decisions.

There are many possibilities.

Decision	Consequences
Continue writing as much per chapter as before.	Too many words. The number of pages will need to be increased and the book will go over budget.
Make the last two chapters much smaller than the others.	The book will be imbalanced. Important material might be left out.
Go back and cut earlier chapters.	This will alter the author's intentions. It might improve the earlier parts by making them more concise. It might mean the removal of useful material.
Shrink or remove some illustrations to make room for the words.	This might make the book less readable or attractive.
Reduce the font size so that more words can be fitted in.	This could make the book more difficult to read.

ACTIVITY

Make a list of other courses of action that might be possible.

From this, it is clear that the model is helpful in the decision-making process, but in the end, other factors must be taken into account before a decision is made.

Factors that differentiate between the decisions

Even in a simple scenario like this one, there are plenty of implications behind each possible option.

Some of the consequences are listed in the table. There are others. If the publisher asks the author to go back over the earlier material and make cuts, he may find that the author is unwilling to do this. There are plenty of reasons why this might happen. The author might be very attached to what he has written and doesn't want to change what he regards as good work. He may simply not have the time. With deadlines approaching, reworking lots of material might simply not be an option.

The decision might depend upon what the author is like. If the author is an unknown or if he has not generated good sales in the past, it may not matter if the publisher upsets him. On the other hand, a successful author might be too valuable to upset by asking him to make big changes.

The cost factor might be so important that extending the size of the book might not be an option. The publisher might be in financial difficulties and committing more funds to a project might be a very bad decision. This is especially so if the success of the book is a big gamble.

Removing illustrations might help in other ways. Each illustration costs money. If it is specially drawn, the artist has to be paid a fee. The publisher could save some money by commissioning fewer art works. But, that might upset the artist who has come to expect a certain level of income from this project. He might not want to work for the publisher again.

Which decision produces the best results?

In this case, the best decision for the publisher is the one that will maximise profits. Publishers, just like any other business, have to be profitable, otherwise they will go out of business. There is no getting away from this simple truth. But, they often do publish books that don't make any money. They survive if their successful books make enough to cover the losses they make on unsuccessful ones. Possibly a few of the loss-making books help to give the publisher a reputation that helps it sell other books. Things are never simple.

Coming to the right decision about what to do comes down to a mixture of:

► experience;
► guess work;
► hunches.

It is not even possible to test for the best decision. Suppose that the publisher decides to increase the size of the book and allow the author to write as much as he wants. This will greatly increase costs and there is no way of knowing if these costs will be recovered by healthy sales figures. This is where experience comes in. The publisher can argue that in similar cases, increasing the size of a textbook does not help sales. Market research in the past might indicate that the users of such books like a concise approach.

In the end, like so many decisions, it is a gamble; although one informed by experience.

What the model does not take into account

This model leaves out a lot of important factors. Mostly, this is because they cannot accurately be included. Some factors are left out because it would simply be too time consuming to find out the data and to work on the model so that it is correctly processed.

It would be very helpful if the effect on sales could be output according to different courses of action but this is mostly unknown.

The model could include the number of illustrations that are planned for the book. It would be easy to work out a relationship between the area of illustrations and the number of words that they replace.

The model does not take into account word length. If the author tends to use longer words than the average, the calculations may be misleading.

At the moment, the model does not consider the problems of translation. The Spanish version of the book will probably be longer than the English original. One reason is because in Spanish, all nouns are preceded by a definite or indefinite article. This can increase the word count by up to 20 per cent.

This model could be made more helpful to the author and publisher if it included costings for extra pages.

The impact of the factors that are not included

As with other decision-making processes, the impact of the missing information can vary and judgements will need to be made.

The increased word count of the Spanish edition could be significant enough to make the translation not worthwhile. On the other hand, the Spanish speaking market might be big enough to absorb the extra costs. Clearly, in this case there is a need for input from market research.

The issue about the length of words used by the author is probably not going to matter much unless there is a very big difference in the case of this particular book. This is an example of where a slight adjustment or a little editing might be all that is required.

ACTIVITY

Have a look at the *Livewires* example that was looked at in earlier chapters.

- Find out which is the most cost-effective solution for *Livewires*. Is it more cost effective to produce quotes with the new system or stick with the old method of simply counting the number of outlets required?
- What alternative methods might *Livewires* consider apart from the two that are used in the model?
- Exactly how do these alternatives differ from the options in the model? You may like to consider how easy would it be to implement these alternatives in a model.
- What factors should *Livewires* take into account apart from immediate costs and profits when deciding on a method for calculating quotations?
- What factors are not taken into account in the existing *Livewires* models? Are these likely to be significant or can they be ignored?

Justifying a decision

Aims

- To make a decision with the help of a spreadsheet model.
- To justify that decision.

Introduction

We have seen that making decisions can be helped by the use of computer models, but in the end, the decision is essentially a human process that takes many things into account including the output from the model. Most decisions are much more complex than they appear to be at first sight. They usually affect more people than just the person who makes the decision. There are nearly always factors that affect the decision that cannot be incorporated into a model. Some factors that were never expected can often have a big effect on the final outcome.

Because others are so often involved in decision-making, it is usually necessary to justify the decisions. This is especially important in a business where everybody's livelihoods are affected by decisions that are made. In the real world, life isn't so easy.

Making a decision

In the *Livewires* example, the model can be used to make a number of decisions. You can factor in changes in labour rates and changes in material costs to see what the outcome will be. However, the main decision that this model was designed to support was the method of producing a cabling quote for a customer.

Remember, the question is do they stick with their old method of basing a quote on the number of points required or do they carry out a larger survey and produce a more finely tuned quote?

The model decided upon was used on two sites. The results were:

Site 1

■ Figure 3.30

	A	B	C
1	Item	Old method	New method
2	Total Costs	£2,669.44	£2,669.44
3			
4	Charges to customer	£3,630.00	£3,749.30
5			
6	Profit made	£960.56	£1,079.86
7			

Site 2

	A	B	C
1	Item	Old method	New method
2	Total Costs	£6,610.90	£6,610.90
3			
4	Charges to customer	£9,195.00	£9,291.13
5			
6	Profit made	£2,584.10	£2,680.23
7			

<table>
<tr><td>

portfolio_tip

It is a good idea to collect the facts together in a computer file. In this case, a spreadsheet or a word processor will do the job adequately. We will need to paste some of the details into a presentation later.

</td></tr>
</table>

In both these cases, there is an increase in profit to be made by using the new more refined method of producing a quote.

On this basis, we shall recommend to the director that the new method be adopted.

We shall need to report all the facts to the director so we shall need to collect some reasons.

The basic figures are the main evidence so far. We can state that in the case of site 1, the increase in profits was found to be 12.4% and in site 2, the increase was 3.7%. The director will probably want to know why there was such a difference and in reality, it would be better if there were more evidence than from just two sites.

Shortcomings

Just presenting these figures is not going to convince anyone. The director will want to know how sure you are about your findings. You should be ready for this.

One thing that will help you to get ready is to try out lots of different scenarios. You can alter the comparisons sheet in order to calculate the percentage increase in profits for any change that you make (see Figure 3.32).

■ Figure 3.32

B8		= =(C6-B6)/B6	
	A	B	C
1	Item	Old method	New method
2	Total Costs	£6,610.90	£6,610.90
3			
4	Charges to customer	£9,195.00	£9,291.13
5			
6	Profit made	£2,584.10	£2,680.23
7			
8	% increase in profit	4%	

One problem that will be brought up is whether the increase in profits is enough to take care of the extra time that it takes to do the survey. Lots of measurements need to be done and someone has to be paid to do this. One way to make sure that you can answer this question is to factor the cost of the survey into the model. You can do this by entering an extra value in the costs sheet. Let's assume a standard cost of £100 for a survey.

■ Figure 3.33

	A	B	C	D
1	Item	Quantity	Cost per item	Total cost
2				
3	Wall boxes	40	£0.50	£20.00
4	Sockets	63	£5.99	£377.37
5	Boxes of cable	11	£49.00	£539.00
6	Boxes of screws	3	£3.99	£11.97
7	Boxes of wall plugs	3	£2.50	£7.50
8	Trunking	40	£1.59	£63.60
9	Labour	55	£30.00	£1,650.00
10	Survey	1	100	£100.00
11	Total cost			£2,769.44

If you incorporate the extra cost and try to recover it from the customer, you will now get a profitability for site 1 of 2.8%.

ACTIVITY

Use the model to find how the profitability is affected on site 2 if the standard survey charge is added to the costs sheet.

What happens if the cost is not charged to the customer? Alter the model to account for that. You will have to deduct £100 from the profit made figure on the comparison sheet

It doesn't look so good now! The director will probably want to know how reliable this model is. For example, are there any chances that unforeseen circumstances might affect its accuracy. What if *Livewires* can get its supplies cheaper from a different supplier?

ACTIVITY

Try changing the cost of a box of cable from £49 to £30 on the material costs sheet. See what happens to the profitability for both sites.

Site 2

Oh dear! If we pay less for cable, our profits go down? That can't be right. We have made a mistake. The model incorporates what we *charge* for materials, not what we pay for them! Change the cost of a box of cable to £60. That's better, we now have a profitability of 20%.

	A	B	C
1	Item	Old method	New method
2	Total Costs	£6,116.90	£6,116.90
3			
4	Charges to customer	£9,195.00	£8,673.63
5			
6	Profit made	£3,078.10	£2,556.73
7			
8	% increase in profit	-17%	

■ **Figure 3.34**

This shows how careful you must be that you really understand what the model is doing. Naming the sheet 'costs' might seem right to the person who created the model but that does not mean the name was a good choice.

portfolio_tip

You will be able to investigate the model used for the examination before you sit it. Make sure you investigate it well.

portfolio_tip

Make sure you investigate it well. As you go through different scenarios, you will be on the lookout for any evidence that will back up your recommendation. One way to do this would be to take screenshots of any circumstances that you want to include. Alternatively, you could copy and paste the relevant spreadsheet pages into a word-processed document.

ACTIVITY

You can try altering the costs of various items and adding in any extra expenses that you think might be possible.
- Keep a record of each change that you make.
- Make only one change at a time.
- Restore each change to its original state before trying the next one.
- Paste the results into a word-processed document each time.
- Find out what combination of circumstances is most likely to convince the management that the new method will always deliver better profits.

Reporting the decision to others

Aims

- To make use of information from a model and from other sources to convince others.
- To make a recommendation for a decision to be taken.

Introduction

Often, the hard part when making a decision is convincing others that it was the right one. You can succeed in convincing others by force of argument and by clearly demonstrating the facts. In real life, you will often convince others simply because they know you and trust your judgement, but it is always easier to convince people if you really know about your subject.

We can use the *Livewires* case study to illustrate some of the things that we can do. IT helps us as well because we have been collecting evidence as we have looked at the situation, and we can use a Microsoft PowerPoint presentation to display our findings. A copy of this presentation is available on the CD.

The arguments can be set out in a presentation. The main details of the research and the decision-making process can be set out on slides. These slides should be brief and to the point so that the company director gets the picture very quickly. Slide shows are used by absolutely everyone these days and many people get fed up with being bored by tedious presentations. So, we shall keep this one brief and to the point.

The first thing to do is to decide upon a 'look and feel' for the slide show. A surprising number of presenters do not realise that a messy slide show with wildly varying styles can distract from the message being put forward. They make shows with lots of different layouts, many different fonts and clashing colours. When people see a badly produced show, they are more interested in what has gone wrong than in the message that the presenter is trying to get across.

The easiest way to get a pleasant but consistent show is to use a design template (Figure 3.35). Microsoft PowerPoint comes with a wide selection. These templates have been carefully put together to look good without being intrusive. You can preview them before deciding. These templates save you time and you will need to save as much of this as you can in the exam.

> **portfolio_tip**
>
> When you draw conclusions from your model in the exam, you will have to communicate your findings very quickly as there is not a lot of time available.

■ Figure 3.35

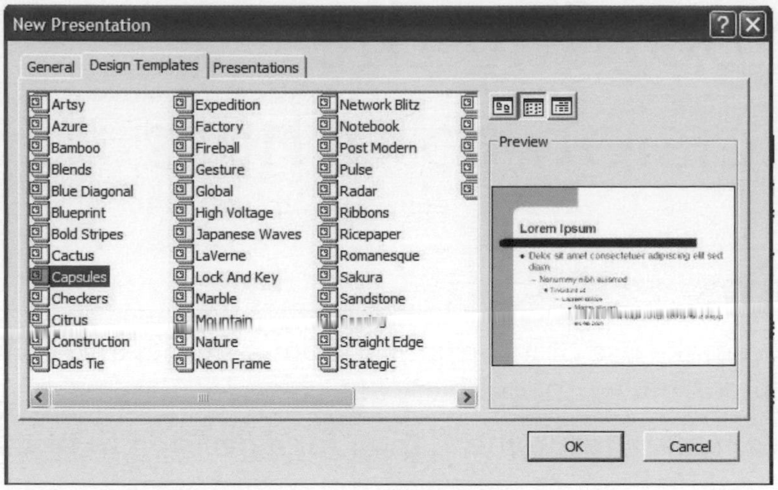

Another tip that helps to make a presentation look consistent is to have a recurring idea on all the slides. This can be done with MS PowerPoint's master slide (Figure 3.36). For example, you can put the name of the company on a footer. This gives the slides a corporate identity.

■ Figure 3.36

Once you have chosen a template and master slide, you use the template to create each new slide and add what you need in the way of comments or illustrations. You can also add multimedia elements if you think they will help. You will need an introductory slide to set the scene (Figure 3.37).

■ Figure 3.37

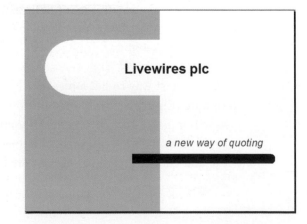

Summary of the current situation

It is always a good idea to remind people of the situation as it stands at present. This gives them something to compare with the new and, you hope, better model. The first slide after the introductory slide should, therefore, be a brief summary of the current model.

Presentation style

You will recall that the current situation is that *Livewires* calculates quotations for customers by simply multiplying the number of computer access points required by the standard cost per point. This causes concerns about profitability. Someone is using the model in order to convince the company director that a change in methods would increase profits for *Livewires*.

Sources and alternatives you considered

The decision is going to be based on the modelling exercise, but it would be a good idea to show that you have thought of a number of solutions. You may have considered:

▶ asking existing customers how they expect quotes to be produced;
▶ asking project managers how well the existing system predicts costs;
▶ checking how the competition produces quotes;
▶ asking the engineers about any difficulties they have had in carrying out installations.

Other factors you took into consideration

The full list of reasons why the current system needs to be looked at can be presented and commented upon. There are many cost factors that can make a quotation unreliable and therefore lose the company money (Figure 3.38).

■ Figure 3.38

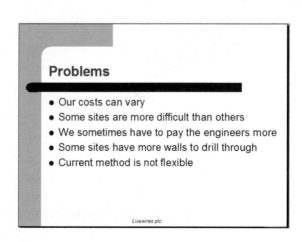

A comment could be made that although a model was used to compare methods, the model did not take everything into account because that would have taken far too long to produce.

The methods you used to reach your decision

The decision was based mostly upon the output from the model. This was applied to data from two sites (Figures 3.39 and 3.40).

The basic working of the model should be explained although the director may not be interested in all the fine details about the formulae and the different worksheets that you used. A summary of the factors taken into account is enough.

The final figures are worth highlighting. That, after all, is the basis for the recommendation to go with the new method.

Results from Site 1

Item	Old method	New method
Total Costs	£2,669.44	£2,669.44
Charges to customer	£3,630.00	£3,749.30
Profit made	£960.56	£1,079.86
% increase in profit	12%	

Livewires plc

■ **Figure 3.39**

Results from Site 2

Item	Old method	New method
Total Costs	£6,610.90	£6,610.90
Charges to customer	£9,195.00	£9,291.13
Profit made	£2,584.10	£2,680.23
% increase in profit	4%	

Livewires plc

■ **Figure 3.40**

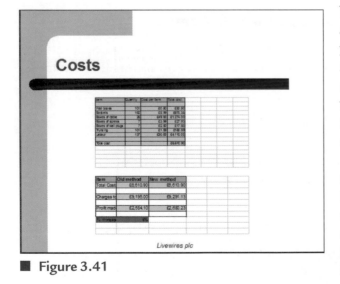

■ **Figure 3.41**

You can make it even clearer to your audience by actually showing some of the 'What if…?' tests that you carried out. You can import spreadsheets into a slide by using the menu sequence `Insert > Object > Microsoft Excel Worksheet`. If you bring in two worksheets, such as the costs and the comparison sheets, you can show the audience how changing costs can affect the profits.

The visual impact can be enhanced by adding a chart or two to the presentation. In fact a 'picture' is often more effective than tables of figures. You can simply copy and paste one from your spreadsheet, but if you add a chart as an object, then you can paste in the data that you want from the spreadsheet and you can then vary the results on the chart 'live and on-screen' as the audience watches. This again will have more impact.

You should make sure that any imported data is big enough to be read easily (Figures 3.42 and 3.43).

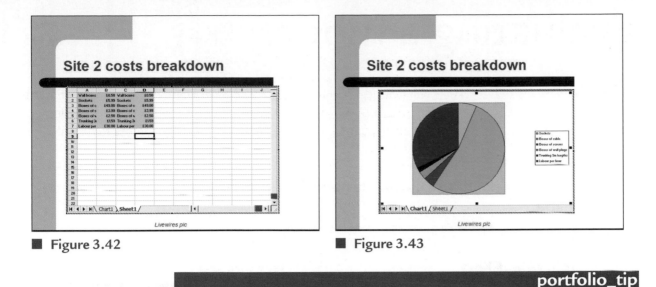

■ Figure 3.42　　　　　　　　■ Figure 3.43

portfolio_tip

If you practise importing data with a few presentations, you will be able to produce a good looking slide show in the exam in very little time at all.

Your decision

In this example, you are recommending a change. You can try to convince the director that this is a good decision by emphasising the likelihood of greater profits by refining the quotation method (Figure 3.44).

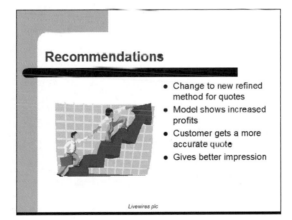

■ Figure 3.44

Justification of your decision

If you have presented all the steps of the decision-making process and made it look neat and professional, the audience should have all the information that they need to decide whether to agree with your recommendation or not.

Be prepared to answer questions. You need to make sure that:

▶ you have all the necessary data to hand;
▶ it is well organised so that you can back up your assertions;
▶ you are fully aware of the issues and can answer without hesitation;
▶ you understand the model and can explain it in simple language to non-IT specialists.

Evaluating a model

Aims

- To assess how well the model has performed in helping a decision to be made.

Introduction

If we are to use a model again, we need to assess how well it has performed. We also need to do this so that we can judge how much we can rely upon its output. Evaluation is always an important part of producing any computer system and there are some standard ways of carrying it out.

The original objectives

The most important aspect of evaluation is to check that the product actually does what it was originally intended to do. This is why it is so important that right from the outset, a set of clear objectives is established. These objectives help throughout the development process to keep things on track. They are central to any evaluation.

The objectives of any system must be clear. If they are just vague aspirations such as 'to produce a user-friendly system', it becomes less easy to evaluate later. You have to rely on opinions and these can vary greatly.

In the case of the *Livewires* model, the objectives were to produce a system that would compare the old method of producing quotations with those of a full survey.

The model was intended:

▶ to show how profitability would be affected if a new method were adopted;
▶ to be able to take account of the materials used;
▶ to take into account the time taken to carry out an installation;
▶ to help arrive at a decision about the best method.

An evaluation can take other aspects into account such as how easy the product is to use.

How well has the model performed?

Accuracy

Technically, there is nothing wrong with the model. It has no errors in it and it will work out what it is supposed to. In other words, it will do exactly what it says. There are no issues of reliability or errors. Calculations are virtually instant so there are no issues of performance.

Ease of use

There is no specially designed user interface on this model. It requires the user to go to different worksheets in order to enter data and look at the output. It would be a lot easier to use if there were a form where costs could be entered or where a data file could be selected and imported into the correct place.

It would be quite easy to do all that, but as this was just a one-off exercise, it probably wasn't worth making all those refinements. It just needed to work. So, it was adequate for the purpose in that respect.

The names used on one of the worksheets was a bit misleading. The sheet labelled 'costs' referred to the charges being made by *Livewires* to customers not the cost to *Livewires*.

Sufficiency of the data

The model takes into account the lengths of cable used and also most of the materials that will be required. There may be some surprises, but most things are taken care of. Where the model falls down is that it does not take into account unexpected labour costs. They are settled at £30 per hour and the time for each job is assumed known.

If there are any problems that cause delay or if the engineers have to work away from home and need to stay in a hotel, these things could throw out the calculations.

If the engineers cause any damage while they are working, they will have to repair that and more time will be lost. For some situations, they will need to be indemnified against causing accidents and an insurance policy needs to be in force. This will be a fixed cost to the company over a year so it is not possible to build this into the model. It is impossible to include everything into a model. If you tried to cover everything, you would never get around to using it. The more complex it gets, the more things will be left out, but even in this relatively straightforward situation, there could be problems.

It has been found that the likelihood of errors increases very rapidly as the complexity of a computer system increases.

portfolio_tip

Look carefully at any model you are given in case there are errors in the data or the logic behind the model.

■ Figure 3.45

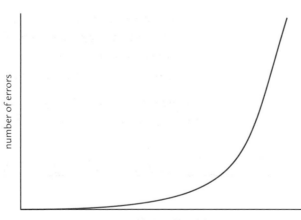

<u>T</u>o what extent has the model helped you make the decision?

We have seen that making a decision always involves much more than just a mechanical adherence to rules or results. We rely on experience and hunches and sometimes just guesswork. Obviously, where one is making decisions about one's livelihood and that of others, you don't want too much guesswork. The model for *Enquirer* is a reasonable compromise between giving us some answers and not trying to do everything.

In other cases, models need to be far more rigorous. If the weather forecast is wrong, that can sometimes lead to economic losses. A farmer might delay a harvest in the expectation of dry weather and then have a year's crop ruined if the weather is wetter than predicted.

A model for designing an aircraft wing or the core of a nuclear reactor has to be very complex so that nothing is left to chance.

A model for assessing how much money a government intends to spend should be as accurate as possible because if it underestimates expenditure, then everyone in the country will be worse off and taxes will rise to cover the mistakes. Financial models are notoriously difficult to get right. There are many completely unpredictable variables so such models have to make use of random functions. Nobody knows how the stock market will perform, otherwise lots of people would make much more money on it.

<u>W</u>hat else would you like to do?

We have already extended the model a little from the original. We added a feature to work out the percentage increase in profitability if there were changed circumstances such as changes in charges to the customer.

It would be helpful if the model were able to take care of differing labour costs because they are likely to change. It is not too difficult to add in some extra rules.

It would be helpful if the model output a graphical comparison between the different methods as well as figures in a table. This, too, would be easy to do.

<u>D</u>oes the model need extending and, if so, how?

Most eventualities have been covered in this model. It does as good a job as we need and we are well aware of the shortcomings. You will be presented with a scenario for the examination and you will need to look at possible extensions.

When you are looking for these, think first of what extra output would be useful. If a model outputs comparisons of call rates for mobile phones, it might be useful to also take into account the cost of the handsets.

If you decide that extra output would be useful, you will have to allow for extra input as well. That will require processing into the model so more formulae and functions will be needed. This will often be best done by putting them on a new worksheet.

Sometimes, the model can usefully be extended by performing some extra comparisons and calculations. For example, a model of traffic flow along a road may be based on factors such as road width, the number of junctions and known information about how traffic responds to hold ups. It could be useful to produce extra calculations to see how the effects of variable speed limits would alter throughput.

ICT skills

Aims

■ To introduce some of the skills needed for Unit 3.

■ To reinforce those skills already demonstrated in previous sections of this unit.

Introduction

This section is essentially a 'how to do it' section. It looks at the skills you will require to use the spreadsheet models for this unit. It also looks at how to report the findings in an appropriate format.

Remember that in this unit you will be assessed using a model provided by the examination awarding body. The model will be a fairly complex one, with some complicated formulae. You will need to test the model, add to it and then make a decision based on your findings. You will also need to be able to evaluate a model and report the findings using word-processing and presentation skills.

The assessment

You will be provided with a scenario and a partly completed model about two or three weeks before the examination day. During this time, you will be able to experiment with the model and become familiar with it. You should try to add data to the model and see what happens. It would be a good idea to spend some time seeing how the model fits in with the scenario and trying to analyse the scenario.

In the examination you will have a clean version of the model and a copy of the scenario. Also, you will be provided with some additional material that you have not previously seen. This could include:

▶ data sets for the model;
▶ another sheet for the model;
▶ further information about the scenario.

You will also have to complete a series of tasks such as summarising the situation, adding data to the spreadsheet, making decisions in the light of the model and explaining these decisions to someone else.

Spreadsheet skills

How to save workbooks in different ways

In a spreadsheet program such as Microsoft Excel, there are many ways that you can save a file as well as simply using the standard `Save` command. If you simply choose `File > Save`, the spreadsheet program will choose a name for you such as Book1 or Book2. It is better if you carefully choose a meaningful file name at this point and not simply accept the default name given. You should choose `File > Save` from the menu and then a file name which is appropriate for you. If you have opened an old spreadsheet file, the `File > Save` option simply saves the sheet using the same name that it had before. This overwrites the original copy that you had on the disk. You will lose the old version.

You have to be fully aware of some 'standard ways of working'. This means that there are some sensible precautions that most computer users take in order to make their lives easier and to protect their data. One of these is to save work at intervals using a different name. You might, for example, have a file called `conversion.xls`. Good practice would normally be to change the name each time you make some changes by adding a version number. For example, if you choose names such as `conversionv1.xls` followed by `conversionv2.xls`, you can always remove the older versions when you are certain that you do not need them any more but it is a good idea to keep at least the last three saved copies. To do this you will need to use the `File > Save As...` option.

■ **Figure 3.46**

There are also other formats in which you might be required to save a file. Perhaps you need to save it as a web page or in CSV format.

The options available in Microsoft Excel and other common spreadsheet programs allow you to save your work in a variety of ways. The `Save As Web Page...` option might be suitable if you need to let someone else view your spreadsheet who does not have Excel. If it is saved in this way it can be viewed in any web browser.

In Section 3.4, you saw a file of numbers saved as a CSV file and imported into a worksheet in order to give it meaning (Figure 3.9). The CSV file can be created by using the `Save As...` command and choosing the CSV file type option (Figure 3.47). CSV stands for Comma Separated Value.

■ **Figure 3.47**

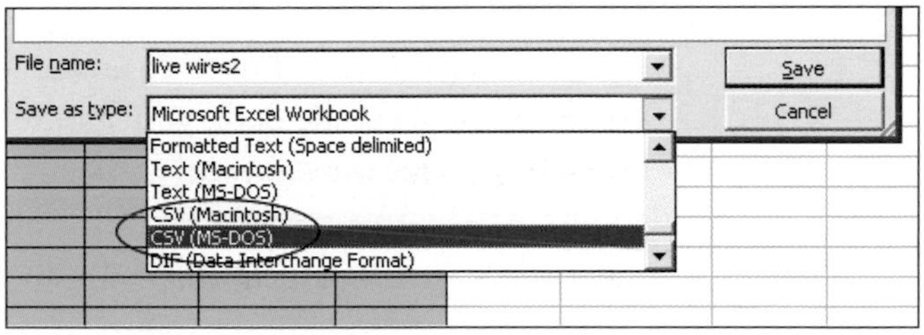

The CSV file looks like this:

```
Run number,Distance (m),Sockets,Time mins,cable used
1, 35, 2, 73, 70
2, 66, 2, 88, 132
3, 25, 2, 70, 50
4, 33, 1, 72, 33
5, 82, 1, 96, 82
6, 04, 2, 97, 168
7, 85, 1, 98, 85
```

Each value is separated from the next by a comma. This type of file can be used to export data to other applications such as a database management system, a word processor or another spreadsheet program that cannot use Excel files.

The difference between workbooks and worksheets

In Microsoft Excel, when you open the spreadsheet you are starting a **workbook**. Just like an ordinary book, this contains separate pages. A workbook can contain several **worksheets**. These are single pages within a workbook.

When you first run a spreadsheet program such as Excel, you start off with three worksheets (Figure 3.48).

■ **Figure 3.48**

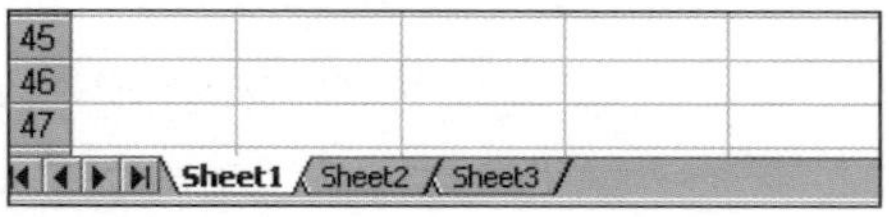

You should always give your worksheets a name that has a sensible meaning. This is another standard way of working. If you look at the example workbook in the *Livewires* model, the names look like Figure 3.49.

■ **Figure 3.49**

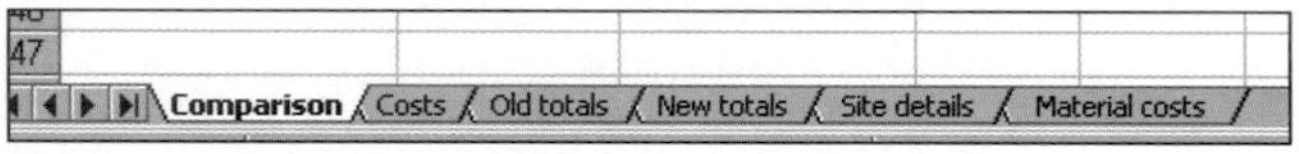

Using names like this means that most people who look at the workbook will be able to get some ideas of the thinking behind the system that you have used.

How to add a worksheet and name it

At some stage, you will need to add a worksheet to a workbook. If you are asked to import some data, you should look at the sheets that exist already. It might be that the data will go easily into one of them, or it might need to be imported into a new sheet.

To add a new sheet, simply right click on one of the name tabs for the existing sheets and choose `Insert...`. A new worksheet will be added. You should always then give it a suitable name by choosing `rename` from the same menu. It is easy simply to accept the default sheet name which will just be 'Sheet' plus a number, but it is always worth the trouble to rename it (Figure 3.50).

Format cells to match data types

In Section 3.7 you looked at the example of Steve the plumber. You saw how to format cells as currency and a percentage. Setting the cell data type is an important step in the refinement of a spreadsheet. If you leave it up to the spreadsheet then odd things might happen. An example is if you enter a telephone number such as `0123457654222` the spreadsheet will change it to `1.23458E+11`.

Because the spreadsheet assumes it is a number, it removes the zero from the beginning. Then, because the number is a long one it changes it into something called **standard form** (otherwise known as scientific notation). Clearly this is no use for displaying a telephone number. If you need to store a telephone number, then you should format the cell to hold **text**.

There are many choices in Excel for the formatting of data. To format a single cell, right click the cell and choose `Format Cells...` from the shortcut menu. To format a range of cells, first highlight the range required then choose `Format Cells...` from the shortcut menu.

■ Figure 3.51

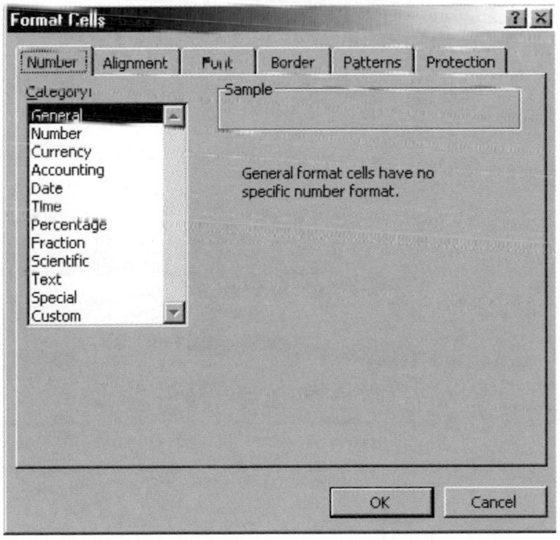

Figure 3.51 shows the range of formats available in Excel. Some of these are:

▶ **General** has no specific format, this is the default, and the program tries to pick what it decides is the best format.
▶ **Number** defines the data as a number. This allows you to choose how many digits come after the decimal point.
▶ **Currency** defines the cell as holding a money value. The default in the UK is to use a £ sign and two decimal places. This means that £2.50 is displayed correctly and not 2.5.
▶ **Accounting** lets you choose the currency symbol. You might not want £s and the standard number of digits after the decimal.

▶ **Date** allows you to store dates in a variety of formats. People from different countries have different ways of writing dates so there are several formats to choose from. You can also do calculations with dates, such as working out how many days there are between two dates.

▶ **Time** allows hours, minutes and seconds to be entered and then to be used for calculations.

▶ **Percentage** lets you use the number as a percentage without dividing by 100 every time.

Formatting colours

Shading is another useful way to make a spreadsheet easier to read. Colours make the rows and columns stand out on screen. The *Livewires* sheet is an example of this.

It is also possible to use borders to make the cells stand out as needed.

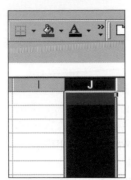

■ **Figure 3.52**

Headers and footers

You should normally include headers and footers in your coursework. You must use these on all your printouts in any exam. It is good standard practice to put them on any document before you print so that the document can easily be identified.

In Microsoft Excel, headers and footers are available from the View menu (Figure 3.53).

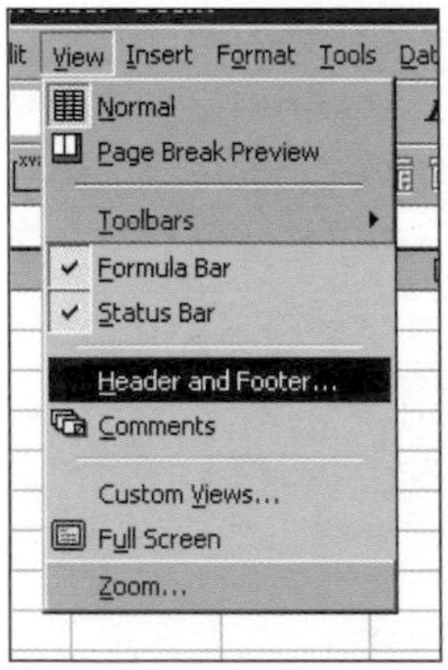

■ **Figure 3.53**

■ **Figure 3.54**

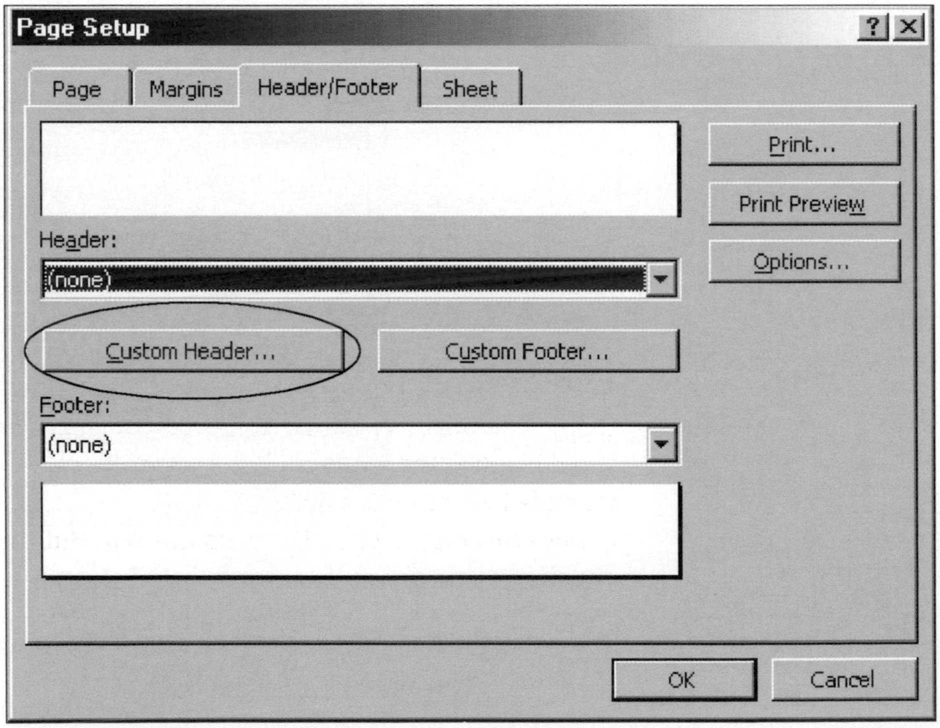

To add your own header or footer, click a **Custom** button (Figure 3.54).

When the custom header of footer box appears (Figure 3.55), you can add things such as your name, candidate number and centre number. All of these are very useful additions to your examination work.

■ Figure 3.55

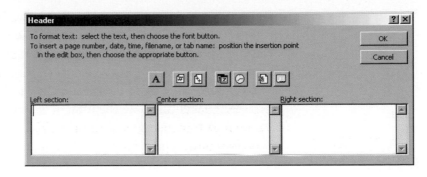

Formulae and functions

Entering formulae

Formulae are entered into cells in order to process data in some way. Always press the = (equals) key to let Excel know that what follows is a formula, otherwise it will treat it as text and just put it into the cell as it is.

In the models you are given, there will be some quite complex formulae to work with. You will not need to create ones that are so complicated but you should be able to understand them.

Modifying formulae

To change a formula, you first select the cells and then edit the formula in the area below the toolbar (Figure 3.56).

■ Figure 3.56

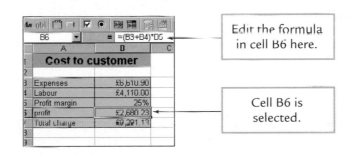

Checking formulae

It is always important to check the results of any formula. To start with, you should look at the answer and ask yourself whether is it reasonable. For example look at Figure 3.57.

Does this total look right? Of course not. But this one is easy to spot. It is not always that obvious!

Another way is to look at a column of figures and see if you can see a pattern and if any cell stands out because it does not fit the pattern.

The next example (Figure 3.58) was first discussed in Section 3.6.

	scores
	15
	12
	23
Total score	12365847

■ Figure 3.57

■ Figure 3.58

	B	C	D	E	F	G	H
1	Mile reading	litres	p/litre	£	petrol p/l	saved	miles
2	34378	26.3	33.5	£8.81	79.9	£12.20	
3	34610	40	33.5	£13.40	79.9	£18.56	232
4	34785	27.5	33.5	£9.21	79.9	£1,276.00	175
5	34822	8.5	33.5	£2.85	84.9	£4.37	37
6	34872	7.5	33.5	£2.51	79.9	£3.48	50
7	34993	21.4	33.5	£7.17	79.9	£9.93	121
8	35177	28	33.5	£9.38	79.9	£12.99	184
9	35294	22	33.5	£7.37	76.9	£9.55	117
10							

You may remember that one way to check this was to turn on the formula view. Take a look at page 00 to recall how to do this.

You will need to be able to print out sheets in formula view for your examination.

Functions are used to do things such as calculate totals. For example, =SUM(A3:A23) will calculate the total of all the cells in the range A3 to A23. It is less effort than using =a3+a4+a5+a6 … +a23 and is better practice.

Functions always have names and they expect **arguments**. These are the values that they need to work on. sum is a function. (A3:A23) are the arguments.

If you are stuck and do not know how to use a function then you can use the function help facility. See Section 3.7 to find out how to do this.

Validating and checking data

It is also necessary in any model to check that the data is reasonable. It is possible to get the spreadsheet to do this for you by setting up validation rules.

Validation checks see if the data that you input matches certain conditions that you have set for a particular cell.

For example, to set cell A1 to accept whole numbers between 1 and 10 only:

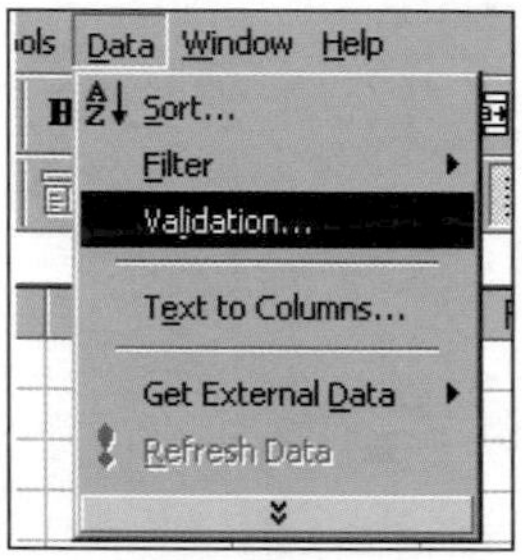

1 Select cell A1.
2 Choose Data from the menu bar and then Validation...φ (Figure 3.59).
3 Fill in the Data Validation dialogue box that follows with the Validation criteria, so that it matches Figure 3.60.

■ **Figure 3.59**

■ **Figure 3.60**

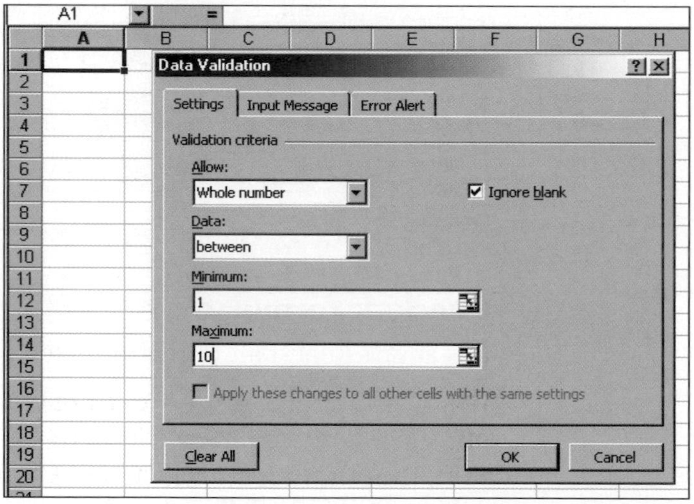

The other tabs on the form allow you to set a message to appear when the cell is chosen and the **error alert** is the message that appears when the value is wrong.

Replicating (filling) formulae

Filling or replicating a formula is an easy way to reproduce formulae in a column. Not only is it easy but it helps prevent typing mistakes like the one shown in Figure 3.61.

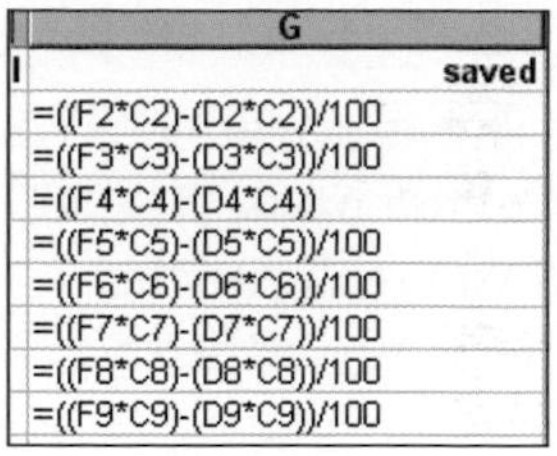

G
saved
=((F2*C2)-(D2*C2))/100
=((F3*C3)-(D3*C3))/100
=(F4*C4)-(D4*C4))
=((F5*C5)-(D5*C5))/100
=((F6*C6)-(D6*C6))/100
=((F7*C7)-(D7*C7))/100
=((F8*C8)-(D8*C8))/100
=((F9*C9)-(D9*C9))/100

■ **Figure 3.61**

■ **Figure 3.62**

If this kind of formula is replicated using the fill feature, then the computer will accurately reproduce the formula and silly mistakes are avoided. You can replicate a formula in any direction, but in most cases you will fill down or across from left to right.

There are two ways to replicate formulae in Microsoft Excel.

Using the menus
Place the cursor in the cell containing the formula, highlight the column area to be filled, then use the edit menu and choose the fill option (Figure 3.62).

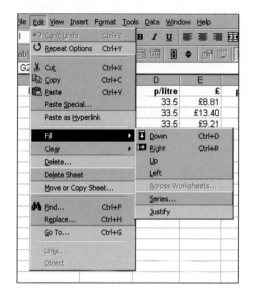

Using the mouse
Select the cell containing the formula and move the mouse cursor over the small square in lower right corner (Figure 3.63). Then, hold down the left mouse button and drag. When you reach the end of the column that you are filling, let the button go and the formula will fill down automatically.

■ **Figure 3.63**

Move cursor over the square (the Full Handle)

When you use this option, the cell references used in the formula change as you go down the column. So if the formula selected is A1+B1 and you fill down, then the next cell will be A2+B2 and the next B3+C3. This continues until you reach the end of the area selected.

Using absolute and relative cell references

The examples above use relative cell references. This means that Microsoft Excel automatically changes the column and row numbers to reflect the new position when you replicate the formula.

Sometimes you do want this to happen. If dollar signs are added to a cell reference, then the reference will not change when copied. If you enter =C2*F3 and fill down the C2 reference will become C3 but F3 will stay the same. This is called absolute cell addressing. You can add the dollar signs very quickly by pressing the function key F4.

See also Section 3.7.

Naming cells

Cells or a range of cells in a table can be given a name. This is useful because you can then use that name in the formula and this saves you having to remember the cell reference where the data is stored. If you replicate the formula the name will copy and not change. You saw this in Steve the plumber's spreadsheet in Section 3.7.

If you give the cell a name that is easy to remember, it makes the formula easy to use. To name a cell or a range of cells, you first select the cell or the area of the sheet you want to name. Then from the Insert menu choose `Name` and `Define...` (Figure 3.64).

■ **Figure 3.64**

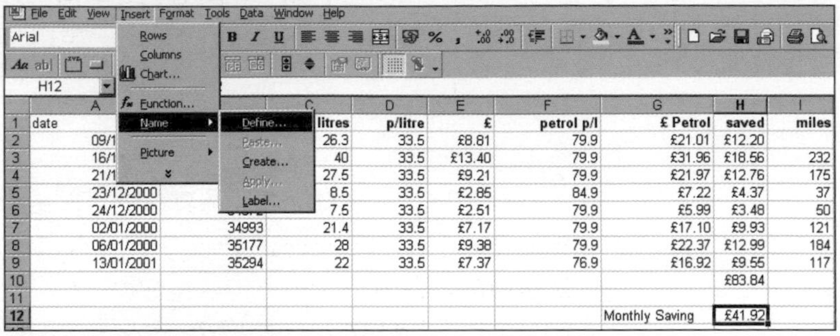

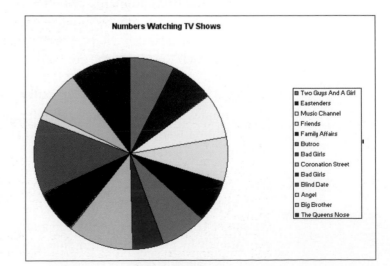

In this example, the cell H12 is about to be given a name.

Sorting data

One way to analyse data is to sort it. This can sometimes reveal a pattern that could not be seen otherwise. Spreadsheets are able to sort data both alphabetically and numerically depending on the contents of a column. The quickest way to sort a table in a spreadsheet is to put the cursor at the top of the column you want to sort and click on a Sort icon on the toolbar (Figure 3.65).

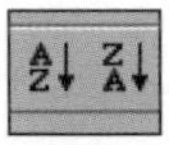

■ **Figure 3.65**

portfolio_tip

Sometimes, your heading might be sorted by the spreadsheet along with the data and appear in the wrong place. If you put headings into bold type then Excel will recognise them as headings and not sort them with the rest of the column.

Presenting graphs and charts

Graphs and charts are a good visual way to present numeric information. Often a chart in a report or presentation gives a much clearer picture of any pattern or trend. It is important however to choose the most appropriate type of chart or graph. For example, pie charts are not much use if there are a lot of different items to show (Figure 3.66).

■ **Figure 3.66**

This data in Figure 3.66 will be much easier to follow as a bar chart as you can see in Figure 3.67.

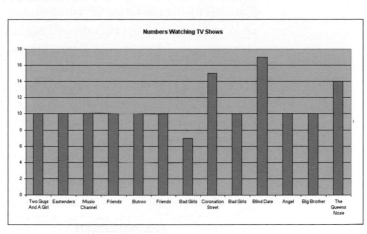

Printing parts of a spreadsheet

When you print a spreadsheet, normally the whole of the current worksheet is printed. Usually this is too much: it wastes paper, delays output and looks confusing. By highlighting the area to be printed, you can choose to print only a part of the sheet. There are two ways to do this.

▶ Choose Print... from the File menu and then the **Selection** option in the **Print what** frame.
▶ From the File menu, choose **Print Area** and then **Set Print Area** (Figure 3.68). This method then prints the highlighted area every time you print until you cancel the command.

■ Figure 3.68

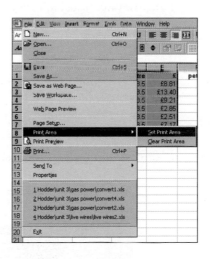

Inserting and deleting rows and columns

Inserting rows and columns into a spreadsheet is easy. Here are one or two tips on how to do it effectively.

When adding rows or columns you need to be aware of how formulae will be affected by your actions. On most occasions the program will update your formula to take account of the additions you have made but there are some exceptions.

For example, if you have produced a total using =SUM(B1:B15) and you add rows between row 1 and 15 then the total will include your new row.

However if your formula for the total was =B1+B2+B3…..+B15 then the new total will not include the added row. You should always use the sum function instead of formulae you make up where you can. When you delete rows or columns, the program will again change other formulae to take account of the changes, but if you delete anything that is needed elsewhere in the workbook, you will find that some calculations will not work and error messages might be produced, so delete with care.

To add a row or column click on the column letter or the row number then right click and choose **Insert** from the shortcut menu.

To delete a row or column click on the column letter or the row number then right click and choose **Delete** from the shortcut menu.

Filters

Filters are a good way to display which data you want to look at. For example, in the *Livewires* model, you might want to look only at the double sockets on a site.

The first step is to set up a filter on the 'sockets' column of the site details worksheet. To do this, click at the top of column C, then from the Data menu choose **Filter** and then **AutoFilter** (Figure 3.69).

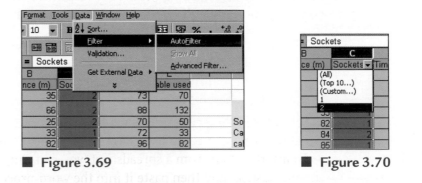

■ **Figure 3.69**　　　　　　　　　　■ **Figure 3.70**

A drop-down box is now available at the top of column C (Figure 3.70). By choosing the '2' in this box, the spreadsheet will only show rows containing the number 2. Figure 3.71 shows this. Notice how the row numbers have gaps in the sequence (4, 7, 9, 11). The missing rows do not meet the filter criterion.

■ **Figure 3.71**

	A	B	C	D	E
C1			= Sockets		
Name Box		B	**C**	D	E
1	Run number	Distance (m)	Sockets ▾	Time mins	cable used
2	1	35	2	73	70
3	2	66	2	88	132
4	3	25	2	70	50
7	6	84	2	97	168
9	8	45	2	78	90
11	10	14	2	70	28
13	12	45	2	78	90
14	13	78	2	94	156
15	14	75	2	93	150
16	15	58	2	84	116
17	16	45	2	78	90

Word processing skills

At some point in the assessment for this module, you will need to be able to word process a document. It could be in the form of a report on your decision made from using a model or a summary of the scenario.

The aim of this section is to highlight a few of the skills you might need over and above the basic word-processing skills you will already have.

Headers and footers

All documents you produce in the examination **MUST** have your name, candidate number and centre number on them when printed. It is not acceptable to write them on afterwards.

You have already seen how to add these to the spreadsheet. Adding them to a word-processed document is very similar. The instructions assume you are using Microsoft Word.

From the View menu, choose **Header and Footer** (Figure 3.72). A toolbar will appear that allows you to edit the header and footer area (Figure 3.73).

■ Figure 3.72

■ Figure 3.73

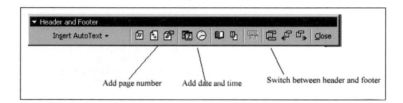

Inserting images

You can greatly improve the appearance and usefulness of a document by suitably inserting pictures, sections of spreadsheets and charts.

To insert a chart from a spreadsheet, you can simply create the chart in the spreadsheet and then paste it into the word-processed document in the appropriate place. However, if you are using Microsoft Word and Excel, it is possible to interact with the chart in Word.

The chart in Figure 3.74 has been produced from the *Livewires* spreadsheet, showing the materials used.

■ Figure 3.74

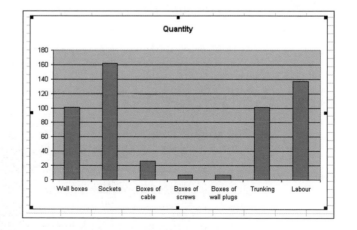

To interact with the chart, right click on the image that has been pasted in and choose **Edit** from the **Chart Object** option on the menu. This may be given as **Edit Active** in later versions of Microsoft Excel.

■ Figure 3.75

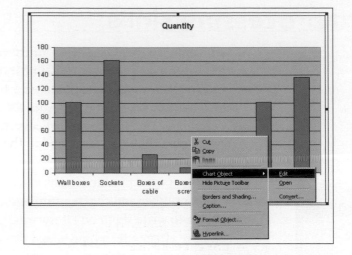

The image will change and tabs appear at the bottom of the image window. Clicking on these allows the data from the worksheets to be viewed (Figure 3.76). This can be useful if you need to make changes to the chart very quickly.

■ Figure 3.76

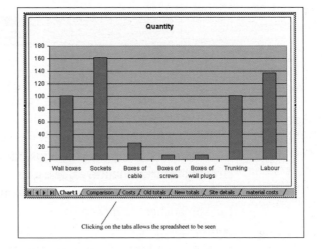

Clicking on the tabs allows the spreadsheet to be seen

Cost to customer	
Expenses	£6,610.90
Labour	£4,110.00
Profit margin	25%
Profit	£2,680.23
Total charge	£9,291.13

■ Figure 3.77

Tables

If you copy and paste part of your spreadsheet, it is imported as a table, and will look just like it does in your original spreadsheet (Figure 3.77).

You can edit the data in the cells if you want to, but the formulae in the spreadsheet are not there, it is simply a table of text and numbers.

Checking documents

You should always check the document that you have produced by careful proofreading. You should do this before printing it. You can check the layout of the document by choosing **Print Preview** from the **File** menu. This will give you a better impression of what the document will look like. You should check the examination paper for any specific instructions at this stage. For example, if the question says 'print on one side of A4' make sure it really does fit on one side or marks will be lost.

Nature of business reports

When writing any report, you should think very carefully about how you are communicating the information. In the case of your examination, you must read the question very carefully to see what you need to communicate and who the audience is. Remember that you have been involved in the process of reaching a conclusion, making a decision and producing recommendations.

Your report should be brief and to the point, but at the same time cover all the required information.

You should:

▶ use paragraphs;
▶ keep paragraphs short;
▶ present evidence;
▶ use images;
▶ meet the needs of your audience;
▶ remember that appearance is important.

Producing presentations

In the examination you may be asked to produce a presentation to inform others of the reason for your decision. The idea of a presentation is to highlight the main points of your findings and communicate these to others in an effective way. Your presentations should communicate effectively and convey information to an audience.

An effective presentation will not have large amounts of text to read. It will highlight the main points using headings and bullet points. In the examination, you will not have a lot of time to produce this, so you should concentrate on communicating the information in the most efficient way.

portfolio_tip

Marks for the presentation are most likely to be for the information you put across and the way you do so, rather than for any fancy backgrounds or clip art. So, concentrate on putting across your points. In Section 3.10, you were shown how to use templates to save time in this way.

Creating and editing presentations

In Section 3.10, you looked at putting together a presentation using a template to format the slides. This is a quick and simple way to format a set of slides to give a uniform overall appearance, however if you want to create the background yourself it is a quick and easy process.

Adding a new slide

When adding a new slide to your presentation, there is a range of layouts already designed for you. If you can use these rather than create your own you will produce good looking slides much more quickly. Figure 3.78 shows some of the styles available to you in Microsoft PowerPoint.

■ Figure 3.78

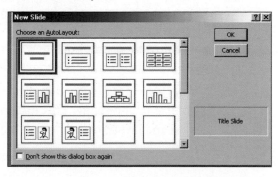

Once you have inserted a new slide, you can add a background of your choice by right clicking the mouse on the background of the slide (Figure 3.79).

■ **Figure 3.79**

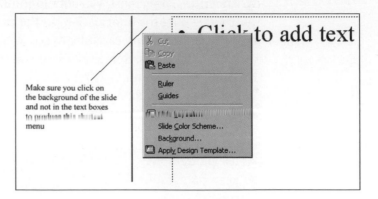

Inserting text

The standard page layouts in Microsoft PowerPoint provide areas for text to be entered. Most of them are setup by default to produce bullet points. Bullet points are the most effective way to get your message across. Remember, a good presentation provides prompts for your audience and should not contain large passages of text.

Pictures and charts

Pictures and charts can enhance a presentation when used well and with care. As you have seen in Section 3.10, a chart can demonstrate trends and patterns in figures far better then words. Pictures can be used to illustrate a point or simply to brighten up a presentation.

Charts can be placed onto a slide in two ways.

The chart wizard will help you construct a chart without leaving the slide you are working on (Figure 3.80).

■ **Figure 3.80**

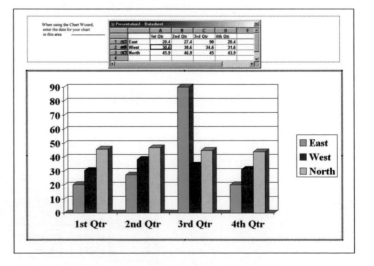

Alternatively you can set up a chart in a spreadsheet application and then paste it into your slide. This method will give you more options for the design and layout of your chart but will be more time consuming.

Checking presentations

When you have completed your presentation, you should check it to ensure that it covers all the points asked for in the examination question and you have designed it to meet the needs of your audience. It is a good idea to check the following:

▶ Spelling
▶ Size of text
▶ Amount of information on each page
▶ The required information is covered
▶ Each slide is clearly laid out.

Standard ways of working

All users of IT should follow some basic principles when they are working. These principles have gradually developed as sensible habits over the years since computers have become so widespread.

They are largely habits that:

▶ make you more effective as a computer user;
▶ help you to avoid legal and other problems.

The examination awarding body has set out a list of habits and actions that you should always try to adopt when working. These are all largely common sense but they will help you to produce the best work possible and to avoid wasting time by losing work or not having the right files easily accessible.

portfolio_tip

Both of the portfolios that you will produce for this qualification have marks available for standard ways of working. You will need to try and show in your work that you have used them.

File Management

These are simple precautions to help you keep track of your work and to protect it against loss.

Save work regularly

We have all lost hours of work because of a glitch that crashes the computer when work is not saved. Even after years of suffering such problems, people still remain careless. The easiest thing to do is to make a habit of hitting ctrl-s every few minutes. You can set the autosave feature to a short interval too. Always work from the hard disk and back up to a memory stick at the end of a session. Make sure you always do things the same way.

Use sensible filenames

Never accept defaults. Choose filenames that really mean something. Make use of the long names that are possible with modern operating systems. *Letter to Mark 20 July 2005* is pretty unambiguous and better than simply *letter*.

portfolio_tip

Using sensible file names is a good way to demonstrate standard ways of working. The external assessor will see these when looking at your portfolio.

Set-up directory/folder structures to organize files

It is always worth putting a lot of thought into your folder structures. It is then easy to reorganize when you need a new category. It also makes backing up so much easier. So, have a folder for all your Applied ICT work, and have sub-folders for Units One, Two and Three. Make further sub-folders for research materials, images etc. Find a method that suits you.

Make backups

This is so fundamental and so easy to forget. Make sure you know that you are backing up the latest version of your files and folders. Everyone has backed up old onto new and lost the latest edits. Use memory sticks or online services. Floppy disks don't hold enough data and they are unreliable.

Choose appropriate file formats

Make sure that you understand these. The main ones you will need to concern yourself with are the various multimedia formats. Choose compressed formats where download speed is an issue. Choose larger uncompressed formats where quality is more important.

Limit access to confidential or sensitive files

You should use passwords to protect folders and documents, especially on networks. You never know who might gain access to your work and plagiarize it or alter it.

Use effective virus protection

New viruses are always appearing. Your network manager will take care of this, but make sure that at home you have an up-to-date subscription to good anti-virus software. Also use a good firewall and run anti-spyware and anti-advert software regularly. Adaware™ is excellent for cleaning out many potential problems.

Use 'readme' files where appropriate to provide technical information

When you make a software or data product you may find it useful to save an associated file to remind yourself, or users, what the requirements are to read or run it. This will normally be in a text file, so use Notepad or something similar, and then any software should be able to read it.

Personal Effectiveness

It is easy to get into sloppy habits and to miss deadlines or waste time when you are in a panic. There are all sorts of tricks to help you to work fast and effectively. Not all of them are technical solutions and many will be your own ideas.

Select appropriate ICT tools and techniques

Use the right tool for the job. There are so many tricks that come with experience but here are just a few ideas:

If you want to make a table to sort out lots of data items, use a spreadsheet, not a word processor. There are far more handy functions that you might need. You can always paste your work into a word processor later, where it will automatically create a new table.

Use automation where you can. You can autoformat a table so that it is the right size. Use styles to make different levels of headings. Record the occasional macro to automate common tasks. Use search and replace so that you can use shorthand when writing. For example, instead of typing an expression such as 'Operating System', type '&' instead then search and replace at the end. Alternatively, use the autocomplete feature.

Don't use a DTP program for writing text or making websites. It is awkward for one and produces dreadful HTML code for the other.

Remember that there is a calculator available in most operating systems such as Windows.

Customize settings

Make life easy for yourself. This is easier on your own computer where settings will be saved. If you find that the word processor black on white setting is making your eyes tired, set it to white on blue instead.

Put commonly used programs where you can best find them – on the desktop or in the start menu. Conversely, get rid of desktop icons that you don't often use.

Make sure that your name is registered in the operating system, so that automated information in new documents defaults to your details.

Create and use shortcuts

Drag icons of commonly used software onto the desktop. Make sure that you know a good selection of keyboard shortcuts such as ctrl-v to paste, ctrl-c to copy, ctrl-b for bold, etc. These save more time than almost any other trick. You can quickly set out paragraph headings with styles by using ctrl-alt-1 or 2 or 3 for three levels of heading. These styles can then be used for automatic contents and indexes. If you are not using Windows, there will be similar shortcuts with other operating systems.

Make macros for repeating tasks, such as inserting your name and other details on documents.

Use templates to save time. They often help you to make a document that looks good without you having to think about it. For example, when you need to communicate your findings in the Unit 3 examination, a presentation template takes all the trouble out of applying a common look to a whole slide show.

Use available sources of help

You should be able to ask your teacher for any details you need to know about what you have to do and get advice about how to carry out your tasks. Don't forget that all software has help just an F1 keypress away. Obviously the big search engines can also help you get information quickly.

If you don't have access to the specification look on the Edexcel web site.

Use a plan to help you organize your work and meet deadlines

Some of us hate planning, but you should organize yourself reasonably well. You may not want to schedule in every last task, although this works for some, but recording the major milestones for producing your coursework is more or less essential. Use a method that works for you. It's not much good if you write down a schedule on a piece of paper then never look at it. Maybe reminders in an online calendar such as the one Yahoo provides will help.

If you use software such as a spreadsheet to record progress (there is an example on the CD), this can help with motivation. It feels good when more and more tasks are ticked off.

Quality Assurance

Use spell check, grammar check and print preview

This is such obvious advice but it is surprising how many students don't bother. No work should ever be handed in that contains spelling mistakes that a spell checker can pick up. The grammar checker often produces very odd results so don't follow all its recommendations. Word, for example, doesn't like your using passive verbs, but these are often what you want to use so ignore the advice if it doesn't suit you.

'Print preview' saves lots of paper and printing out time. If you work at home, it will save expensive ink cartridges too.

> **portfolio_tip**
> Make sure that the work you submit is well presented and spell checked.

Proofread

Read over your work after it is completed. Does it make sense? Could you express yourself better? Are there any typos that a spell checker might have missed?

Seek views of others

You get quite close to your work and do not always see its faults. A fresh pair of eyes will sometimes help to show up problems and inconsistencies. Maybe you use a word or a cliché too often? Maybe your sentences are too long and are difficult to understand? Someone else might see this if you don't.

Authenticate work

You should do your best to make sure that what you write is correct. Take all the usual precautions about what you find on web sites. Some sites take a neutral stand and are well known as being reliable. Others can contain all manner of unsubstantiated opinion and rubbish. Think carefully about who can be trusted and if they have a biased point of view that needs to be taken into account.

Legislation and Codes of Practice

It is easy to fall foul of the law. Even if you are not a criminally minded hacker or virus writer, there are pitfalls to be aware of.

Acknowledge sources

> **portfolio_tip**
> Make sure you include a properly set out bibliography for your work.

If you have 'borrowed' material from someone's web site, say so. You wouldn't like it if someone copied your work without giving you credit, so don't do it to others.

Respect copyright

Copyright law is complex and nobody expects you to know all the subtleties, especially when using an international resource such as the web, where lots of different laws may apply. However, you should be aware that copying a published resource such as a book, music or software might well be illegal. Every so often, the owners of copyright will follow up a case and take it to court 'to discourage the others'.

Avoid plagiarism

If you do use unacknowledged work from others, this can cause quite a few undesirable consequences. Apart from discouraging authors from producing and publishing work, you may be disqualified from your qualification.

Protect confidentiality

It is very easy to pass on facts, comments and opinions when using email or web sites. Be very careful what you include in an email and think hard before clicking the 'send' button. Sometimes, it is a good idea to save emails until the next day, and then re-read them before sending. Be particularly careful when forwarding an email. It may contain details that were meant for you but not for anyone else.

Safe Working

It is so easy to get blasé about safe working – we get used to our surroundings and maybe get careless or forgetful. There are a few things that you should think about from time to time.

Ensure that hardware, cables, seating etc are positioned correctly

People can, and do, get muscle, joint and vision problems from computer use. You may be all right using a cheap plastic chair in the computer room for a week or so but eventually you will probably get backache. If you strain to see the screen, you will probably get neck pains. It really is worthwhile taking a lot of care about your comfort when working.

Ensure that your lighting is appropriate

A nearby window can make focusing on a screen uncomfortable. It is common to get headaches from badly lit rooms, and this will not help your productivity.

Take regular breaks

Many of us take too many breaks when work gets boring, but you should try to factor in periods of time when you are away from the computer. This is another reason why you should not leave things until the last minute. Rest breaks not only help you to avoid aches and pains, they also help you to clear your thoughts.

Handle and store media correctly

This is less of a problem than it used to be. Media such as memory sticks and CDs are less likely to go bad on you than floppy disks. Even so, treat them with care. A scratched CD may not work, so use an envelope or box. It is easy to bend the USB connector on a memory stick. However careful you are, you will occasionally experience data loss, so every so often take extra backups.

Eportfolio

Create an appropriate structure for an eportfolio

Setting up sensible folder structures helps you work. It also helps whoever marks your work to understand what you have done. You don't want to make extra problems for your teacher or the moderator. They may miss something and you will lose credit. Set out your work logically.

Collect all the required information, converting files to an appropriate format if necessary

Have a folder where your raw data accumulates. If you are likely to need it in a different format later, convert it when you collect it. You don't want to waste time converting BMPs to JPEGs when you are putting your ebook together. Anything that saves effort later is worth the trouble at the beginning.

Authenticate your work

Check through your work to make sure that you are confident that it is accurate and that there is no doubt about the sources you have used.

Provide a table of contents, using hyperlinks to locate information easily

Your ebook will use hyperlinks if you do it properly. Make it easy to view your work by having an easy way in for people to understand what is there and find what they want quickly. Usability is always an important factor to consider when making an IT resource.

Test for size, compatibility and ease of use, making sure that the portfolio conforms to the technical specifications

You will lose marks if you do not follow the proper format for presenting your work. Check your work against what is written in the Edexcel specifications. You should really look at the original specifications on the Edexcel web site.

Glossary

ASCII (American Standard Code for Information Interchange): This is a well known code where numbers from 0-255 are interpreted as characters. For example, 65=A, 66=B, and so on.

Page 177

Byte code: a program written in the Java language, which has been partly compiled so that it can be interpreted by a web browser. This makes it platform independent.

Page 5

Corruption: The alteration of data as a result of malfunction or a malicious act.

Page 160

Domain Name System: A standard way of defining and naming resources on the Internet. A limited number of domain name suffixes such as .com and .org are available and users can apply to hold a unique name using one of these.

Page 32

Direct Access: A method of file access where any part of a file can be retrieved without having to read through the rest of it. Direct access is only possible with disk storage, that is, not with tape.

Page 45

Directory: A division of a storage medium which is used to group together files with something in common. Often directories are called *folders*.

Page 53

DSL (Digital Subscriber Line): A means of providing digital broadband connectivity by adding additional channels to existing telephone lines.

Page 67

EFT (Electronic Funds Transfer): The process of handling a cashless transaction such as when paying for goods by credit or debit cards. The funds are transferred from the credit card company or, in the case of a debit card, from the customer's account to the store's account.

Page 123

EFTPOS (Electronic Funds Transfer At Point of Sale): This refers to an EFT transaction conducted at the checkout.

Page 123

GANTT Chart: A graphical representation of how resources are to be used in a project over a period of time.

Page 55

HTML (Hypertext Markup Language): This is a system of coding for web page display. HTML code is interpreted and displayed by some web browser software. It uses 'tags' or markers to instruct the software how to display the web page content.

Page 91

IP (Internet Protocol) Address: The Internet and many internal networks use a set of rules or protocol to allow the connected devices to communicate. Every device has a unique number or address and it is one of the jobs of the protocol to define the exact format of these addresses. IP addresses consist of four numbers, each in the range 0-255, so a typical IP address might be 125.78.86.67.

Page 162

ISDN (Integrated Services Digital Network): This is a dial-up digital service that provides fairly high-speed data links between devices. It is charged by the time that it is open. This is different from a dedicated link where a line is rented and open all the time.

Page 43

JPEG (Joint Photographic Expert Group): A standard for compressing and storing still images. It is the most common image storing standard used for web pages.

Page 91

LAN: a LAN is a Local Area Network. That is a network confined to one site.

Page 10

Modem: A modem (modulator demodulator) is a device that changes a computer's digital signal into the varying voltages (analogue signals) used by most PSTNs (Public Service Telephone Networks) and back again. Even today, many internet users still use slow (56 kbps) modems.

Page 9

MP3: a compression format for audio files. It uses a method called Mpeg 1 Audio Layer 3. MPEG stands for Moving Pictures Expert Group.

Page 45

Patch: An addition to an existing computer program in order to fix a problem discovered after release.

Page 46

PDA (Personal Digital Assistant): A small hand-held computer that has much of the functionality of a PC but is easier to carry around when travelling.

Page 79

PDF (Portable Document Format): A file standard for documents where the document is received exactly as in the original. There is no alteration due to different platforms or different software. The document can be protected if necessary so that legal documents, for example, cannot be altered. PDF is a proprietary standard owned by the Adobe Corporation.

Page 55

Platform: a combination of specific hardware and operating system. Most applications will work on one particular platform. A common example is Intel/Windows XP. They have to be recompiled to work on another platform.

Page 5

Plug-in: a software add-on that adds a new feature to an existing software package.

Page 6

Real Time: A mode of interaction between a user and a computer system where the computer output happens almost immediately, thus allowing the user to modify the next input.

Page 123

Search String: The words that you enter into a search engine for it to look up web sites, news groups or images.

Page 52

Spam: this is unwanted and unsolicited email. It is always a nuisance and getting rid of it can waste hours. It sometimes carries viruses, Trojan horses, spyware and other 'malware' (malicious software) that can damage your data or invade your privacy.

Page 33

Trojan Horse: Malicious software that is disguised as something else, possibly a program that you want.

Page 62

Usenet: A worldwide bulletin board system that can be accessed through the Internet.

Page 34

Validation: the checking of data by the software as it is being input, to prevent the entry of unreasonable data.

Page 117

Virus: A computer program that is designed to copy itself. It may attach itself to other programs or it may be a stand-alone program, when it is then called a *worm*. Viruses often cause harm to a computer system.

Page 62

VPN (Virtual Private Network): A private subsection of a larger network or part of the Internet to which only certain individuals have access. A VPN can provide a worldwide private space where individuals can collaborate on a project.

Page 55

Index

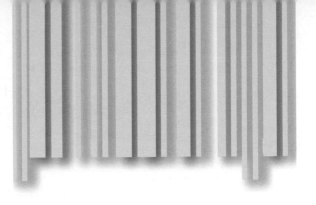

South Sefton
6th Form College

information &
communication
technology

for edexcel applied AS level single award

chris.guy_sean.o'byrne

Hodder Murray
THE HODDER HEADLINE GROUP

The Publishers would like to thank the following for permission to reproduce copyright material:
Photo credits
© Astrid & Hanns-Frieder Michler / Science Photo Library (page 17 top); © David Woods/Corbis (page 203); © fStop / Alamy (page 12); © Goodshoot / Alamy (page 17 middle); © Peter Macdiarmid/Reuters/Corbis (page 28); © Steve Chenn/Corbis (page 43); Steve Connolly (pages 17 bottom, 25, 36, 56); © Swerve / Alamy (page 150); All other images are author supplied.

Acknowledgements
This product contains Free Comersus Cart, developed by Rodrigo S. Alhadeff (http://www.Comersus.com/). Copyright © Comersus Open Technologies LC. All rights reserved.

A full listing of the Comersus copyright details can be found on the licence.txt documents in the accompanying CD-ROM.

Every effort has been made to trace all copyright holders, but if any have been inadvertently overlooked the Publishers will be pleased to make the necessary arrangements at the first opportunity.

Although every effort has been made to ensure that website addresses are correct at time of going to press, Hodder Murray cannot be held responsible for the content of any website mentioned in this book. It is sometimes possible to find a relocated web page by typing in the address of the home page for a website in the URL window of your browser.

Orders: please contact Bookpoint Ltd, 130 Milton Park, Abingdon, Oxon OX14 4SB. Telephone: (44) 01235 827720. Fax: (44) 01235 400454. Lines are open 9.00–6.00, Monday to Saturday, with a 24-hour message answering service. Visit our website at www.hoddereducation.co.uk

Typeset in by Pantek Arts Ltd, Maidstone, Kent
Printed in Italy for Hodder Murray, a division of Hodder Headline, 338 Euston Road, London NE1 3BH

A catalogue record for this title is available from the British Library

ISBN-10: 0340907282
ISBN-13: 978 0340 907283